Linc

P9-CMB-222

561 Highland Pl.
Bellevue, Pa.

THE MAKING AND MEANING OF THE
NEW TESTAMENT

BY
JAMES H. SNOWDEN

THE BASAL BELIEFS OF CHRISTIANITY
THE WORLD A SPIRITUAL SYSTEM
CAN WE BELIEVE IN IMMORTALITY?
THE COMING OF THE LORD
IS THE WORLD GROWING BETTER?
THE PERSONALITY OF GOD
A WONDERFUL NIGHT
A WONDERFUL MORNING
SCENES AND SAYINGS IN THE LIFE OF CHRIST
THE PSYCHOLOGY OF RELIGION
A SUMMER ACROSS THE SEA
THE TRUTH ABOUT CHRISTIAN SCIENCE
THE MEANING OF EDUCATION
THE ATTRACTIONS OF THE MINISTRY
THE CITY OF TWELVE GATES
JESUS AS JUDGED BY HIS ENEMIES
SUNDAY SCHOOL LESSONS, THREE ANNUAL VOLS.

The Making and Meaning of the New Testament

BY

JAMES H. SNOWDEN

New York

THE MACMILLAN COMPANY

1923

All rights reserved

PRINTED IN THE UNITED STATES OF AMERICA.

COPYRIGHT, 1923,
By THE MACMILLAN COMPANY.

Set up and electrotyped. Published October, 1923.

BROWN BROTHERS, LINOTYPERS
NEW YORK

2259.
Sn6

The words that speak unto you, they are spirit, and
they are life.—*Jesus.*

Religion cannot be said to have made a bad choice in
pitching on this Man as an ideal representative and guide
to humanity; nor even now, would it be easy, even for
an unbeliever, to find a better translation of the rule of
virtue from the abstract into the concrete, than the endeavor so to live that Christ would approve our life.—
John Stuart Mill.

Look on our divinest Symbol: Jesus of Nazareth and
His life and His biography and what followed therefrom.
Higher has the human thought not yet reached; this is
Christianity and Christendom, a symbol of quite peren-
nial, infinite character: whose significance will ever de-
mand to be anew inquired into and anew made manifest.
—*Carlyle.*

I thoroughly believe in a university education for both
men and women; but I believe in a knowledge of the
Bible without a college education is more valuable than
a college course without the Bible. For in the Bible we
have profound thought beautifully expressed; we have
the nature of boys and girls, of men and women, more
accurately charted than in the works of any modern
novelist or playwright. You can learn more about human
nature by reading the Bible than by living in New York.
—*William Lyon Phelps.*

All Scripture is given by inspiration of God, and is
profitable for doctrine, for reproof, for correction, for
instruction in righteousness; that the man of God may
be perfect, thoroughly furnished unto all good works.
—*Paul.*

42889

INTRODUCTION

BOOKS AND THE BOOK

Books are boats loaded with cargoes of ideas, the most valuable goods and vital wealth in the world. They come floating down the stream of time, it may be from distant days and far lands and various climes, and bring us freight infinitely more precious than the silks of India, or the spices of Araby, or all the ivory and diamonds and gold of Africa. Yet are they so plentiful and cheap that no one is so poor but may be rich in this treasure.

Books are the fossilized brains of thinkers that are gone. The ideas that glowed in Plato's luminous brain or soared in Shakespeare's imperial imagination kindle their fires or spread their wings in our minds and hearts. They are vital arteries through which the thoughts and deeds, visions and victories of men of genius pour into us and throb in our pulses. They crowd the glorious consciousness of these gifted souls into our minds so that we see through their eyes and think with their thoughts and are strong with their strength and rise on the wings of their spirits.

Words, the first and oldest human invention, are still the most magical things in the world, incomparably surpassing all our modern wonders. Loom and locomotive, telephone and wireless radio are small achievements compared with the wizardy of words. The sign which consists of only a few strokes of a pen or a mere puff of breath yet comes nearer to being the incarnation of the soul and the very life of the spirit than any other device of man. It distills and condenses and crystallizes the living content of one soul and transports it to and dissolves it in another so that two minds think the same thought and two hearts beat as one. A single word may thus diffuse ideas around the world, compel multitudes to think and act together, and shape the history of coming centuries.

Beware of a word: a thousand thinkers and a hundred generations and countless heroes and martyrs may have distilled their life-blood into it, and at its call they may awake and come forth to fight for it and with it. It may seem impalpable and impotent as so much empty air, but its few innocent-looking letters may contain more condensed potency than all the dynamite on the planet. It may unify and electrify a nation, make a million bayonets think and conquer the world. The simple word democracy has in modern times put kings out of business, overturned all despotic thrones and uprooted some of the most ancient special privileges and most sacrosanct customs among men. The sceptres of kings and emperors are puny playthings compared with these magic wands.

Books are battalions of words that in their massed might are charged with mysterious and almost miraculous power of molding and merging many and even millions of minds into one thought and purpose and life. They resurrect the past, create the present and foreordain the future. They are the great university and contain all ideas and visions and carry in their bosoms the promise and potency of all achievements.

Of all the books in the world the Bible is incomparably the greatest and best. It was slowly produced, as diamonds are distilled and crystallized atom by atom, through a thousand years at the convergent and crowded crossroads of the ancient world where all civilizations and languages and religions met and flowed into it. Not only was Palestine compressed into its pages, but so also were Babylon and Egypt and Greece and Rome. All the world was taxed and rifled of its treasures to compose and enrich it. A great many-sided literature of the most gifted people religiously, it is the expressed essence of their history and experience. Historian and psalmist, prophet and poet emblazoned its pages with their pictures of the march of God through time, tossing impenitent nations out of his path, and with the most glorious visions and colors of their inspired imagination. The Hebrew was the most richly endowed child of God and yet also was the most wilful and wayward and passed through the deepest waters and the fiercest fires. He poured his burning, throbbing soul into this book so that it flames with his ardent dreams and hopes, is jubilant with his joyous triumphs, smeared and stained with his sins and tears, darkened with his tragedies, and sobs with his sorrows.

No other book is so varied and picturesque and colorful, so surcharged and saturated with the distilled essence of human nature, so woven of the very palpitating fibres of the human soul. It is at once the most human and the most divine book in all the vast library of the world's books; and like an old rose jar it will ever retain and emit its precious divine aroma; out of its ancient moss-covered rock will ever gush forth living streams of life. It has been and is the most prolific soil and seed-bed of other books, and out of it have grown vast forests of literature. It can never pass out of human interest and become obsolete, any more than can the majesty of mountains and the mystery of the sea, the beauty of the Parthenon, the plays of Shakespeare, or the soul of Lincoln. It is rooted in the religious nature of man and will endure as one of the permanent and perennial interests and values of our human world.

The New Testament is the best part of this greatest and best book. The New is the blossom and fruit of which the Old is the root. It contains the most precious truth distilled out of the richest and most sensitive spiritual souls and brings it to our minds and dissolves it in our hearts. It comes to us out of the greatest period of human history, the First Century of the Christian Era which still overtops all the centuries. It is full of picturesque scenes and stirring stories and dramatic moments. It grows out of a great background and is full of great biographies. It is written in everyday speech in simple words level to the common people and to children, and the simplicity and beauty and majesty and music of its style have been the charm and praise of all the Christian centuries. Translated into no fewer than seven hundred and seventy languages no other book has come near it in circulation over the entire globe. It is read on every continent and island and is incomparably the best seller in the world today. It is a profound book in whose depths scholars may lose themselves, and yet it is a popular book and the common people read it gladly.

It is a highly composite book, produced by many writers and containing various kinds of literature, history and doctrine, gospel and epistle, parable and prose-poem and panoramic apocalypse, and yet it blends this wide variety into a rich unity. Woven of many notes and chords and melodies, it yet all melts into harmony and makes one music. It gathered honey from all the fields and flowers of the ancient world. It considered nothing human foreign to it and taxed all the world for its own enrichment. An Oriental book, it is yet equally understood in the Occident. It crosses all continental and racial and linguistic lines and is everywhere familiarly at home. While deeply colored with the soil and ideas and customs of Palestine its pictures are true to the life of every land. It speaks to the universal human soul and sweeps all the mystic chords of the human heart. Never can it grow old and out of date, nor can custom ever stale its perennial freshness and infinite variety. One of the oldest books which we know, it is yet one of the most modern and matches and meets all the experiences and needs of our day and life.

All its lights are thrown upon its central Figure and supreme Personality. It sets in its frame a Portrait unique and unapproachable in all other literature which no human pen ever produced out of imagination or myth, but which was simply drawn from life and brings us face to face with the living Reality. So realistic and modern is the Picture that Jesus seems to step right out of these pages into our homes and streets and marts and all our life.

The New Testament is an intensely human book, and yet it is none the less but all the more divine. It is not easy to separate and define this divine element, just as it is not easy or possible to draw the dividing line between the human and the divine in providence or in our own consciousness. But this divine element is present as a golden thread woven into all its web, or as a flame that burns all the way through it, or as a relish that is found in all its pages. The book is earthly clay fused with celestial fire, human flesh filled with divine spirit. Its vessel is earthen, but its treasure is heavenly. The breath of God is blowing through this book: nothing else will explain it.

To know this book is in itself an education. It broadens the brain, kindles the imagination, purifies the heart and transforms the life. More than any other book it has shaped and colored the history of these nineteen Christian centuries, and with every cycle of the sun it is infiltrating its teaching and spirit more deeply into the highest and finest civilization. But as yet it is sadly true that only dimly and slightly is its light seen and its power felt and its truth transmuted into life, and its great days and deeds are yet to come.

There is vastly more light to break out of this book. Countless seeds and innumerable harvests yet slumber in its soil. When these seeds have been sown around the world and are sprouting on every shore and blossoming in every heart, when all its truth has been turned into bread and assimilated into the life-blood of the race it will be seen and experienced that its words are spirit and life.

TABLE OF CONTENTS

PART I

THE BACKGROUND OF THE NEW TESTAMENT.

CHAP.

INTRODUCTION vii

PAGE

I. THE JEWISH BACKGROUND 3
1. The Land of Palestine 3
2. The Jewish People 6
    (1) The History of the Jews 6
    (2) Racial Characteristics of the Jews . . 8
    (3) The Religious Nature of the Jews . . 9
3. The Old Testament 11
4. Conditions in Palestine in the Time of Christ . 14
    (1) Political Conditions 14
    (2) The Religious Worship and Life of the Jews 15
    (3) Religious Parties among the Jews . . 19
    (4) Religious Doctrines of Judaism . . 20
II. THE GREEK BACKGROUND 22
1. The Greek Genius 22
2. The Spread of Greek Civilization . . . 23
3. The Greek Language 24
4. Greek Contributions to the New Testament . 26
III. THE ROMAN BACKGROUND 29
1. The Roman Genius 29
2. The Roman Empire 30
3. Pagan Religions in the Roman Empire . . 31
4. Roman Contributions to the New Testament . 33
IV. THE FULNESS OF TIME 35

PART II

THE BOOKS OF THE NEW TESTAMENT.

I. INTRODUCTION 41
II. GENERAL CHARACTERISTICS OF THE GOSPELS . . 44
1. The Historicity of the Gospels 44
2. The Interrelations of the Gospels . . . 47
3. Can the Gospels Be Harmonized? . . . 50

CHAP.   PAGE
    4. The Dates of the Gospels 53
    5. Why Four Gospels? 55
    6. Miracles in the Gospels 56
    7. The Chronology and Outline of Events of the
       Life of Jesus 59
       (1) Chronology 59
       (2) Outline of Events 59
III. THE FOUR GOSPELS 62
    1. The Gospel According to Matthew . . . 62
       (1) Authorship 62
       (2) Characteristics 63
       (3) Contents 64
    2. The Gospel According to Mark 66
       (1) Authorship 66
       (2) Characteristics 67
       (3) Contents 68
    3. The Gospel According to Luke 69
       (1) Authorship 69
       (2) Purpose and Characteristics . . . 69
       (3) The Preface 70
       (4) Contents 72
    4. The Gospel According to John . . . 73
       (1) Authorship and Date 73
       (2) Purpose and Characteristics . . . 74
       (3) Contents 75
IV. THE ACTS OF THE APOSTLES AND THE EPISTLES OF PAUL 77
    1. The Acts of the Apostles 77
       (1) Authorship and Date 77
       (2) Purpose and Characteristics . . . 77
       (3) Contents 80
    II. The Epistles of Paul 80
       (1) Authorship 80
       (2) Circumstances and Characteristics of the
          Epistles 81
       (3) Chronology of Paul's Life and Letters . 83
       (4) Contents of the Epistles 84
          Romans 84
          I and II Corinthians 85
          Galatians 86
          Ephesians 88
          Philippians 80
          Colossians 90
          I and II Thessalonians 90
          I and II Timothy 92
          Titus 94
          Philemon 94
       (5) Review of the Epistles 95
V. THE CATHOLIC EPISTLES AND REVELATION . . 99
       Hebrews 99

TABLE OF CONTENTS

XV

CHAP.

PAGE

James 101
I and II Peter 102
I and II and III John 103
Jude 104
Revelation 105
VI. THE CANON AND TRANSMISSION OF THE NEW TESTAMENT 107
    1. The Canon 107
    2. Manuscripts 108
    3. Translations 109

PART III

THE LIFE OF JESUS.

I. INTRODUCTION 115
II. THE THIRTY SILENT YEARS 117
    1. The Genealogy of Jesus 117
    2. A Holy Mystery Revealed 118
    3. The Birth in Bethlehem 120
    4. Angels and Shepherds 121
    5. Worshipping Wise Men 123
    6. The Childhood at Nazareth . . . 125
    7. The Carpenter 129
III. FIRST YEAR: THE EARLY JUDEAN MINISTRY . . 131
    1. A Great Revival Meeting 131
    2. The Baptism of Jesus 133
    3. The Temptation of Jesus 134
    4. How the Kingdom Started to Grow . . 137
    5. Water Turned into Wine 141
    6. First Cleansing of the Temple . . . 143
    7. A Distinguished Night Visitor . . . 146
    8. A Convert from Low Life 148
IV. SECOND YEAR: THE GALILEAN MINISTRY . . . 152
    1. A Prophet Driven out of His Own Town . 153
    2. Preaching and Fishing at Lake Galilee . 156
    3. A Busy Day in Capernaum . . . 158
    4. A Missionary Tour through Galilee . 162
    5. Strange Things 164
    6. Jesus at the Pool of Bethesda . . . 167
    7. The Choosing and the Mission of the Twelve
       Disciples 169
    8. The Sermon on the Mount—The Beatitudes . 172
    9. The Sermon on the Mount—The Lord's Prayer 175
    10. Jesus Heals a Centurion's Servant . . 178
    11. How Jesus Dealt with John's Doubt . . 180
    12. Jesus Teaching by Parables . . . 184
    13. A Storm on Lake Galilee 187
    14. The Tragedy of the Black Tower . . . 190
    15. Five Thousand Fed 192

16. Jesus Breaks with the Pharisees . . . 195
17. The Interview at Cæsarea Philippi . . . 198
18. The Transfiguration 201
V. THIRD YEAR: THE LATER JUDEAN MINISTRY . . 205
1. The Man Born Blind 205
2. Mary and Martha 208
3. The Triumphal Entry 212
4. Certain Greeks 215
5. The Lord's Supper 217
6. Gethsemane 221
7. The Trial 223
8. The Crucifixion 227
9. The Resurrection 230
10. The Great Commission 233
11. The Ascension 236

PART IV

THE SPREAD OF CHRISTIANITY

I. INTRODUCTION 243
II. THE CHURCH IN JERUSALEM 245
1. The Day of Pentecost 245
2. The Martyrdom of Stephen 248
III. THE GOSPEL SETS OUT ON ITS WORLD MARCH . . 253
1. The Gospel in Samaria 253
2. The Conversion of Paul 256
3. Peter and Cornelius 260
4. First Council at Jerusalem: Shall Gentiles Be
Received into the Church? . . . 263
5. The Gospel in Antioch 265
IV. PAUL'S MISSIONARY JOURNEYS 269
1. Paul's First Missionary Journey . . . 269
2. Second Council at Jerusalem: Must Gentile Converts Submit to the Mosaic Ceremonies? . 273
3. Paul's Second Missionary Journey: From Antioch
to Berea 276
4. Paul at Athens and Corinth 280
5. Paul's Third Missionary Journey . . . 283
6. Paul at Jerusalem and Cæsarea . . . 286
7. Stormy Voyage and Shipwreck . . . 289
8. Paul in Rome 292
INDEX OF SCRIPTURES 299
INDEX OF SUBJECTS 303

PART I

THE BACKGROUND OF THE NEW TESTAMENT

THE MAKING AND MEANING OF THE NEW TESTAMENT

CHAPTER I

THE JEWISH BACKGROUND

Christianity is an historical religion and its roots run down into the land of Palestine and back through Hebrew history and still further back into ancient Egypt and Babylon and then out through the wide Gentile world.

The books of the New Testament are historical documents and follow the laws of such records in their origin, authorship, contents and purpose. They sprang out of concrete historical conditions, and they can be fully understood only as they are viewed in the light of their original environment.

It will, therefore, be necessary to begin this study of the New Testament by sketching the background out of which it grew.

The New Testament is primarily a Jewish book and therefore it must be viewed as an outgrowth of Jewish history.

1. THE LAND OF PALESTINE

Palestine, the home of the Bible, is physically one of the smallest countries of the world, but historically and religiously it bulks larger than some continents. It is a mere strip of country only about 145 miles long and on the average about 70 miles wide so that it is not larger than some American western counties.

It runs north and south along the eastern shore of the Mediterranean and consists of four sections: the maritime plain, the central mountain range, the Jordan valley, and the mountain plateau east of the Jordan bordering on tne desert.

The maritime plain, about 20 miles wide, was originally the land of the Philistines, from which word was derived the name of the country. It was and still is the most fertile part of Palestine.

The central rocky ridge runs up through the middle of the land like a spinal column, and at the plain of Esdraelon, which cuts across the country from the sea to the Jordan, the mountain range turns to the west and buries its rocky roots in the blue Mediterranean. North of the plain of Esdraelon rise the mountains of Lebanon and Hermon.

The Jordan valley, or gorge, is one of the most remarkable chasms on the planet. It is a geological "fault" or slip in the rock strata of the earth which, at the deepest point at the bottom of the Dead Sea, is 2,600 feet below sea level. The Jordan rises in the mountains of the north and descends to a small lake, the Waters of Merom, near sea level, plunges down in less than nine miles to Lake Galilee, 680 feet below sea level, and then descends in 65 miles to the Dead Sea, 1,300 feet below sea level, the Dead Sea itself being 1,300 feet deep. From the summit of Hermon, 9,000 feet high, to the Dead Sea is a fall of 10,300 feet and a change in climate from perpetual snow to tropic heat.

The plateau east of the Jordan rises higher than the mountain range west of the river, and fades out into the desert sand, and is the region known in the New Testament as Perea.

Palestine is thus remarkable in the range of its climate and vegetation from the intense heat and tropic palms and pomegranates of the lower Jordan to the snow and the hardy oaks and pines of the northern mountains. Packed into this small area is a greater variety of meteorology and botany than probably can be found within the same limits anywhere else on the earth. It is a crowded museum of geography and is one of the wonders of the world. On account of this diversity it abounds in picturesque scenery and magnificent views.

Palestine is now generally barren, having been swept of forests and being meagerly supplied with water, but in ancient times it was remarkably fertile and produced grains and fruits in great abundance. Its chief industries were farming and vineyards and olive orchards, and fishing on Lake Galilee which was incredibly prolific in fish, and, in the days of Jesus, 4,000 fishing boats plied their trade on its waters.

The principal cities and towns in the time of Christ were Jerusalem, the ancient capital of splendid renown, near the southern end of the central mountain range, Capernaum on Lake Galilee, Bethlehem south of Jerusalem, Samaria between Jerusalem and the Esdraelon valley, Nazareth in the hills to the north, and Caesarea and Joppa down on the Mediterranean.

An important fact about Palestine was its geographical and strategic location on the highways between Babylon and Egypt and between Asia and Europe, so that it lay at the crossroads of the ancient world. This subjected it to attack on every side and made it a battle ground between the empires of ancient history; and as the main trunk lines of travel and trade ran through it, it was exposed to foreign influences and absorbed cosmopolitan culture from every quarter.

This central location also made it a strategic point from which it could radiate its light out in every direction upon the world. Especially was this true in the time of our Lord and in the early days of Christianity when Palestine was in direct communication with all countries and the first apostles and missionaries found roads running out to points all around the then known world.

The Jews loved Palestine with passionate devotion, and in their long exile from it they have ever cherished the desire and the dream of returning to it as their homeland. This desire has survived to this day and is the objective of the Zionist movement, which has acquired new strength and practical meaning as the result of the Great War, which after many centuries has thrown Palestine back into Christian hands.

The Bible is deeply saturated and richly colored with Palestine from beginning to end. It was the promised land which for centuries lured the Hebrews onward as the star of their hope. All its places and scenes became consecrated and dear to them with accumulated sacred and patriotic associations. Here they developed their religious institutions and wrought out their destiny until their final exile from it and dispersion among the Gentiles.

Almost every page of the Bible reflects some aspect of this land. Its mountains and valleys, springs and rivers and lakes, the hot desert and snow-crowned Hermon, the steep rocky roads running down to the Jordan and the blue mountains of Moab, wheatfield and olive orchard and vineyard, palm and pine, flowers and birds, all the varieties of climate and scenery and vegetation that are crowded into this little country add their picturesqueness and color to this wonderful book.

The New Testament was born in this country and much of it was written on its soil. Jerusalem and Capernaum, Bethlehem and Nazareth, the busy shore of Lake Galilee and its fleet of fishing boats, the plunging Jordan and the blue Mediterranean, the green hillsides and flower-embroidered plains and the clear Syrian sky, all its historic places and varied scenes meet us on these pages. It is the constant background of the Gospels and of the greater part of the New Testament. It is still the most sacred land in all the world and contains

> those holy fields,
> Over whose acres walked those blessed feet
> Which, nineteen hundred years ago, were nailed
> For our advantage on the bitter cross.

2. THE JEWISH PEOPLE

The Jews are as remarkable and unique among the peoples of the world as Palestine is among the countries of the earth.

(1) A brief sketch of the history of the Jews will be in place at this point. The ancient roots of this race run back into Babylonia in the east and down into Egypt in the south.

Abraham, "the father of the faithful," a member of the Semitic branch of the human family, is the starting point of the race. He was a dweller in Mesopotamia in the Euphrates valley, a land of gross idolatry, and he was called to go out as an emigrant to the west that he might be delivered from idolatrous religion and worship the one true and living God. He "followed the gleam" and "went out, not knowing whither he went," and wandered over Palestine, living a nomadic life.

Abraham's descendants were Isaac and Jacob. Jacob and his sons, under the pressure of famine, were forced down into Egypt where they settled in a state of servitude that became practical slavery, and where their descendants remained under the Pharaohs during a period of about 400 years.

Out of the bondage in Egypt the Israelites were delivered under the inspiring leadership of Moses and were conducted to Mt. Sinai, where they received the Ten Commandments and other legislation of Moses and were organized into a nation.

After forty years of wandering in the wilderness the Israelites entered Palestine under the leadership of Joshua, the successor of Moses, and conquered the land by the extermination or subjugation of the Canaanites.

The period of the Judges extending to 400 years ensued. The Judges were local rulers, and it was a time of unsettled government and insecurity of property and life when law was loose and rough customs prevailed.

Samuel was the last judge, and he inaugurated the monarchy with Saul as the first king of the nation. David succeeded Saul, Jerusalem was made the capital, and the kingdom was extended over the whole land and greatly strengthened. Under Solomon, David's son and successor, the kingdom rose to its greatest height of power and splendor, the temple was built in Jerusalem, and the ceremonial system of worship under the priests was established.

Under Solomon's son and successor, Rehoboam, a weak and insolent king, the ten northern tribes revolted under the leadership of Jeroboam and set up the northern kingdom of Israel with its capital at Samaria, and the southern kingdom of Judah remained with its capital at Jerusalem.

A succession of kings followed in both of these rival kingdoms. A few of these rulers were wise and good, but most of them were corrupt and wicked and many of them came to a violent end. Idolatry and social corruption developed in both kingdoms, though the southern has a better record than the northern kingdom. This degeneracy proceeded in spite of the opposition and brave words and solemn warnings of such prophets as Elijah and Elisha, Amos and Isaiah and Jeremiah.

The Syrians and then the mighty Asyrians began to attack both kingdoms and finally both their capitals fell and their inhabitants were carried into captivity, Samaria in 722 B. C., and Jerusalem in 568 B. C.

After an exile of 70 years in Babylon, remnants of the Jews returned to Jerusalem under Zerubbabel and Ezra and Nehemiah, aided by the Persian kings of Babylon, and rebuilt the city with its walls and temple and restored the former worship. The exile in Babylon thoroughly cured the Jews of idolatry and broadened their mental horizon and thus prepared them for their world mission.

Palestine fell under the rule of Alexander the Great in 322 B. C., and continued under his Greek successors. In 167 B. C. the Jews revolted and regained their independence under Judas Maccabaeus, and maintained their national existence until 65 B. C., when Pompey captured Jerusalem and Palestine became a Roman province.

At the division of the Roman Empire into the Eastern and Western Empires, Palestine became a part of the Eastern Empire. It fell into the hands of the Mohammedans in 636 A. D., and remained in their control, with brief interruptions during the Crusades, until it passed into the power of the Turks in 1516 A. D., where it remained until in the Great War it was taken out of their hands and is now a mandate of the British Empire.

(2) The racial characteristics of the Jew stamp him as the most unique and persistent type of man known to history, and his checkered career and manifold sufferings and tragic fate have made him the pathos of the world. His peculiar physiognomy looks out at us from Babylonian bricks and Egyptian hieroglyphics and Roman monuments, and it is one of the most distinctive among men and has endured with little change through thousands of years. No one would fail to pick him out in any company or crowd.

He played a great part in his ancient homeland in government and literature and religion, and then he became a wanderer and has entered all lands and left no shore untrodden by his foot. He has been an actor or a spectator in history since it emerged from primeval mists. He has witnessed the rise of every empire and then has seen it decline and has stood at its grave. There are few fields of achievement in our modern world in which his genius has not exhibited its versatility and power. He has been the best hated and most universally persecuted man in the world, and yet, he has also been highly esteemed and at times greatly exalted. History has focused the light of all the centuries upon him and there he stands revealed, sometimes wearing the purple robes of wealth and distinction, but often clothed in rags, crowned with honor or crucified on a cross. Yet in spite of his persecutions and poverty he has rarely been a beggar but has rather been the banker of the world.

The most ubiquitous man in the world, he has been everywhere and seen everything and absorbed everything into his life and spirit. Without a homeland of his own he has made himself at home in all lands, and mingling with all peoples he has yet identified himself with none.. He has so inwoven himself into the entire web of the world's civilization that we cannot touch a single thread of it without involving him. Whether we are for him or against him, there is no escaping the Jew. We cannot even date a letter, newspaper or contract without doing him an honor; the very calendar proclaims his central place in history. The most rabid Jew baiter and the bitterest anti-semitic propagandist bow to him in the very act of persecuting him.

This many-sided and wonderful man stands in the background of the entire Bible and especially of the New Testament.

(3) The outstanding and supreme characteristic of the Jew is his religious nature. The peculiar genius of a people is a spirit so subtle and elusive that it is difficult to catch it in a definition or cage of words, but every great race is marked by such a spirit which it is easier to feel than to describe.

Among the upstanding peoples of the past, the Jew obviously stands loftiest and purest in spirituality. He specialized in religion. He was not a universal genius, but his nature was peculiarly sensitive to the things of the spirit. He stood closer to heaven than any other man and earliest caught the light of eternity and reflected it down upon and out over the world.

The Jew was the first to see the one true and living God rising above the multitudes of polythestic and idolatrous gods that crowded the ancient world. This was the gleam that Abraham discerned and followed and that led him out into the light of monotheism that finally became the light of the world.

The Jew had a strong sense of the righteousness of God. Moral character bulked larger and was infinitely worth more in his sight than physical might, and an unethical god was abhorrent to his soul. His fundamental question and faith was, "Shall not the Judge of all the earth do right?"

This Jewish sense of the righteousness of God was accompanied with a corresponding sense of the guilt of sin and the obligation and necessity of personal righteousness. The Ten Commandments comprise an ethical code unapproached by any other people in the ancient world, and though falling short of his ethical idealism the Jew imposed this divine law upon his own heart and life.

The Jew had a masterful faith that trusted God in the most dreadful day and darkest night. Though subjected to repeated captivity and exile, defeat and retribution, and unprecedented sufferings and sorrows, so that more than any other he "was a man of sorrows and acquainted with grief," yet he never lost faith but would sing songs in the night and exclaim, "Yea, though I walk through the valley of the shadow of death, I will fear no evil: for thou art with me."

The Jew was preëminently a prophet, sensitive and quick to catch the breath of heaven and the light of God's face. He was ethically the most susceptible soul in the world to which God could communicate his revelation; the loftiest peak which was earliest illumined by the rising sun of inspiration; the most spiritually harmonized race through which God could breathe his music.

Therefore it was that while other races were endowed with other gifts, the Greeks with a sense of beauty and the

Romans with administrative ability, the Jews were endued with religious sensibility so that they became the revealers of God to the world.

This spiritual achievement is the precious and priceless legacy the Jew has bequeathed to us. It has fertilized and enriched our modern world immeasurely beyond the contributions of any other people. "If it had not been for the Jews," said Romanes, "the human race would not have had any religion worth our serious attention."

The soul of the Jew as quickened by the breath of the Holy Spirit of God is the soil out of which grew the Old Testament and blossomed the New, which contains the ripened seed of Christianity that is now being scattered around the world.

3. THE OLD TESTAMENT

All this history and genius of the Jews were embodied in the Old Testament, which is the literary background of the New.

The essential religious history of the Jews, their wanderings and vicissitudes, development in their promised land, division and captivity, exile and return, are recorded in its pages. The Old Testament is itself a highly composite book, not only containing various documents older than itself, but also tinctured in its teachings and colored in its pages with ideas and words derived from other ancient sources, notably Egypt and Babylon. Our fundamental religious ideas are very old and go back beyond the beginning of recorded history.

The germinal roots and the growth of Hebrew religious ideas and doctrines and ordinances are unfolded in the progressive revelation of the Old Testament. We see the Ten Commandments expanded into the fuller ethical life and legislative enactments of the law, the tabernacle give way to the temple, and the simple services and sacrifices of early ages grow into the elaborate and splendid ceremonies of later times.

The doctrines of God's unity and sovereignty, spirituality and righteousness and universal Fatherhood and love and providence; of sin and salvation; of growing ethical obligation and social responsibility and righteousness; and

the expression of these in an increasingly elaborate ritual-
ism, are portrayed in these books. The teachings of the
great prophets, declaring the will of God as the pre-
eminent preachers and statesmen of their time and seeing
splendid visions and uttering eloquent words for all time,
are conspicuous in these records. Especially did they
catch views of the coming Messiah in the light of his rising
sun as it fell upon their inspired vision and flooded the
whole horizon of the future with prophetic glory.

The psalmists voiced the aspiration and worship, penitence and faith, prayers and songs of the Jews in their
ancient hymn book that is still a precious treasury of sacred
poetry and song to the whole Christian world.

The lapses into unfaithfulness and sin, the sorrows and
tears, and the retribution and tragedies of the chosen people stain and color these pages with somber hues and
mournful beauty.

It is true that the Old Testament in its early pages reflects low ethical ideas and is blotted on many a leaf with
the barbarous deeds of barbarous days or the wickedness
of a corrupt age. But this is because it is an honest book
in its records and starts with the rude civilization of
primitive times and advances through progressive revelation and purer ethical ideals to higher levels of doctrine
and life; and in the New Testament these lower levels are
outgrown and left behind.

Taken as a whole the Old Testament is a mass of national
literature that ranks as one of the richest literary treasures
of the world. Even apart from its religious value its loss
would leave a large and irreparable gap in the library of
the world's great books, and its spiritual contents and its
ministry of preparation for the birth of its more richly
endowed child make it one of our most useful and precious
deposits of religious experience.

All these lines of history and doctrine and ritual, prophecy and song, led towards the culmination and climax of
the Old Testament in the New, as the seed leads towards
the blossom and fruit, or as the dawn ushers in the day.

The New Testament roots itself back in the Old at every
point; all its fibres and rootlets run down into the Old and
draw their nourishment from its soil. The New Testament

derives from the Old all its essential doctrines of God and man, sin and salvation as seeds which it then expands into flower and fruit. The New is thus concealed in the Old, and the Old is revealed in the New. It is no more possible to understand the New Testament apart from the Old than it is to understand the second volume of a two-volume work apart from the first.

The supreme connection between the Old Testament and the New is that the sacrifices of the Old prefigure the supreme sacrifice of the cross, and the Messiah of the Old is the Christ of the New.

There are 275 quotations from the Old Testament in the New, which are so many visible threads directly binding the two books together, or roots running out of the one into the other, besides the innumerable filaments that interlace them.

The Gospel of Mark, the earliest written gospel, opens with a quotation from the Old Testament, so that the new gospel connects itself up with the old gospel in its very first sentence. All the evangelists and especially Matthew conjoin their gospels with the Old Testament by numerous quotations from it.

John the Baptist opened his ministry with a text from Isaiah, and Jesus chose the text of his first sermon from the same book. Jesus expressly declared that he came not to destroy but to fulfill the law and the prophets, and he gave a new commandment which he affirmed was a complete expression and fulfillment of the old commandments of Moses.

Peter preached his great sermon on the day of Pentecost from a text from the prophet Joel and declared "this is that," the new message was identical with and the fulfillment of the old truth.

Paul wove numerous quotations from the Old Testament into his Epistles to show the continuity of his teaching with the teaching of the prophets.

Christ and his apostles and all the writers of the New Testament appeal to Moses and the prophets to confirm their teaching and to show that they are simply carrying out and fulfilling the Old Testament. And one New Testament book, Hebrews, has for its special and direct object the demonstration that the old dispensation of Moses is more gloriously fulfilled in the new dispensation of the gospel of Christ.

If we were to strike out of the New Testament all the quotations from and allusions to and all the doctrines drawn more or less directly from the Old Testament, the New would be riddled to pieces and rendered unintelligible, or its foundation would be removed and it would fall apart.

These two volumes of the Word of God are indissolubly united, one principle and spirit of unity pervades them, one heart beats in them and one spiritual blood courses through them. They have been divinely joined in the history of redemption, and what God hath joined together let not man put asunder.

The Old Testament, then, can never fall out of date and become obsolete, but it is still alive with vital spiritual truth, and it is necessary as the soil and seed, the framework and background of the New.

4. CONDITIONS IN PALESTINE IN THE TIME OF CHRIST

The conditions existing in Palestine in the time of Christ are important factors in the background of the New Testament.

(1) The political state of Palestine was that of a Roman province. The country fell under the Roman rule when Pompey captured Jerusalem in 65 B. C., and in 40 B. C. Herod the Great became king under Roman control. His death occured in 4 B. C., and he was on the throne when Jesus was born.

Herod at his death was succeeded by three of his sons, Archelaus, Antipas and Philip. Archelaus became king of Judea, but was deposed in 6 A. D., and Pontius Pilate became procurator in 26 A. D. and was in office at the time of the trial and crucifixion of Jesus. Herod Antipas became tetrarch of Galilee, and Philip became tetrarch of Perea.

Palestine at this time was divided into Judea, Samaria, Galilee, and Perea. Samaria lay between Judea and Galilee, and the Samaritans were the descendants of the mixed races that settled in the region after the fall of Samaria and the deportation of the Jews to Assyria in 722 B. C. Because of these racial and religious differences the Jews had "no dealings with the Samaritans," and this fact plays a part in the New Testament history.

Perea lay on the east side of the Jordan, and it was the custom of the Jews in traveling between Judea and Galilee to cross the river and thus avoid passing through Samaria.

The aristocratic and ruling classes of the Jews mostly lived in Judea in and around Jerusalem, the capital and the seat of the temple worship and of education in the two chief schools or colleges, conducted by the rival teachers or professors, Hillel and Shammai, and the center of wealth and fashion and social life; and Galilee was a rural district which contained no large city and was inhabited by farmers and fishermen and was provincial in spirit and uncultivated in manners. Judea, however, was more conservative and traditional and less open to progressive ideas than was Galilee that lay more directly on the highway between the East and West, and was more exposed to cosmopolitan liberalism.

(2)   The religious worship and life of the Jews at this time centered in Jerusalem where sacrificial worship was restricted to the temple. Herod the Great had built this temple, which was an imposing structure with marble walls and flashing gilded roof, a mass of snow and gold.

The temple service was held daily and consisted of bloody sacrifices and incense offerings administered by white-robed priests and was accompanied by an antiphonal choir composed of singers and players on instruments and with the blowing of silver trumpets, and altogether it was an elaborate and splendid ceremony.

The Jewish sacrifices were of three kinds: 1. For the individual, the burnt-offering (Lev. 1:2-3), the sin-offering (Lev. 4:1-12), and the tresspass-offering (Lev. 5:1-6). 2. For the family, the Passover (Ex. 12:1-27). 3. For the people, the daily morning and evening sacrifice (Ex. 29:38-46), and the scapegoat-offering on the great day of atonement (Lev. 16:5-10).

The religion of Judaism had developed beyond the system of the Old Testament and been elaborated and hardened into a system of legalism which had grown up around

the law. This law was the system of teaching and commandments which was chiefly contained in the Pentateuch
but had been expanded by noted rabbis. Not only were
the commandments and ordinances of the Mosaic law binding on the people, but these had been extended and
"fenced" by additional rules and regulations which had
accumulated into a highly complicated set of minute injunctions and prohibitions that were almost impossible of
obedience and hampered and burdened life to an incredible
degree.

These ceremonial restrictions of the most complicated
and rigid nature were spun around life at every point. The
"washings" so often referred to in the Gospels were not
the ordinary cleansing of the hands but were religious rites
for the removal of ceremonial impurity. They were un-
believably numerous and meticulous and were applied not
only to the hands and body but also to the dishes and fur-
niture. The clothing was regulated, especially the robes,
and the phylacteries or leather straps with small boxes
containing prescribed texts of Scripture, which were bound
around the arm or forehead, were also subject to countless
rules.

The Sabbath, which was such a frequent occasion of
friction and collision between Jesus and the Pharisees, was
especially hedged around with restrictions that made it a
burden upon life. The command to do no work on this
day had been drawn out into a thousand petty prohibitions.
"Grass was not to be trodden upon, as being akin to harvest work. Shoes with nails were not to be worn, as the
nails would be a 'burden,' and a 'burden' must not be
carried. A tailor must not have his needle about him
towards sunset on Friday, for fear the Sabbath should
begin while he was yet carrying it." In the same way,
"plucking grain was wrong because it was kind of reaping, and rubbing off the husks was a sin because it was a
kind of threshing."

These traditions, which were elaborated into an astound-
ing system of complexity and trivialiy, acquired an authority far exceeding that of the law of Moses. "It is a greater
offense," said the Mischna, the Jewish book containing
these additional laws, "to teach anything contrary to the

voice of the rabbis, than to contradict Scripture itself."
"The Bible was like water, the Traditions like wine, the
Commentaries on them like spiced wine."

These were "the traditions of the elders" with which the
scribes made "the word of God of none effect" (Mark
7 : 13). These were the "heavy burdens and grievous
to be borne," which they laid "on men's shoulders,
but they themselves" would "not move them with one of
their fingers" (Matt. 23 : 4), for they resorted to all sorts
of ingenious subterfuges to evade them.

No doubt these complicated rules were invented with
good motives as a means of serving God more minutely and
perfectly, and many sincerely pious Jews derived good
from such religion. But it was a highly external and
mechanical system and could assume ostentatious and
pompous forms in public and yet inwardly hide hypocrisy
and pride and selfishness and even gross corruption, a
"whited sepulcher" concealing "dead men's bones." This
danger ever attends ritualistic religion.

Jesus came into frequent collision with this ritualistic
and legalistic religion, as we shall see, and it was the chief
occasion of his break with the priests and Pharisees and of
their hostility to him that culminated in their sending him
to the cross.

The religious life of the Jews was further centered and
concentrated in Jerusalem in the yearly feasts, of which
the principal ones were Passover, Pentecost, Tabernacles,
and Dedication. The Passover was celebrated in the spring
of the year and was in commemoration of the deliverance
out of Egypt. It began with the sacrifice of the Pascal
lamb and continued for a week. Pentecost, so-called because it came fifty days after Passover, celebrated the first
fruits of the harvest and was a joyous festival. In the fall
the feast of Tabernacles, so-called because the people lived
in tabernacles or booths out in the open, celebrated the
ingathered harvests, and was a national thanksgiving week.
The feast of Dedication came in December and celebrated
the purification of the temple in the time of Judas Maccabaeus in 165 B. C.

There were other minor feasts and fasts, such as Purim,
celebrating the deliverance of the Jews in the days of

Esther, and the Day of Atonement, which was a day of fasting and humiliation.

It was required of all Jews that they attend these feasts at Jerusalem so that they drew great multitudes to the capital. They were not only religious meetings but were also social and festive and patriotic gatherings that served to bring and mingle the people together and thus to conserve and intensify their religious and national life.

Jesus is reported in the Gospels as being present on several occasions at these feasts and it is probable that he regularly attended them as he observed the requirements of the Mosaic law.

In addition to this centralized worship at Jerusalem, there was the worship that was everywhere carried on in the synagogue, which corresponded with our local church. The synagogue was found in all the cities and towns and villages, as well as wherever Jews were settled in foreign countries.

The service in it consisted in reading selected portions of the Scriptures, chiefly of the law and prophets, together with an exposition of a passage or a sermon and prayer. A collection was taken for the poor. Each synagogue was governed by a board of elders, of whom one presided as "ruler," but there was no minister in our sense of the word and any one might read the Scripture or speak, so that the service was a social one after the manner of our prayer meeting. A curious feature of the synagogue was that ten men were each paid a shekel to attend every service so that a quorum might always be present.

The local common school was also held in the synagogue, either in the building or in one connected with it, and attendance was compulsory on all Jewish children, beginning at the age of six years. The synagogue school was thus the precursor of our public school. The local law court or police court was also held in the synagogue, so that it was the center of the religious and educational and civil life of each community. The supreme court of the Jews was the Sanhedrin, consisting of 71 members, scribes and priests, which sat in Jerusalem and had jurisdiction over religious matters and the more important civil and criminal cases.

It was in the synagogue in Nazareth that Jesus worshipped and went to school, and during his ministry he frequently taught in the synagogue at Nazareth and in other places.

(3) Several religious parties had grown up among the Jews, dating from the time of the Maccabees, and these play an important part in the Gospels.

The Sadducees were the high priestly and court party. They were wealthy aristocrats who stood in with the Herodian and then with the Roman government and had political and social prestige; and they usually had the office of high priest, which was the principal position of religious and political influence. The temple administration and services were in their hands.

As regards doctrines, they held to the Mosaic law as it was contained in the Old Testament and rejected the traditional additions to it that had grown up into such burdensome complexity. But they also rejected belief in angels and spirits and the resurrection of the dead and were doubtful of immortality (Acts 23:8). They emphasized the freedom of the will as opposed to the determinism of some extremists known as Essenes and a middle position of the Pharisees.

Altogether they were the worldly party among the Jews, supporting the government which was so unpopular with the people, holding to formal religion and occupying ruling positions in the church, but lacking in the spirit of piety.

Over against the Sadducees were the Pharisees, who were the party in opposition to the government and were the orthodox religious people. The name means "separatists" and designates their position and character as separated from the less scrupulous defenders of the Jewish religion. They were the traditionalists who had elaborated the law of Moses into all its minute rules and regulations, and they were punctilious and ostentatious in enforcing these regulations on others and yet were expert at evading them in their private practice.

The scribes were men of learning who studied and wrote upon the law and mostly belonged to the Pharisees. They were traditionalists and were generally joined with the Pharisees in their opposition to Jesus and along with them came under his condemnation. The "lawyers" occasionally mentioned are practically the same as the scribes.

Two smaller parties mentioned in the Gospels are the "Herodians" (Matt. 22:16), and the "zealots," to whom Simon, one of the twelve disciples, belonged (Luke 6:15). The former were supporters of the Herod government and family, and the latter were intense and radical nationalists who advocated violent measures against the Romans and, during the various Jewish rebellions against the hated pagan power, committed many excesses.

(4)   The religious doctrines of Judaism consisted in those of the Old Testament, such as the unity and sovereignty and righteousness of God, salvation from sin through sacrifice and faith; but in addition to these two others were specially prominent and dominant in the time of Christ.

The first of these was the doctrine as to the Messiah. The prophets predicted the coming of the Messiah under various names and aspects, sometimes as the conquering King and at other times as the suffering Servant. Various were the views and hopes of the Jews as to the Messiah, but by the time of Christ, the prevailing view had fixed on the idea and hope of a conquering king who would come in the greatness of his strength and put down the enemies of the Jews and exalt them in power.

Corresponding with this idea of a Messiah was the Jewish doctrine and hope of the kingdom of God. The Jews were impatiently waiting and passionately longing for this kingdom in the days of Christ. Various views were also held of the kingdom, some interpreting it in spiritual terms as the righteous rule of God over men in his gracious truth and love.

But the prevailing view was that of an earthly kingdom to be established by the wrath and power of the Messiah breaking in pieces the Gentile kingdoms, especially hated Rome, and setting up a world kingdom with Jerusalem as the capital and themselves in the chief offices.

This hope of a conquering Messiah and an earthly kingdom established by his power was the passionate desire of the Jews in the time of Christ. It found expression in the "apocalypses" of the Jews, books which represented history as a drama in which enemies were destroyed and the kingdom of God was set up by sudden divine power. Daniel and Revelation are two such apocalyptic books, but the Jews had many others.

By this time the Jews had turned all the symbolical representations of the Messiah and his kingdom found in the prophets into literal materialistic reality. They wanted another kingdom like the Roman Empire with another Caesar, only they wanted its capital to be Jerusalem instead of Rome and themselves to sit on Caesar's throne in place of Augustus and Nero.

These prevailing views and hopes as to the Messiah and his kingdom are a prominent fact and feature in the background of the New Testament and play an important part in the life of Jesus. It was because he was not the kind of Messiah they were looking for and was not setting forth the kind of kingdom they wanted that they rejected him and sent him to his cross.

CHAPTER II

THE GREEK BACKGROUND

The background of the New Testament is much wider than the country of Palestine, and the religious history of the Jews; it really is rooted back in Babylon and Egypt in the ancient world, and in the time of Christ it ran its roots out widely through the Greek and Roman world. The New Testament was largely shaped and colored by Greek life and thought and owes much to this wonderful people.

1. THE GREEK GENIUS

The Greeks were an Aryan people who came down from the north in early times in successive waves of immigration and settled in Greece and its adjacent islands and shores, and there through a thousand years developed their racial life.

From the sixth to the fourth centuries B. C. the Greek genius blossomed into its fullest glory, but its fading splendors lasted down into the Roman Empire. This was the age of its great statesmen and orators and artists, poets and philosophers, Pericles and Demosthenes and Phidias, Pindar and Aeschylus and Euripides, Socrates and Plato and Aristotle, names that are imperishable in the history of the human race.

The genius of the Greeks, like that of any other great people, is complex and subtle, and different students have analyzed it differently. It had a supreme sense of beauty and produced architecture and sculpture of which the very ruins and fragments are now guarded as priceless treasures. The Greeks had intellectual depth and brilliance and their historians and poets produced literary masterpieces that in these fields have rarely been equalled and probably never surpassed; and the Greek philosophers thought profoundly on all the great questions that still perplex us. If it be true, as has been said, that the ancients stole all our best thoughts, then the Greeks got the larger part of them, for it is surprising how modern their books are.

Other factors in the Greek genius that have been noted were their originality, their freedom, their intense curiosity, their humanism and their versatility. And of course they were deeply religious and Athens swarmed with gods so that, not to miss any god in their worship, they set up an altar ''To the Unknown God,'' which attracted Paul's attention and became the text of his memorable sermon on Mars' Hill.

2. The Spread of Greek Civilization

The Greeks lacked political cohesiveness and never built up a great state at home, but after their decline had set in they burst their own narrow boundaries in a notable adventure that profoundly affected the ancient world.

Alexander the Great started out in 334 B. C. and cut his way into the heart of Asia, mowing down Asiatic hordes in his path and reaching India. Death by fever cut short his meteoric career at Babylon in 323 B. C., and his Greek generals divided up his empire, Ptolemy taking Egypt, and Seleucus taking Syria, including Palestine. Palestine thus remained under Greek rule, with the exception of the brief Maccabean independence, until it fell under the rule of Rome.

Many Greeks following in the train of Alexander settled in Syria and other regions along the track of his march. These Greek settlements became centers of Greek life and culture and sowed seeds that fertilized these regions and produced widespread and lasting effects. The conquest of Alexander thus broke up the immobility and stagnation of the East and mixed with it the ideas and energies of the West and opened a new era in history.

Many Greeks settled in Palestine and affected its life and thought. Many Greek names of individuals and towns and regions occur in the New Testament. Decapolis (Matt. 4 : 25) was a region lying east of the Esdraelon valley containing ten Greek cities, as the name means, which had been founded by Greeks following in the wake of Alexander. Greeks came up to the feasts at Jerusalem, and on one occasion several of them wished to see Jesus (John 12:20-22) and first made known their desire to Philip, probably because he bore a Greek name. The ''Grecian Jews'' (Revised Version) mentioned in Acts 6:1 and 9:29, commonly called ''Hellenists,'' were Jews who spoke Greek and thus were deeply saturated with Greek culture.

3. THE GREEK LANGUAGE

The Greeks developed one of the most flexible and expressive and beautiful of human languages, in many respects the highest achievement of human genius in this field. It has a wealthy vocabulary and a wonderful power of expressing ideas in all their shapes and shades and it is rarely rhythmical and musical. The tongue of Homer and Demosthenes remains to this day as a master instrument of the human soul, capable of voicing its great heights and depths, and is still one of our richest means of culture.

Such a language easily proved its superiority by overspreading the ancient world and becoming a universal speech. As formerly French was and now English is a world language by which culture and trade and travel compass the earth, so in the days of Greece the Greek language was the instrument of universal communication and life and thought. Cicero said in 62 B. C.: ''Greek is read by practically the whole world, while Latin is confined to its own territory, which is narrow indeed.''

Greek, then, overran Palestine and was generally used and understood in the cities and towns by many if not most of the people. By the time of Christ Hebrew had ceased to be a vernacular language and had grown into the Aramaic, as the Anglo-Saxon developed into our English tongue. Aramaic was generally the common speech among the Jews, although many of them also understood Greek.

Jesus no doubt was reared in the Aramaic language and commonly spoke it in his life and used it in his public ministry. A few of his Aramaic words are preserved in the Gospels. In his sorrow in the garden of Gethsemane he said, ''Abba,'' Father, which was possibly the first word his infant tongue uttered; and in his cry on the cross,

"Eli, Eli, lama sabachthani," he reverted to his childhood speech.

Yet we may be sure that Jesus knew Greek and could use it on occasion. He must have talked with the Greeks, who came to see him (John 12 : 20), in their own language, and his trial before Pilate probably was conducted in Greek.

The Old Testament was early (285 B. C.) translated into Greek and was widely read in this Septuagint version; there were many Greek towns and Greeks as well as Greek-speaking Jews in Palestine, Paul was reared in a Greek city, and of course the apostles, when they went out as missionaries, preached in Greek.

The outstanding fact at this point is that the New Testament was written in Greek. One and only one book of the New Testament, the Gospel of Matthew, may have been originally written in Aramaic, according to an early tradition, but if so written it was soon translated into Greek, and all the others were originally written in this language.

It is an astonishing fact that while the Gospel of Christ came from a Jew and through the Jews, yet it was not given to the world in the Jewish language: this immortal honor was conferred upon the Greek tongue. The whole story of the life and ministry of Jesus, the Sermon on the Mount and his parables and all the recorded words that fell from his lips went out to the world and have come down to us in the Greek language.

The reason for this, of course, was that Aramaic was only a provincial and short-lived language and was not a fit and sufficient vehicle to carry the gospel out over the world. The Greek, being the universal language of the time, was the only proper channel for the transmission of the universal religion. Jesus Christ was no parochial schoolmaster, but the Prophet of humanity and he must needs speak in a world language. The language was fitted to the message of good news, and the good news was worthy of the language, and so the two were divinely wedded together in a union that has not been sundered to this day.

The particular idiom or kind of Greek in which the New Testament was written was not the classical Greek of the writers of the palmy days of Greece, but the speech of

the common people of the time of Christ. Recent discoveries in the sands of Egypt and elsewhere have un-
earthed Greek papyri or letters and other writings of this
period which show that the everyday speech of the Greeks
was practically identical with the Greek of the New Testament, and these writings are throwing much fresh light on
the meaning of New Testament words and teachings. Such
books as Professor Adolf Deissmann's *Light from the
Ancient East,* containing these discoveries, are an illum-
inating commentary on the New Testament.

4. GREEK CONTRIBUTIONS TO THE NEW TESTAMENT

The New Testament, being written in Greek, necessarily
derived from that language something more and much
more than the mere words in which it was expressed. The
words of any language not only convey their primary sig-
nifications but also carry with them subtle associations and
suggestions and implications that cannot be divested from
their express contents. When words are chosen as vehicles
to convey ideas these marginal or atmospheric implications
or overtones go along with them and mingle with the expressed ideas.

Not only the Greek language poured into the New Testament, but along with it slipped in a stream of Greek ideas
and suggestions that helped to shape and color the book.
Any important Greek word in it is thus more or less saturated or tinctured with Greek thought.

A notable instance of this is the word Logos translated
Word in the opening verses of John's Gospel. This word
was in use in the Greek city of Alexandria as a designation
of divine reason in action or deity expressing itself in
creation, and thus John found it shaped to his use and
applied it to Christ. As a word is the revelation or expression of the mind, so is Christ the Logos or Word or
revelation of God, or God in action.

The word translated "propitiation" in Rom. 3:25, a
critical word in connection with Christ's atoning death,
has recently had fresh light thrown upon it from its use
in Greek worship in which it was applied to a sacrifice
offered to God to appease or satisfy him.

Not only did Greek words, however charged with Chris-

tian meanings, necessarily carry Greek implications into
the teaching of the New Testament, but Greek principles
of theology and philosophy were also incorporated in it.
Paul's letters are especially tinctured and colored with
these foreign ideas more or less derived from pagan cults.
Christianity has a native affinity with any and all truth
and selects and absorbs and assimilates it from any source,
and so as it went out through the world it appropriated
and transformed ideas and customs from Greek thought
and Roman law and pagan religions; and in its march
down through the centuries it has continued this process
to this day. It has an enormous digestive capacity and
has thus grown and enriched itself through its whole history.

Never was this selective and absorbent affinity and process more active than in our age. By this principle our
modern knowledge is being constantly digested by and
assimilated into our religious thought and life. As Paul
said to the Corinthians (1 Cor. 3: 21-22), "For all things
are yours, whether Paul, or Apollos, or Cephas, or the
world, or life, or death, or things present, or things to
come; all are yours," so may we say that all truth is ours,
whether of Copernicus and Newton, or of Milton and
Tennyson, whether of astronomy and geology, or of philosophy and poetry, all are ours to incorporate in our
religious thought and interpretation of the Scriptures.
There is no escaping this psychological necessity of doing
all our thinking in the terms and under the limitations
of the language and ideas and life of our day.

The fact, then, that the New Testament was originally
written in Greek was one of tremendous importance. This
involved it deep and subtle consequences as it abandoned
its own mother speech and domiciled itself in a new tongue,
for every Greek word it used carried with it Greek associations and implications and overtones that entered into
and modified its own meaning. "This change meant at
once a change of race and home; the cradle of the religion
ceased to be its nursery. So it forgot the tongue of its
birthplace and learned the speech of its new mother-
land." We know how deeply a change of language goes
into any one's whole thought and life, and the New Testa-

ment did not and could not escape the consequences of this epochal fact.

The result of this change of base was not the narrowing and impoverishment of Christianity but its enlargement and enrichment. It gave up a meager, provincial and rapidly vanishing tongue for one of the richest, most powerful, most expressive and most beautiful organs of human communication in the world. The New Testament, the most vital, dynamic and creative book ever given to humanity, did not lose but immensely gained in thought and life and power because it spoke to the world and to the ages in the marvelous Greek tongue. And although the New Testament, along with the Old, has been translated into many hundreds of languages and thus is given to most of the peoples of the world in their own speech, and although it stands translation and carries its thought and message over into other languages better than most other books, yet the Greek New Testament remains as the original and standard of the inspired Word of God.

CHAPTER III

THE ROMAN BACKGROUND

Behind and around the New Testament stands a vastly wider background than the Jewish and the Greek worlds, the Roman Empire. This is the majestic frame that hems in Palestine and all its doings as mountains encircle a plain.

1. THE ROMAN GENIUS

The Romans were an Aryan people closely related to the Greeks, the Latin and Greek languages being kindred tongues, but they had a characteristic racial genius that was in marked contrast with that of the Greeks and that of the Jews. The Jews were intuitive and mystical, along with all Semitic peoples, the Greeks were artistic and philosophical, but the Romans were practical and political.

The Romans had immense common sense and always took hold of things at the practical end. They borrowed their arts and philosophy, but they conceived and built their own roads and bridges and buildings and government. While they imported a good deal of Greek art and philosophy, yet these never passed into their blood and circulated in their system, but remained as a thin veneering on their civilization.

Their philosophy was materialistic and tended downward into the flesh. They endured hardship as soldiers in gaining their conquests, and then, feasting on the fruits of their victories, they relapsed into ease and luxury and sensuality. They were as hard-hearted as they were hardheaded, and never was a great people more insensible to human suffering. They were pleasure mad, and "bread and the circus" were the demand of the populace and were the two things that would keep them quiet. The Colos-

seum, whose mournful ruin is the most majestic monument
of the Roman Empire and stands as its most significant
tombstone, typified its life and spirit as it was filled to
overflowing with 80,000 people frenzied with excitement
and shouting over the scenes down in the blood-stained
sand of the arena where thousands of men lost their lives
in mortal combat to make a Roman holiday.

The most prominent feature of Roman genius was administrative ability. The Roman was strong where the
Greek was weak, and weak where the Greek was strong.
The Greek had philosophical acumen, but he lacked execu-
tive ability. He could build a system of metaphysics and
mould marble, but he could not build a political fabric
larger than a city state because he could not join and weld
city states into permanent cohesion.

The Roman lacked philosophical insight and depth of
thought, but he was tremendous in execution. He had a
will to govern and political adhesiveness to cement his
conquests into coherence and stability. Thus, while the
Greek instructed the world as its schoolmaster and charmed
it with his art, only the Roman could impose upon it an
imperial will.

2. The Roman Empire

And so it came to pass that the Roman built the mightiest political structure that had ever been erected on the
earth and that has hardly yet been surpassed or even
equaled in the world. From the Golden Milestone in the
center of his capital city he swept a far-flung circumference
around the western world and shut up within its mighty
rim the motley multitudes of peoples from the Atlantic to
the Euphrates and turned the Mediterranean into a Roman
lake. From one hundred to one hundred and fifty millions
of human beings were housed under this vast roof, a greater
mass of population that had up to that time been gathered
under one government. Within this territory were many
races and peoples speaking many languages which had
hitherto been in a state of chronic mutual warfare and confusion, and Rome reduced all this chaos of tongues and
strife into law and order and hushed it into peace.

With his strong sense of the practical, the Roman built

roads running out from his capital in every direction to
the rim of the empire so solidly constructed that some of
them are in use to this day; and he made trade and travel
by land and sea as safe as they are in our modern world.
The Roman legions marched everywhere with their glittering helmets and flashing spears and golden eagles, and their
mere presence was enough to secure order and quiet.
Roman officials were generally honest, though many of the
petty ones were grafters, and they were efficient and fearless and terribly severe in enforcing law and justice.

The Roman boundary of the empire protected the West
against the Asiatic hordes of the East and against the
barbarians of the North. The world had grown weary and
exhausted with the wars of the closing years of the Re-
public, and welcomed the peace of Augustus Caesar and
his successors, despotic as it was, with a profound sense
of relief and thankfulness. Under the mighty wing of
Rome the world recovered its exhausted energies and began
to build up its agriculture and industries and to grow in
prosperity and wealth. Greek culture also spread under
the same protection and the higher and finer things of life
began to grow and flourish.

For two hundred years after Augustus this peace endured, and to Rome was given the mission of saving the
ancient world from chaos and of holding it together in
peace and preparing the way for the advent and spread
of Christianity.

3. Pagan Religions in the Roman Empire

Paul's opening sentence in his sermon on Mars' Hill,
"Ye men of Athens, in all things I perceive that ye are
very religious," might equally well have been addressed
to the whole ancient world. Man is constitutionally and
incurably religious, and his religious nature is the soil
which over the whole earth from the most primitive times
has sprouted into innumerable religions which have sought
to know and worship the God of heaven.

The Roman world swarmed with gods in countless numbers. The Greek mythological gods, Jupiter and Venus
and their whole company that were supposed to occupy
Mount Olympus and were once sincerely worshipped, by

the time of Christ had become pale specters and myths
that were no longer believed in by thoughtful people and
were generally made the objects of ridicule and jest.

A horde of Asiatic cults, religions that worshipped the
sun and fire and other forms of nature, and mystery religions with their secrets imparted only to their initiates,
all with their priests and rites, had invaded Rome, and
each had its little coterie or larger group of followers.
Many of these cults were immoral in teaching and practice, and one temple of such worship had 6,000 young
women devoted to its impure rites. Most of these religions
were decadent and dying, but some of them were vigorous
and militant with the missionary spirit, and one of them,
Mithraism, was at one time a threatening rival of Christianity that was not overcome and crowded out of the
field until the second century of the Christian era.

All these pagan religions headed up into the worship of
the Roman Emperor, whose very name as an object of
worship struck terror or inspired confidence throughout
the empire. Rome was tolerant of all faiths, but, while
permitting them to exist, compulsorily imposed upon all
its subjects the worship of the Emperor, which was offi-
cially and might be perfunctorily performed by dropping
a little incense on the altar of Caesar in acknowledg-
ment of his divine authority. The object of this worship was not simply the gratification of the Emperor,
but chiefly the binding of the empire into unity and
solidarity.

When this formal act of worship was rendered, the wor-
shipper was free to worship any other god or gods, but
when this act was refused the consequences became grave,
for this was regarded not only as an act of impiety, but
also of treason. It was this Emperor worship that precipitated the fateful break and collision between Christianity and Rome that brought upon the early Christians
the terrible doom of ten dreadful persecutions and that
plays so prominent a part in the lurid pictures of the Book
of Revelation.

Underneath all these pagan faiths was a great hunger
for God and a great deal of sincere piety. By means of
these cults their followers sought to satisfy their religious

needs, especially for guidance and courage and comfort, and these multitudes of souls were seeking after God if haply they might find him; and through these dim faiths some light glimmered into their minds from "the true light which lighteth every man that cometh into the world." However misguided they often were, yet

> There were longings, yearnings, strivings,
> For the good they comprehend not.
> And the feeble hands and helpless
> Groping blindly in the darkness,
> Touched God's right hand in that darkness,
> And were lifted up and strengthened.

4. Roman Contributions to the New Testament

While there was not given to the Roman such a glory as fell upon the Greek, that of contributing to the New Testament his language, yet the Roman contributions to the book are large and important.

Rome furnished the political framework and world background for Christianity. It prepared the world at large and hushed all its clamorous confusion into quiet so that the gospel could be heard. It built the roads and bridges over which it could travel and made the sea safe over which it could sail.

It also furnished ideas that passed into the New Testament. The idea of law that is so fundamental in the gospel, while not a distinctive Roman contribution, was yet greatly deepened and broadened by the background of Roman law. And the vast overshadowing presence and power of the Roman Empire lent its powerful influence and impetus to the ideal of the kingdom of God.

Paul was a Roman citizen as well as a Greek scholar and a Hebrew rabbi, and so these three backgrounds, the Jewish, Greek and Roman, met and blended in him, and something from each of them passed through him into his Epistles. Roman ideas and customs, some of them connected with the pagan religions, by various methods and means percolated into the New Testament and colored its pages in ways which the ordinary reader may little suspect but which the critical scholar can detect. Christianity has not hesitated to adopt and adapt elements from pagan religions, transforming and transfiguring them to its own teaching and spirit and use.

The Book of Revelation especially is set in the framework of the Roman background and is deeply colored by Roman Emperor worship and Roman persecution.

Thus the New Testament is a highly complex book. It has many roots running down into and back through many continents and countries, races and religions, languages and literatures, cities and civilizations. Babylon, Egypt, Palestine, Persia, Greece and Rome, all sent streams into this book. It is composed of and colored with elements, ideas, customs, doctrines, ordinances contributed from every quarter of the world. A providential decree went out that all the world should be taxed for the enrichment of this sacred volume.

These diverse and widely separated human origins and elements do not detract from its divine origin and inspiration, but all the more enhance its value. These were the "sundry times and divers manners" at and in which "God spake in time past unto the fathers by the prophets." The book is therefore the distilled essence of the religious life and experience of many lands and peoples. The most gifted spiritual geniuses, the loftiest souls closest to God and quickest to catch the light of his face, poured their light into these pages. It is because of this highly composite nature, gathering its materials from many sources, that it so completely matches our experiences and meets our needs. It is the sifted sum and supreme summit of the religious literature of the race, and thereby is incomparably the most vital and precious book in the world.

CHAPTER IV

THE FULNESS OF TIME

Why was it that the Saviour of mankind was not brought into the world until so late a period in its history, after so long a delay in which many prophets grew weary of waiting for his coming, and generation after generation passed without ever hearing his voice? Why did he not come in the beginning and get an early start in saving the world? The question must ever surprise and startle us when we come to think of this long delay.

And yet the answer is not far to seek. Preparation must always precede execution, as plowing must go before planting and planting before reaping. Even a great man of genius cannot be brought into the world until all things are ready for him. It would have been of no use to bring Sir Isaac Newton into the world in the 17th century B. C.; he would then have died unknown without any worthy accomplishment; the soil was not ready for the peculiar seed of his brain. And so his coming was delayed until the 17th century A. D. when all things were ready for him.

In a still greater degree the world had to be got ready for the coming of Christ. God did not drop this precious "corn of wheat" into the ground until the soil was prepared for it and its summer was near.

The various backgrounds we have been sketching were so many converging paths of preparation for the coming of Christ and the writing of the New Testament. The Jewish people were endowed with religious genius and disciplined through their varied history and experiences to receive the Messiah. They were drilled in the great doctrines of the one true and living, sovereign and righteous God; of sin and sacrifice, penitence and faith; of the spirituality of religion and of increasing revelation through the prophets.

35

From Babylon through Egypt and Palestine and down into exile and back to Jerusalem they were traveling towards the advent of their Messiah; and however blindly and perversely they missed seeing him in his true light when he came, they did prepare the way for his coming and his mission and kingdom.

At the same time a parallel process of preparation was going on out in the universal Gentile world. Greek genius was developing its thought for the enrichment of Christian doctrines and was fashioning and finishing its flexible and facile language for the New Testament. Rome was also suppressing disorder in the world and binding it into unity and quieting it into the stillness of a vast amphitheatre in which the gospel could make its voice heard. It was building roads and casting up highways along which the gospel could travel and sweeping the sea of pirates and making it safe. It was enforcing principles of law and maintaining a universal empire that were powerful reënforcements to the kingdom of God.

And all pagan religions, while they were pathetic and often sincere efforts to feel after God if haply their groping fingers might touch his hand in the darkness, yet had proved the utter impotence of unaided man to save himself by all the altars he could build and all the sacrifices he could offer and all the tears he could shed. It would seem that God left the world largely to itself for so long a time to show it and bring home to the very bosom and heart of men that only his truth and grace could redeem the world from sin and restore it to his fellowship.

At this crisis all the stars of pagan faith were fast fading into a night of black despair. The Roman Empire, while it suppressed disorder, was yet a terrible burden of despotism and cruelty on the world. Slavery cast its deep pall over its vast domain, and the rich were exploiting the poor without mercy. Never was the human heart more cruel and hopeless. The world was really sick at heart and seemed to be reeling to its doom.

> On that hard pagan world disgust
>   And secret loathing fell.
> Deep weariness and sated lust
>   Made human life a hell.

And yet at this time the world stood expectant. Strange rumors were abroad of a coming Saviour, in the Gentile as well as in the Jewish world, and in many souls were deep forebodings of his advent. The universal human heart was weary of the burden of sin and was receptive of some more sure word of prophecy.

At this critical juncture the angels announced to Judean shepherds the birth of the Babe of Bethlehem. Hebrew and Greek and Roman had done their work of preparation, and the great hour struck. God did not wait a day too long to bring his Son into the world, but ushered him in at just the right moment. The world stage was set, and the calendar of the centuries marked the exact hour. The divine philosophy of history is that "when the fulness of the time was come, God sent forth his Son."

It is in the light of this grand background only that we can understand the New Testament, and we are now ready to examine its books.

PART II
THE BOOKS OF THE NEW TESTAMENT

CHAPTER I

INTRODUCTION

Christianity, being an historical religion, early committed itself to writing and embodied itself in books that are still its foundation and fountain. The Bible, consisting of the Old and the New Testaments, is at once its history and charter and constitution.

The New Testament contains twenty-seven books as follows: the four Gospels, the Acts of the Apostles, thirteen Epistles of Paul, Hebrews, James, two Epistles of Peter, three Epistles of John, Jude, and Revelation. These are only a selection out of a much larger body of literature which arose in connection with the beginnings of Christianity, but which, with the exception of the New Testament books, has perished. Luke in the preface to his Gospel refers to some of these writings which he had in hand, and many books of later date, such as the apocryphal gospels, have survived; but the books forming our New Testament were the only ones which were selected to constitute the Canon.

It is an important fact that the New Testament did not create Christianity, but Christianity created the New Testament. These books are only the record of things said and done, and are the consequence and not the cause of the history they relate. They are bits of literature floating on the stream of early Christianity that issued out of the ministry and especially out of the resurrection of Christ, and they no more created this stream than all the books written about Niagara have created that river and its cataract, or than any history creates the facts it records.

Christianity began before there was any single book about it; and it would have gone on had no book about it ever been written. Of course without the aid of the New

Testament, Christianity would not have come down to us
in the same certainty and clearness, volume and power,
but its living tradition would have carried it far down the
stream of time; just as the British Empire has no written
constitution, but it does have a deep and powerful stream
of national tradition and life that carries it through the
centuries.

It startles us even yet to recall the fact that there was
no book or line of the New Testament in existence during
all the earliest years of Christianity. Although Jesus is
the central fact and figure in the New Testament and it
is all written about him, yet he wrote not a word of it and
had no Bible but the Old Testament. We have no record
of his writing anything except a few words in the dust
which some passing foot or breeze quickly obliterated. He
seemed to be quite careless about his words, tossing them
out upon the air and letting others catch them up and put
them on record.

Peter on the day of Pentecost did not have a page or
word of the New Testament but chose his text from an Old
Testament prophet.

The apostles all went forth preaching the gospel without
any one of the four Gospels in their hands or possibly without any written record at all. They simply told the story
of the life and teaching and resurrection of Jesus from
memory, speaking as eyewitnesses and declaring "That
which was from the beginning, which we have heard, which
we have seen with our eyes, which we have looked upon, and
our hands have handled, of the Word of life" (I John
1:1). Paul never quotes or alludes to any one of our Gospels or any New Testament book because no one of them
was in existence until near the end of his ministry. These
first Christians and preachers had the gospel in their
minds and hearts and were themselves living gospels, and
the living truth was at first the only form of the truth.

Yet the New Testament now contains the teachings and
life and work of Christ and the early history of the gospel, and these are the foundation on which Christianity
rests and the fountain out of which it flows, and these
books bring the gospel to us in its original form in which
it is still fresh and vital with its original life. The New

Testament is our most fruitful and powerful means of grace and blessing and is therefore incomparably the most important book in our hands. More than any other book its words are spirit and life.

It surprises many readers of the New Testament to discover that the order in which its books are now arranged was not the order in which they were written. It is commonly thought that Matthew's Gospel was written first, and so on in the present order until Revelation, which was written last.

But this was not at all the order in which these books were produced. It is obvious that some of Paul's Epistles were written before any of the Gospels, because he was converted and began his missionary work a few years after the resurrection and ascension of Christ, before any of the Gospels had appeared.

Scholars are not agreed as to the order in which these books were produced, but they generally agree that either Paul's Epistle to the Galatians or his First Epistle to the Thessalonians was the first New Testament book to be written. But various orders of arrangement were in use in the second and third Christian centuries, and it was not until the fourth century that the Canon was finally settled and the present order became fixed.

There is a great justification for the present arrangement of these books in that they follow the general historical order. The Gospels necesarily come first in the order of their events and then the Acts and then the Epistles, because this follows the order of their chronology. It is confusing to the ordinary reader or student to break this arrangement up and adopt another, and therefore we shall follow this natural and familiar order in our study of these books.

CHAPTER II

GENERAL CHARACTERISTICS OF THE GOSPELS

The Four Gospels are the root of the New Testament, the fountain of its essential facts and faith, and all the other books are the expansion and fruitage of this root, the broadening stream of this fountain. We begin their study by considering some of their general characteristics.

1. THE HISTORICITY OF THE GOSPELS

The question of the historical trustworthiness of the Gospels confronts us at the threshold of our study. The final decision of this question logically comes after we have gone through them and critically examined them; but we can take a preliminary general look at them and get a broad impression of their truthfulness.

The question is, Are these books late productions, written long after the events they record and evidently the outgrowth of tradition and legend? If so, their historical value is greatly reduced.

But they are not late books. There is good ground for believing, as we shall see, that Mark, the earliest Gospel, was written within twenty-five or thirty years after the death of Christ, and still earlier writings derived from eyewitnesses were in existence, as is seen by Luke's preface to his Gospel. This date is close enough to the events to give us a trustworthy history of them and too close for the growth of legend and myth.

But at present we are concerned chiefly with the general impression these Gospels make upon us; for we can judge much as to the consistency and reality and trustworthiness of a narrative from the mere reading of it.

Let the student read one of them through, say the Gospel of Mark, which can be read at a single sitting.

How does it impress us? As sober history keeping down on the ground of reality. The writers of these Gospels impress us as having competent knowledge of the facts, either as eyewitnesses or as investigators who were close to the facts, and as being men of honesty and sound judgment, insight and sincerity, who had no other motive or purpose than to tell us the simple truth. Seldom do we read writers that are so free from subjective influences and so transparent in their truthfulness. While no one of them was a learned scholar and one was a tax collector and another was a fisherman, yet they were men of sanity and sound sense who were fully competent to judge and record plain matters of fact.

These narratives have all the telltale self-evidencing marks of reality. They give details of persons and places and dates, events and incidents, in their due order and connection. None of the stuff of invention and imagination, legend and myth, is woven into their web. The things that would almost certainly have been pushed into prominence in an invented story are conspicuous by their absence. Facts are recorded which would have been carefully glossed over or suppressed in a partisan account or fictitious narrative. The most damaging facts, such as that the disciples at first disbelieved and ridiculed the reports of the resurrection of Jesus as an idle tale, are boldly written down on their pages.

The outstanding feature of these narratives is that they have none of the inescapable marks of vision and ecstasy, invention and legend, which are careless of order and system, causes and consequences, and unmindful and unconscious of contradictions and impossibilities as they weave all sorts of incongruities and absurdities into the subjective fabric of desire. These writers and witnesses do not lose touch with the earth and take to the wings of fancy; on the contrary, due allowance being made for the supernatural events they are relating, they keep close to sober reality and concrete details, follow the necessary connection of things, and observe the order and unity and harmony of normal human experience and historic fact. We are familiar with the glowing pictures that are produced when imagination works with palette and brush.

Such artistry is absent from these narratives. In a word, the Gospels have all the simplicity and artlessness of un- affected truth, and these inimitable signs of veracity are so many seals authenticating their trustworthiness.

Another general impression may be derived from the life of Jesus as depicted in the Gospels. The portrait of his life and ministry and character is there as an existing fact. How did it get there? It must be accounted for. We must suppose either that it is a transcript of a reality, or else that in some way it was an invention of later days.

But who could have invented such a portrait, so life- like and wonderful, composed of such various features, some of which, such as the contrasted virtues of meekness and manliness, justice and love, are difficult of consistent composition, and yet are combined and blended into perfect proportion and harmony? Where was the genius that could create out of imagination or weave out of tradition and myth a portrait of such remarkable verisimilitude and appealing beauty and compelling power which for near two thousand years has put a spell upon the world as a reality? It is easier to believe that the picture of Christ is in the Gospels only because these writers, humble un- lettered men devoid of literary training and art, simply painted the portrait from life and told what they saw.

On the general historicity of the Gospels we here give one of the latest and most authoritative deliverances of critical scholarship. The Rev. Arthur C. Headlam, D.D., now Bishop of Gloucester, but formerly Regius Professor of Divinity in the University of Oxford, in his recent *Life and Teaching of Jesus the Christ,* sums up the results of his long study of the Gospels as follows: "I have aimed, in the first place, at showing that, accepting the results of modern criticism, there is every reason to think that the subject-matter of the first three Gospels represents the traditions about the life and work of Jesus of Nazareth as they were current in the earliest years of the Christian church. Then, secondly, that it harmonizes with all that we know of the times when Jesus lived and the environment in which he taught. Thirdly, that the teaching of Jesus is harmonious throughout, natural in its language and form to the circumstances and representing a unity of thought transcending anything that had existed before. And then, fourthly, that the life as narrated forms a consistent whole. The result of these investigations is to satisfy myself, at any rate, that we have a trustworthy account of the life and teaching of Jesus.''

From this preliminary view we may accept these Gospels as trustworthy historical documents, but this conclusion will be strengthened as we proceed with our study.

2. The Interrelations of the Gospel

The problem of the interrelations of the Four Gospels is one of great interest and importance.

In order to compare the Gospels, it is best to study them as they are arranged in parallel columns in a harmony, such as Stevens and Burton's *Harmony of the Gospels*, which will be used and referred to in this connection.

We soon discover that the Gospel of John stands apart from the first three Gospels in that there is missing in John's column much that is present in the others, while there are many passages and sections, and even whole pages that are peculiar to John. Evidently the Fourth Gospel covers a special field and has a special object in view in its narrative of the life of Christ.

Examination soon discloses the fact that John deals more in interpretation of the words of Jesus and is especially interested in his inner life as compared with the other Gospels. The first three Gospels keep to plain matters of fact, while the Fourth breathes a mystical spirit in tone and temper. John takes us more closely into the inner thought of Jesus and his confidential relations with the disciples. The Fourth Gospel is also of much later date than the others. For these reasons this Gospel may be set aside for the present, and we proceed with the special interrelations of Matthew, Mark and Luke.

These three Gospels give an outline or synopsis of the life of Jesus, and are therefore called the Synoptic Gospels or the Synoptics. How are they related? Did Matthew in writing his Gospel have Mark's or Luke's Gospel, and did Mark have Matthew or Luke, and did Luke have Matthew or Mark? Did each one write entirely independently of the others, or did each have one or both of the others?

This question was for a long time an unsolved problem, and all possible combinations and solutions have been tried out. Yet the key to the problem, which has been discovered only in modern times, is simple enough when we once see it.

A study of the *Harmony* will disclose the secret. It will be observed that Matthew begins his Gospel with the genealogy of Jesus, and proceeds to give the annunciation to Joseph, the birth of Jesus, the visit of the wise men, the flight into Egypt and the return to Nazareth.

Luke has a different order and only at three points does he touch Matthew's order as they are arranged in parallel columns. Luke begins with his preface and proceeds to give the promise of the birth of John the Baptist, the annunciation to Mary, Mary's visit to Elizabeth, the birth of John the Baptist, the birth of Jesus with the accompaniments of the angels and the shepherds, the circumcision of Jesus and his presentation in the temple, and the childhood and youth of Jesus at Nazareth.

The only three points at which they touch and run parallel in the same events are the genealogies, which are yet different in the two, the birth of Jesus at Bethlehem, and the childhood at Nazareth. The two narratives are not at all contradictory, but it is plain that each follows its own order and selects its own events, and the three parallel columns coincide in only three brief widely-separated sections.

But as soon as we arrive at the opening of Mark's Gospel the three columns appear and run side by side in general continuity until we reach the end of Mark, when Matthew and Luke again part company and each follows his own order and tells his own story to the end.

What is the evident explanation of this remarkable fact? It is just this that Matthew and Luke had Mark in hand in writing their Gospels and followed his order and used his materials. We may accept with confidence the conclusion that Mark was the first Gospel written and that Matthew and Luke wrote later and used Mark.

This conclusion is strengthened by a closer examination of the parallel columns in the *Harmony*. Two thirds of Mark's Gospel is reproduced in both Matthew and Luke, and of the remaining one third, all but 30 verses is found in either Matthew or Luke. All of Mark except 55 verses is found in Matthew, and all except 129 verses is found in Luke, and 74 of these are found in one passage, 6 : 45—8 : 26. The only explanation of these facts is that Matthew and Luke had Mark and utilized his material.

There is also a considerable body of material common to Matthew and Luke which is not found in Mark. Some of these passages are specially important and include the preaching of John the Baptist (Matt. 3 : 7-12; Luke 3 : 7-9); the temptation of Jesus (Matt. 4 : 3-10; Luke 4 : 3-13); and the Sermon on the Mount (Matt. 5-7; Luke 6). About fifty of these passages that are common to Matthew and Luke but are not found in Mark have been noted.

The probable explanation of this fact is that Matthew and Luke also used some other common document besides Mark. This unknown common source is called by scholars Q, being the contraction of the German *Quelle,* meaning source. It is true that this common material may have been drawn by Matthew and Luke from more than one source, and the problem at this point begins to grow complex and uncertain. As we know from Luke's preface that other writings or gospels were in existence which he used, it is not surprising that Matthew and Luke had one or more such common sources.

Attempts have been made by piecing together the passages that constitute Q to reconstruct this document, but with small success, as the passages are evidently fragmentary. An examination of these passages, however, makes it appear that this source was mainly composed of the sayings and sermons of Jesus.

We may then conclude that Mark's Gospel was written first, and that Matthew and Luke used his Gospel in writing theirs and that they also used one or more other common sources.

Another question at this point is, Did Matthew have Luke, or Luke have Matthew? The evidence on this point strongly indicates that these two Gospels are independent of each other, the writer of each having no knowledge of the other.

3. CAN THE GOSPELS BE HARMONIZED

As we look at the Gospels arranged in the *Harmony*
the question forces itself upon us, Can they be harmonized?
The question assumes two forms.

First, what is the meaning of these gaps in the columns
where the several narratives do not coincide and one has
matter which one or more of the others omit? How does
it come that only Matthew and Luke have the genealogies
and the virgin birth of Jesus, that only Luke has the account of the angels and shepherds, and that only Matthew
has the visit of the wise men and the flight into Egypt in
connection with his birth, and so on to the end? How can
it be that Mark says nothing of the birth and early years
of Jesus and starts right off with his public appearance
and ministry? Why is it that so important a matter as
the Sermon on the Mount is entirely absent in Mark and
John, and that many parables and miracles are found in
one and not in another Gospel? How did it happen that
Luke has a long section extending through nearly eight
chapters (11-18 : 8) that no other evangelist records? And
especially how can we account for the fact that John so
seldom has material in common with the three synoptics
and that so much of his narrative, including some of the
most important and precious portions of the Gospel, such
as John 14-17, is peculiar to himself? These facts look
surprising if not startling.

And yet the explanation is not difficult. This explanation is that each evangelist had access to different sources
or had a larger body of material than he used, and he
selected and incorporated in his Gospel such portions as
suited his point of view and purpose. No one of these
writers was attempting a full biography of Jesus in the
modern sense, but each one was giving an impressionistic
account with a particular end in view, which will appear
later in this study. It is not strange, then, but quite in
accordance with their purpose and with literary art that
these writers should produce narratives of the same life
that coincide only in sections and at points.

We see the same fact in books of biography and history
written today. No two biographers or historians of the
same personage or period will follow the same outline and

give the same facts. Open two or four or a dozen Lives of Lincoln and the same apparent lack of continuity and identity in the narratives is conspicuous; and if they were arranged in a harmony in parallel columns they would show gaps and difficulties as great as or greater than, what we find in the Gospels. Yet the many Lives of Lincoln do combine into one consistent picture of the man that is fuller and richer than any Life by one author can be.

So these four brief Lives of Jesus, each of which is incomplete and fragmentary and gives only glimpses of him from a special point of view, do fit together and complement one another so as to give a composite but consistent and lifelike portrait of the one Person who is the common subject of them all. And the portrait is all the richer because it is composite.

A second question relates to the harmony of the Gospels in so far as they do run parallel. Seldom is the parallel so close as to be a coincidence, but there are thousands of verbal variations, even when the evangelists are reporting the words of Jesus. Such verbal variations, however, are of small importance and do not affect the validity of the narrative.

More important are variations that seem to involve inaccurate and inconsistent statements. Reference has been made to the 275 quotations from the Old Testament in the New, but rarely are these quotations verbally exact and are often only loose paraphrases and accommodations of the originals. Mark begins his Gospel with a quotation which is stated to be from Isaiah, yet the first part of it is from Malachi and only the second part of it is from Isaiah. But, to say nothing of the mistakes of copyists, the explanation of such facts is that the common usage did not require ancient writers to be exact in their quotations as it does with us, and the evangelists simply conformed to the literary rules of their day.

Other variations may be magnified into more serious differences. The different evangelists often locate the same events and teachings at different times and places, or they state them differently. The Sermon on the Mount is located differently by Matthew and by Luke, but possibly Jesus repeated the substance of it on different occasions.

The Lord's Prayer is given in a longer and a shorter form, but the same explanation may apply to this.

Matthew says that two blind men appealed to Jesus as he was going out of Jericho, but Mark and Luke mention only one, and Luke says the incident occurred as Jesus was drawing nigh to the place. But there is little difficulty in such a case, for if there were two blind men, then there was one. Such differences do not disturb us in other books.

One of the most serious of these variations relates to the accounts of the resurrection of Christ. Much has been made of different statements in the narratives of this event as though they amounted to irreconcilable contradictions. Mark mentions three women as going to the tomb on the morning of the resurrection, Matthew mentions two, and John mentions only one. But again we may say that if there were three, then there certainly were two and also one. All the evangelists give an account of the appearances of Jesus at Jerusalem, but it is said that only Matthew and John know of his appearances in Galilee. Yet these differences are harmonized if he appeared in both places.

One gets the impression, when these differences are fairly considered, that they have been overstrained in order to magnify them into contradictions. Again we must emphasize the fact that the evangelists were not composing a systematic and complete history of these events, and are not even trying to arrange and set forth the facts so as to prove them, but are only giving personal experiences and impressions from their different points of view. And hence we have only disconnected incidents and fragments of the entire story, and it is not surprising that we cannot put these broken pieces together so as to make them fit around the ragged edges when other parts are missing that might complete and harmonize the whole.

These differences also are generally such as should be found in independent accounts. If all these writers related the story in precisely the same way, this would throw suspicion on them all as having been in collusion or as simply copying one another. No two men will tell their experience of an event in just the same words. While they relate substantially the same story, yet they will differ in their points of view and shading and emphasis, one relating one incident that another omits, or setting it in a different light.

These individualistic variations in the Gospels are strong indications of truthfulness. It is mostly such differences that exist in these narratives. It is not at all strange that the evangelists that were eyewitnesses of the risen Christ had each one more vivid recollections of some of the happenings of that wonderful day, surcharged with the excitement of unexpected and unbelievable events, than of others and that some of them have emphasized the appearances at Jerusalem and others those in Galilee. They may differ widely and even seriously at such points, and yet all be telling the truth, which fuller light would make plain to us. There is such substantial agreement among them that we feel sure of their testimony to the essential facts. Such agreement satisfies us in historical matters.

Let it be admitted that there are variations and discrepancies in the Gospels, some of which have not yet been reconciled, yet these are unimportant in comparison with their general agreement and do not impair the substantial truth and value of their testimony.

Our conclusion then is that the Four Gospels stand the light of examination and are shown to be trustworthy historical documents. They have been under the fiercest test of criticism for centuries and have held their place in the field of scholarship and in the faith of the Christian world. Scholars are not unanimous in their views in all these points, and there are yet unexplained remainders to be cleared up in New Testament criticism, but we have solid ground on which to hold that these Gospels are not cunningly devised fables but are an honest record of things that were not done in a corner and are not afraid of the light of day.

4. THE DATES OF THE GOSPELS

The three synoptic Gospels are so interrelated and linked together, as we have seen, that their dates become a common problem, while the date of the Fourth Gospel, being much later, can be set aside until we come to its particular study. If we can fix the date of one of the synoptics we can draw some conclusions as to the dates of the others.

A base line at this point is the date of the Acts of the Apostles. The author of this book is Luke, the traveling companion of Paul, who appears in the narrative at chapter 16:10 where he includes himself with Paul under the designation "we." The Acts from this point on is practically the biography of Paul by Luke, and Luke closes it with Paul under arrest in Rome waiting for his trial, which probably did not occur until after his release and further work as a missionary and his second arrest and final trial and execution.

The inference is therefore direct and strong that Luke wrote the Acts before the final trial and death of Paul; for if he completed his biography of Paul after this event he would certainly have given an account of it. We cannot think of a biographer of Lincoln, writing after his death, concluding his book without a reference to this tragical event.

Paul was executed in Rome under Nero, who died in 68 A. D., and the death of Paul has been placed at 64 and the date of the Acts at or near 62. But Luke wrote his Gospel before he wrote the Acts, as we learn from his preface to the Acts, and its date must be placed near 60. Mark's Gospel is still earlier than Luke's, as we have seen, and therefore, its date falls between 55 and 60. This line of reasoning and these dates have behind them the weighty authority of Harnack and many other scholars.

This date of Mark is supported by the contents of the Gospel, especially by the fact that it was clearly written before the destruction of Jerusalem by the Romans in 70, as it contains no reference to that cataclysmic event except Christ's prophetic prediction of it. The date of Matthew comes after Mark, but cannot be so clearly fixed. It was probably written in its original form before or near the destruction of Jerusalem and may have undergone some later editing.

We may then date the synoptic Gospels at from 55 to 70 A. D., and this takes them back of the region of legend and myth into trustworthy historical connection with their contents and with eyewitnesses.

5. Why Four Gospels

The question arises how there came to be just four Gospels. Fanciful reasons for this fact were given in early times, such as that they correspond with the four seasons or the four winds of heaven, and so on. There is, however, nothing mysterious or even remarkable in the fact. Every great man has many biographies written of him, and the same historical and literary instinct prompted "many to set forth a declaration of those things" which were surely believed among the first Christians, as Luke says in his preface to his Gospel. Our Four Gospels, then, are a selection from a much larger number which have been lost. It is not impossible that one or more of these lost Gospels may yet be found.

It is a fortunate event that we have these Four Gospels, for we thus have as many separate portraits of our Lord that complement and complete one another. The absence of any one of these would be an enormous loss and impoverishment to our knowledge of Jesus, and it takes all of them fused into unity to give us anything like a full and rich and adequate appreciation and apprehension of him. For these evangelists did not simply reproduce or copy one another, but each one wrote from his own point of view out of his personal experience and for his own purpose. They thus give us so many supplementary views and interpretations of the same Person. They pass the manifold contents and colors of the life and ministry of Jesus through the prisms of their peculiar minds and give us combined a more glorious spectrum of his person and character; or their superimposed pictures combine and blend into a composite portrait that is fuller and richer.

Each evangelist wrote for his own audience and with his own object in view, as will appear later. Matthew wrote more especially for the Jewish converts to convince them that Jesus is the Messiah of the old Testament. Mark wrote in Rome under the direction of Peter to present Jesus to the Gentiles as a mighty worker and Saviour: Luke wrote primarily to convince a Roman friend of the certainty of the things of the Gospel, but being a physician and scholar and a Greek, he addressed a wider audience. John wrote for the church to give an interpretative portrait of Christ as the Word who abides in mystical union with believers.

These four points of view are distinct yet are complementary, and no one of them could be missed without marring the composite picture in a serious degree: fused together they present that wonderful Life that is the praise of the ages and has put its spell on all these Christian generations.

The Christian centuries and world have been largely guided and shaped and inspired by these four brief pamphlets, any one of which can be read through at a sitting. But brief as they are, they are charged with infinitely precious significance. Many a classic of Greek and Roman literature has been lost and buried in the dust of the ages, but these four little writings have come down through all the vicissitudes of the centuries that have convulsed continents and wrecked empires unscathed and are as fresh and vital as ever. There is something in them that the world will not let die. When the early Christians connected these Four Gospels with cosmic agents such as the seasons and the winds they were guided by a true instinct, for they are human in form yet superhuman in contents and are the power of God unto salvation.

6. MIRACLES IN THE GOSPELS

There are accounts of miracles incorporated in all the Four Gospels and it may be well to dispose of the question of their reality in this place.

A miracle may be defined as an event in the physical world not explainable by known natural laws or human agency, wrought for a worthy religious object, and therefore to be attributed to the special act of God to authenticate his redemptive presence and work among men.

That there are such signs recorded in the Bible is plain enough, but they are not nearly so plentiful as is commonly supposed. Many appear to think that the Bible is full of miracles and that they just dripped from the fingers of Jesus. But they are comparatively few and scarce in the Bible, and only about thirty are attributed to Jesus and about one third of these are instances of healing, some of which may not have been strictly miraculous but within the bounds of natural agencies. Not every "wonder" or "sign" was a miracle, and it is not always easy to draw the line between where the natural leaves off and the supernatural begins.

Jesus was possessed of extraordinary powers of personality and did not ordinarily draw upon his supernatural power to accomplish his purposes, but kept well within his human limitations, as is illustrated in his temptations in the wilderness. He used miracles charily and kept them in the background and refused to permit them to be exploited as mere wonders. Yet that, according to the Gospels, he did work miracles in the supernatural sense is a plain matter of record.

These miracles were never spectacular or absurd and silly performances, such as the alleged miracles attributed to Jesus in the apocryphal gospels, but they were sober and sane, keeping close to the ground of nature and were fitting and worthy works of the Son of God. His miracles were always proper manifestations of his divine personality and power and were wrought as illustrations and activities of his redemptive presence and purpose. That they did authenticate his divine person and mission was only an incidental object and result. They were integral parts of his message and mission and are not to be separated from them.

The miracles of Christ must not be dissociated from this framework and background of worthy purpose. A mere wonder, however supernatural it might seem, that was unrelated to any such worthy end, would be difficult if not impossible of proof; but the miracles of our Lord fit into his divine character and mission and are consonant therewith. Any historical event is rational and capable of proof very much in proportion to its congruity with its environment in time and place and purpose, and in the light of this principle the miracles of Jesus are appropriate to him as leaves to a tree or as light to the sun, and therefore they present themselves to us as rational events capable of proof, and this proof is the main question to be considered.

The writers of the Gospels do not show any conscious anxiety or intention to prove the miracles of Jesus by

direct evidence and argument with one outstanding
exception: the resurrection of our Lord. This is pushed
out into the light of publicity and supported by many
witnesses and much evidence and direct argument and is
thus attested "by many infallible proofs" (Acts 1:3).
The evangelists all narrate it with fulness and particularly, and Paul expressly argues it and stakes the whole
Gospel upon it (1 Cor. 15:1-20). This miracle stands as
the central pillar and support of the supernatural in the
New Testament, and as long as it stands the other miracles
will stand with it. He who could raise himself from the
dead could also with perfect mastery and ease heal the
sick and still the stormy sea. The detailed examination
of this epochal event in the life of Christ will come up
later in our study, and it is here adduced as a central
support and proof of the miraculous element in the
Gospels.

While specific proof is not given for other miracles in
the Gospels, yet many of them are so interwoven with the
entire web of the account that they could not be dissected
out without dismembering and destroying the whole narrative. If any such conversation as is recorded in John 9
with reference to the restored blind man took place, then
the miracle of opening his eyes must also be historical.

The relation of miracle to natural law calls for a word.
A miracle is not a violation of natural law but only the
intervention of a higher power to turn natural law to its
own purpose. The human will is constantly interposing
its presence and purpose in the world of natural law and
thereby effecting results that nature itself would never
accomplish. One cannot close a window or lift his hand
without doing something that is strictly supernatural; and
what man can do in his finite degree and way, God and
God in Christ can do in his perfect way.

Perhaps the chief difficulty the modern mind feels in
connection with miracles is that nature is viewed as a
closed and rigid system of mechanical action which must
proceed in its determined operations and cannot be interrupted at any special point in any special way.

But philosophy views nature, not as a closed and complete world in itself, but as a part of a larger spiritual

system or living organism in which God is immanent, or as the mode of the divine activity, and then physical laws are habits of the divine will and are still subject to special divine purposes. On this view, miracles are such special acts and fall within the sweep of wider laws and higher ends. In such a world the miracle of the resurrection of Christ violated no law but fulfilled a high spiritual end and was a supremely rational event. As all physical laws continue in their operation while we turn them to our use and ends, so the miracles of Christ did not violate or arrest any natural laws but only caused them to move in the larger orbit of his plan and purpose as the revelation of God and the Saviour of the world.

7. THE CHRONOLOGY AND OUTLINE OF EVENTS OF THE LIFE OF JESUS

Before examining the Gospels it may be well to fix their general chronology and the outline of events in the life of Jesus.

(1) Chronology. It was not until the sixth century, A. D., that the birth of Jesus was adopted as the initial date of our calendar, and therefore it is not surprising that this event was placed four years too late. Jesus was born under Herod the Great and he died in 4 B. C., and therefore Jesus must have been born in or before this year, which is the commonly accepted year of his birth.

As Jesus began to teach at the age of thirty (Luke 3 : 23), he entered upon his ministry in 26 A. D. The duration of his ministry depends on how many Passover feasts he attended, and this depends on whether the unnamed feast of John 5 : 1 was a Passover. The view is generally accepted that it was a Passover, making four he attended (John 2 : 13; 5 : 1; 6 : 4; 12 : 1), and this would make his ministry extend to three years and the ascension would fall in the spring of 29 A. D. There are elements of uncertainty in these dates, but they are approximately correct.

(2) Outline of Events in the Life of Jesus. The life of Jesus falls into two main parts, the thirty silent years, and the three years of the public ministry.

Of the three years of the public ministry, the first was

60 THE MAKING AND MEANING

spent chiefly in Judea and has been designated by Dr. James Stalker the year of obscurity; the second was spent in Galilee and was the year of growing popularity; the third was spent chiefly in Perea and Judea and was the year of increasing opposition. These years are not to be taken strictly as one year each, as the early Judean ministry was probably less than a year, and the Galilean ministry extended to considerably more than a year, but the three periods into which the public ministry falls may be approximately designated as years.

The chief events of the life of Jesus may be arranged in the following outline, which is the framework into which we shall fit the contents of each Gospel. We cannot always be sure of the chronological order, but this general arrangement cannot be far from the facts and will serve our practical purpose.

PART I
THE THIRTY SILENT YEARS
B. C. 4—A. D. 26

1. The genealogies.
2. The annunciations of the births of John the Baptist and of Jesus.
3. The birth at Bethlehem.
4. Angels, shepherds and Wise Men.
5. The quiet years at Nazareth.

PART II
THE PUBLIC MINISTRY
B. C. 26—A. D. 29

FIRST YEAR
Early Judean Ministry: Year of Obscurity
1. The ministry of John the Baptist.
2. The baptism of Jesus.
3. The temptation.
4. First disciples of Jesus.
5. First miracle.
6. First cleansing of the Temple.
7. Discourse with Nicodemus.
8. The coöperation of Jesus with John.
9. Departure from Judea.
10. Discourse with the Woman of Samaria.

SECOND YEAR
Galilean Ministry: Year of Popularity
1. First rejection at Nazareth and removal to Capernaum.

2. Itinerant preaching in Galilee.
3. Calling the Twelve and the Sermon on the Mount.
4. Many miracles.
5. John the Baptist's last message.
6. Many parables.
7. Second rejection at Nazareth.
8. The feeding of the five thousand.
9. Break with the Pharisees on eating.
10. Renewed controversy with the Pharisees.
11. Retirement to the north: Peter's confession.
12. The transfiguration.
13. Discourse on humility.

THIRD YEAR

Later Judean Ministry: Year of Opposition

1. Arrival in Judea.
2. The mission of the seventy.
3. Jesus foretells his death.
4. Incidents on the way to Jerusalem.
5. Anointing of Jesus by Mary in Bethany.
6. Triumphal entry into Jerusalem.
7. Second cleansing of the Temple.
8. Questions and controversies.
9. Discourse concerning the destruction of Jerusalem.
10. The conspiracy between the priests and Judas.
11. The Last Supper.
12. Christ's farewell discourses.
13. Gethsemane.
14. Betrayal and arrest.
15. The trial.
16. The crucifixion.
17. The burial.
18. The resurrection.
19. The appearances and ascension.

CHAPTER III

THE FOUR GOSPELS

We now proceed to an examination of each of the Four Gospels.

1. THE GOSPEL ACCORDING TO MATTHEW

(1) Authorship. The title, "The Gospel According to Matthew," does not necessarily mean the Gospel by Matthew or written by him, but the gospel story as he reported it. There is evidence that Matthew's report of the gospel was an earlier writing than our Matthew. Papias, Bishop of Hierapolis early in the second century, is quoted by Eusebius, a church historian of the third century, as follows: "Matthew, in the Hebrew dialect, compiled the Logia, and each one interpreted them according to his ability." "Logia" means words or speeches, and this early book by Matthew, consisting of the sayings and sermons of Jesus, was written in Hebrew or Aramaic, and was then translated and used together with Mark's Gospel by the author or editor of our Matthew.

This view is borne out by the fact that 411 verses, or two-fifths, of Matthew consist of the reported words of our Lord. There is then back of our Matthew an earlier Matthew, but the name of the apostle rightly stands in connection with our Gospel as being "The Gospel According to Matthew."

As Matthew was a tax collector (Matt. 9:9), he was used to gathering facts and statistics and to reducing them to tabular form and writing, and this was literary training that fitted him for collecting materials for and composing his Gospel. It is thought by some scholars that he shows a fondness for numerical combinations, such as groups of three, five, seven or ten incidents or topics, and this may have grown out of his habit of tabulating matters in his tax reports. His business methods would unconsciously creep into his writing.

No information is available as to his place of residence at the time of writing the Gospel, or of his career and death as an apostle. Eusebius says of him: "For Matthew, after preaching to Hebrews, when about to go also to others, committed to writing in his native tongue the Gospel that bears his name; and so by his writing supplied, to those whom he was leaving, the loss of his presence."

(2) Characteristics. Matthew's point of view and purpose is plain: he is writing to the Jews to show that Jesus is the Messiah of the Old Testament. This purpose begins with the genealogy and continues through the visit of the Magi and runs through the whole teaching that the gospel fulfills and expands the law of Moses, down to the form of the inscription on the cross and the great commission (Matt. 28 : 18-20) as carrying out the Messianic predictions of the prophets. "Think not that I am come to destroy the law, or the prophets: I am not come to destroy, but to fulfill" (5 : 17) is a principle in the teaching of Jesus that Matthew never lets his readers forget.

Matthew quotes the Old Testament more frequently than any other evangelist, giving twenty-nine such quotations, of which ten are peculiar to himself. When we compare Matthew with parallel passages in Mark, we find that often when Mark makes a simple statement of fact Matthew confirms and enriches it with a quotation from the Old Testament. Thus, when Mark states that Jesus and his disciples "went into Capernaum" (1 : 21), Matthew states that this was done "that it might be fulfilled which was spoken by Isaiah the prophet" (4 : 14), and quotes Isa. 9 : 1-2. "To Mark's simple statement that Jesus withdrew himself to the sea after the collision with the Pharisees, occasioned by the healing on the Sabbath of the man with the withered hand (Mark 3 : 7), the first evangelist attaches a fine prophetic picture, as if to show readers the true Jesus as opposed to the Jesus of the Pharisaic imagination (Matt. 12 :15-21). From these instances we see his method.

He is not inventing history, but enriching history with prophetic emblazonments for apologetic purposes, or for increase of edification'' (*Expositor's Greek Testament*, Vol. I, p. 41).

Matthew is thus on every page connecting the gospel with the Old Testament and showing that the teaching of the Old Testament is fulfilled in the person and mission and kingdom of Jesus as the true Messiah and is thus removing doubts and misgivings from the minds of Jewish converts and confirming them in the Christian faith. It is difficult for us to realize how great was the transition from the old to the new, what a wrench and shock it gave to Jewish loyalty and faith to seem to give up the one for the other, and how earnest were the efforts of the New Testament writers to show the Jewish Christians that they were not sacrificing their old faith, but were only fulfilling and enriching it in receiving the new faith. This was Matthew's special purpose and it is deeply stamped upon every page of his Gospel.

That Matthew is the Jewish Gospel is also seen in the fact that it is more deeply impregnated and richly colored with the soil of Palestine than any other Gospel. He is minutely acquainted with Jewish history and custom and assumes that his readers understand these. The seven parables in chapter 13 show acquaintance with Jewish farming and fishing, housekeeping, the fondness for and traffic in jewels and other matters, and while Jesus spoke these parables only Matthew records them all and thereby shows his keen interest in them. He knew his own country and people and wrote for them a Gospel that must have touched more native chords in their hearts and appealed to them more deeply than any other of these narratives.

(3) Contents. Matthew, as well as the other evangelists, does not always follow a chronological order, especially in the teachings of Jesus, but groups together detached sayings and larger portions of discourses delivered at different times. However a general progressive plan may be plainly traced, and we can fit the chief portions of Matthew into our Outline of Events in the life of Jesus as follows:

PART I: The Thirty Silent Years, 1–2.

1. The genealogy, 1:1–17.
2. The birth at Bethlehem, 1:18–2:23.
3. The quiet years at Nazareth, 2:23.

PART II: The Public Ministry, 3–28.

I. First Year: The Early Judean Ministry, 3–4:11.
   1. The ministry of John the Baptist, 3:1–13.
   2. The baptism of Jesus, 3:13–17.
   3. The temptation of Jesus, 4:1–11.

II. Second Year: The Galilean Ministry.
   1. Departure from Judea and settlement at Capernaum. 4:12–17.
   2. Call of the Four and itinerant preaching in Galilee, 4:18–23.
   3. Controversies with scribes and Pharisees, 9:1–17, 12:9–14.
   4. Calling the Twelve, 10:2–4, and the Sermon on the Mount, 5–8.
   5. John the Baptist's last message, 12:2–19.
   6. Warnings to the scribes and Pharisees, 12:22–45.
   7. The true kindred of Christ, 12:46–50.
   8. Many parables, 13, and miracles, 8:23–34, 9:18–34.
   9. Second rejection at Nazareth, 13:54–58.
   10. The mission of the Twelve, 9:36–11:1.
   11. Death of John the Baptist, 14:1–12.
   12. The feeding of the five thousand, 14:13–23.
   13. Break with the Pharisees on eating, 15:1–20.
   14. Journey to the region of Tyre and return, 15:21–31.
   15. Feeding of the four thousand, 15:32–38.
   16. Renewed controversy with the Pharisees, 15:39–16:12.
   17. Retirement to the north: Peter's confession, 16:13–20.
   18. The transfiguration, 17:1–20.
   19. Discourse on humility, 18.

III. Third Year: The Later Judean Ministry, 19–28.
   1. Arrival in Judea, 19:1–2.
   2. The mission of the seventy, 11:20–30.
   3. Jesus foretells his death, 20:17–19.
   4. Incidents on the way to Jerusalem, 20:20–34.
   5. Anointing of Jesus by Mary in Bethany, 26:6–18.
   6. The triumphal entry to Jerusalem, 21:1–11.
   7. Second cleansing of the Temple, 21:12–17.
   8. Questions and controversies, 21:23–23.
   9. Discourse concerning the destruction of Jerusalem, 24–25.
   10. The conspiracy between the chief priests and Judas, 26:1–5, 14–15.
   11. The Last Supper, 26:17–30.
   12. Christ's farewell discourses, 26:31–85.
   13. Gethsemane, 26:36–46.

14. Betrayal and arrest, 26:47-56.
15. The trial, 26:57-27:31.
16. The crucifixion, 27:32-56.
17. The burial, 37:57-66.
15. The resurrection, 28:1-10.
16. The appearances, 28:16-20.

Matthew omits the events in the first year of the ministry of Jesus after his temptation, recorded only in John, gives in fuller detail than any other evangelist the Galilean ministry, and concludes the final scenes with the appearance of the risen Christ in Galilee and omits the ascension.

2. The Gospel According to Mark

(1) Authorship. Mark first appears in the New Testament in connection with the release by an angel of Peter from prison in Jerusalem, when Peter went to "the house of Mary the mother of John, whose surname was Mark" (Acts 12:12). It would appear that his mother owned the house and was a woman of some means. Mark then became associated with Paul who took him with him as a helper on his first missionary journey.

The earliest testimony to his authorship of the Second Gospel is again that of Papias writing about 125 A. D. "Mark," he says, "having become the interpreter of Peter, wrote down accurately everything that he remembered, without, however, recording in order what was either said or done by Christ. For neither did he hear the Lord, nor did he follow him; but afterwards, as I said (attended) Peter, who adapted his instructions to the needs (of his hearers) but had no design of giving a connected account of the Lord's oracles. So then Mark made no mistake, while he thus wrote down some things as he remembered them; for he made it his one care not to omit anything that he heard, or to set down any false statement therein."

This statement that Mark wrote as the disciple of Peter is borne out by the fact that Peter is prominent in this Gospel, often in unimportant matters, especially as it becomes more specific in details when Peter appears upon the scene in the first chapter; and it bears the impress of Peter's urgent spirit and direct rough speech.

Mark was also a traveling companion of Paul in his first missionary journey, and some critical readers think they discern something of the spirit and teaching of Paul in the Second Gospel.

We have already seen reasons for dating this Gospel between 55 and 60 A. D., and this date is borne out by its contents, especially by the fact that it was evidently written before the fall of Jerusalem in 70 A. D.

(2) Characteristics. Mark's immediate purpose is to set forth Jesus as the Son of God, the note he strikes in the very first verse: "The beginning of the gospel of Jesus Christ, the Son of God." In Matthew Jesus is the mighty Speaker, but in Mark he is the mighty Doer. On every page he is doing great deeds that show forth his divine power and Saviourhood. It does not appear that Mark is writing specially for either Jews or Gentiles, but is proclaiming to all believers that Jesus is mighty to save. He appeals especially to men of action.

Mark's Gospel is marked by characteristics that sharply distinguish it from the others. It is *realistic* in the direct vision and apprehension of the facts of the life of Jesus and graphic in its style. Mark sees and says things just as they are without any effort or thought of smoothing them off or toning them down. A rapid reading of the book gives one a vivid impression of this feature. He calls Jesus a "carpenter," has the people on first hearing him at Capernaum exclaim, "A new teaching!" and tells how his family declare of him, "He is beside himself," or is crazy. These realistic touches appear on every page.

There is also an urgency in the book that is characteristic. The words "straightway" and "immediately" occur more than forty times and indicate the rapidity and eagerness with which Jesus passes and almost rushes from one point or work to another. Once while hastening to one work of mercy he dropped another by the way (chapter 5). This urgency is characteristic of the impulsive nature of Peter and reflects his spirit in the narrative.

The frequent use of the present tense in the narrative is another mark of its realistic style, the author telling events as though they were present before him as he writes.

These characteristics are indications of the historicity of the book as being inimitable, and also accord with its being the earliest Gospel written under fresh knowledge and vision of the facts before reflection and tradition had begun to pale their colors and dim their sharp outlines. They are indications that Mark saw through the eyes and wrote with the hand of Peter.

(3) Contents:

PART I: THE THIRTY SILENT YEARS, omitted.

PART II: THE PUBLIC MINISTRY, 1–16.

I. FIRST YEAR: The Early Judean Ministry, 1:1–13.
    1. The ministry of John the Baptist, 1:1–8.
    2. The baptism of Jesus, 1:9–11.
    3. The temptation of Jesus, 1:12–13.

II. SECOND YEAR: The Galilean Ministry, 1:14–9.
    1. Call of the Four and itinerant preaching in Galilee, 1:16–45.
    2. Miracles and controversies, 2:1–3:12.
    3. Calling the Twelve, 3:13–19.
    4. Warnings to scribes and Pharisees, 3:19–30.
    5. The true kindred of Jesus, 3:31–35.
    6. Many parables and miracles, 4–5:43.
    7. Second rejection at Nazareth, 6:1–6.
    8. The mission of the Twelve, 6:7–13.
    9. Death of John the Baptist, 6:14–29.
    10. The feeding of the five thousand, 6:30–46.
    11. Break with the Pharisees on eating, 7:1–23.
    12. Journey to the region of Tyre and return, 7:24–30.
    13. Feeding the four thousand, 8:1–9.
    14. Renewed controversy with the Pharisees, 8:10–21.
    15. Retirement to the north: Peter's confession, 8:27–30.
    16. The transfiguration, 9:2–29.
    17. Discourse on humility, 9:33–50.

III. THIRD YEAR: The Later Judean Ministry, 10–16.
    1. Arrival in Judea, 10:1.
    2. Various teachings, 10:2–31.
    3. Jesus foretells his death, 10:32–34.
    4. Incidents on the way to Jerusalem, 10:35–52.
    5. Anointing of Jesus by Mary in Bethany, 14:3–9.
    6. The triumphal entry to Jerusalem, 11:1–11.
    7. Second cleansing of the Temple, 11:15–19.
    8. Questions and controversies, 11:27–12:40.
    9. Discourse concerning the destruction of Jerusalem, 13.
    10. The conspiracy between the chief priests and Judas, 14:1–11.

11. The Last Supper, 14:12–26.
12. Christ's farewell discourses, 14:27–31.
13. Gethsemane, 14:32–42.
14. Betrayal and arrest, 14:43–52.
15. The trial, 14:53–15:20.
16. The crucifixion, 15:21–41.
17. The burial, 15:42–47.
18. The resurrection, 16:1–11.
19. The appearances, 16:9–20.

Mark in the oldest existing manuscript breaks off abruptly in the middle of a sentence in verse 8 of the last chapter: "for they were afraid of," leaving the meaning incomplete. The ending to the chapter found in our versions was supplied by a later hand and is no part of the genuine Gospel. Probably the end of the roll of the manuscript was worn or broken off; and as the Gospel also begins abruptly without any account of the birth of Jesus it has been suggested that the first end of the manuscript roll may also have been worn or torn off and thus the original Mark may have been mutilated at both ends.

3. The Gospel According to Luke

(1) Authorship. Luke is directly mentioned only twice in the New Testament, both times as the companion of Paul: "Luke, the beloved physician, and Demas, greet you" (Col. 4:14). "Only Luke is with me" (II Tim. 4:11). But he appears in Acts 16:10 as one of Paul's companions in his second missionary journey: "And after that he had seen the vision, immediately we endeavored to go into Macedonia." There are four of these "we passages" (16:10-18, 20:5-16, 21:1-18, 27:1—28:16) that indicate the presence of Luke with Paul, so that he is writing Paul's biography from personal knowledge.

Uniform ancient tradition ascribes the Third Gospel to Luke. Irenæus, writing about 180 A. D., says, "Luke, the companion of Paul, recorded in a book the gospel preached by him," and Justin Martyr, writing thirty years earlier, quotes from the book. We have already fixed its date at near 60 A. D.

(2) Purpose and Characteristics. Luke addressed his Gospel to a single individual, the "most excellent Theophilus," a Roman knight or man of rank, to whom he

subsequently addressed the Acts (1:1). It was therefore written for a Gentile and no doubt was intended through him to reach a wide circle of Gentile readers. Yet this Gospel is not adapted specially to any particular class, but is suited to all readers and has in view its declared purpose that Theophilus "might know the certainty of those things" that are set forth in it.

The Gospel of Luke, pronounced by Renan "the most beautiful book ever written," having for its author a physician was composed by a professional scholar and is the most literary of the Gospels in style and finish and, in fact, is the most literary book in the New Testament with the possible exception of the Epistle to the Hebrews. The Greek is smooth and the construction is that of an artistic biography.

The Gospel is characterized by the spirit of humaneness, as befits the nature and work of a physician. The author notes that they were "gracious words" that proceeded from the mouth of Jesus at Nazareth (4:22), and graciousness marks his narrative all the way through. He alone gives us such beautiful humanitarian parables as the Good Samaritan and the Prodigal Son, and he very noticeably smooths down the faults of the disciples, as is seen in his omitting the rebuke to Peter, "Get thee behind me." He notes the specific features of disease, such as "a great fever" (4:38), and "full of leprosy" (5:12), and he notes "the only son" (7:12), and an "only child" (9:38). Many are the little touches that show the quick eye and tender hand and sympathetic heart of "the beloved physician." Thus the human charm and healing ministry of Jesus shine out in special splendor upon his pages.

(3) The Preface. A specially important part of Luke's Gospel is his preface. The author of a book in his preface usually gives us information about it that is interesting and helps us to understand it and yet does not fall within the book itself, such as telling us his purpose in writing it and indicating his sources and his competence for his task. This is just what Luke does; and his preface is so valuable that we here reproduce it from Moffatt's *New Translation* that will give us a more literal and a fresher view of it:

Inasmuch as a number of writers have essayed to draw up a narrative of the established facts in our religion exactly as these have been handed down to us by the original eyewitnesses who were in the service of the Gospel Message, and inasmuch as I have gone carefully over them all myself from the very beginning, I have decided, O Theophilus, to write them out in order for your excellency, to let you know the solid truth of what you have been taught.

This brief preface, worth many times its weight in gold, is one of the most important historical documents in the Bible and in all the literature of the world. It lets us see right into the heart of the process by which Luke prepared the materials for and wrote his Gospel. It takes us into his literary workshop and shows us the author at work. And we find there, no romancer or mere repeater of rumors and traditions and legends coming down from a distant day, but a careful and conscientious historian proceeding in accordance with the laws of trustworthy historical investigation and composition.

Luke first collected his data and documents that were close to the facts, having been written by those who had received them from eyewitnesses, and there were many such sketches which he had in hand. This gives us a glimpse of the Gospels before our Gospels, many of which have long since perished. However, we know of one of them, for we have seen that Luke and Matthew used not only Mark but also another document now known as Q.

Having collected his data Luke says, "I have gone carefully over them all myself from the beginning": that is, he sifted and digested his data and put them through the whole process of systematic examination. He did not simply copy them, but he tested them and reduced them to the consistency of truth.

He then set about writing his narrative in a methodical form, producing an orderly and logical history or biography. And all this was done that his noble friend might "know the solid truth of what you have been taught." He had a practical purpose in view and with him truth was in order to goodness.

Luke thus based his Gospel on contemporary witnesses and documents after the manner of the most approved methods of the modern scientific historian. This is the immense value of this preface, and though all the Gos-

pels were dated very much later yet would these four introductory verses assure us that the author of the Third
Gospel had first-hand documents and take us back to
eyewitnesses of these tremendous events.

(4) Contents. Luke has considerable material peculiar
to himself, including such parables as the Good Samaritan, Selfish Neighbor, Unjust Judge, Prodigal Son, Unjust
Steward, Lazarus and Dives, and the Pharisee and Publican. These parables and much other material peculiar
to Luke are found in a long passage extending from 9: 51
to 18: 14. The main portions of this Gospel can be fitted
into our Outline as follows:

THE PREFACE, 1:1–4.

PART I: THE THIRTY SILENT YEARS, 1–2: 52.
1. The genealogy, 3: 23–38.
2. The annunciations of the births of John the Baptist and
   of Jesus, 1: 5–38.
3. The birth at Bethlehem, 2: 1–2: 39.
4. The quiet years at Nazareth, 2: 39–52.

PART II: THE PUBLIC MINISTRY, 3–28.
I.   FIRST YEAR: The Early Judean Ministry, 3–4: 13.
   1. The ministry of John the Baptist, 3: 1–20.
   2. The baptism of Jesus, 3: 21–23.
   3. The temptation of Jesus, 4: 1–13.
II. SECOND YEAR: The Galilean Ministry, 4: 14–9: 50.
   1. Departure from Judea and settlement at Capernaum,
      4: 1–3, 31–41.
   2. Itinerant preaching in Galilee, 4: 42–44, 5: 12–16.
   3. Controversies with scribes and Pharisees, 5: 17–6: 11.
   4. Calling the Twelve, 6: 12–19, and Sermon on the Mount,
      6: 20–49.
   5. John the Baptist's last message, 7: 18–35.
   6. Warnings to the scribes and Pharisees, **11: 14–36.**
   7. The true kindred of Christ, 8: 19–21.
   8. Many parables, 8: 4–18.
   9. Many miracles, 8: 22–56.
   10. The mission of the Twelve, 9: 1–6.
   11. Death of John the Baptist, 9: 7–9.
   12. The feeding of the five thousand, 9: **10–17.**
   13. Peter's confession, 9: 18–21.
   14. The transfiguration, 9: 28–43.
   15. Discourse on humility, 9: 46–50.
III. THIRD YEAR: The Later Judean Ministry, 9: 51–24.
   1. Arrival in Judea, 9: 51.

2. The mission of the seventy, 10:1-24.
3. The Good Samaritan, 10:25-37.
4. Various discourses, 11:1-13, 37-13:9.
5. A woman healed on the Sabbath, 13:10-21.
6. Further discourses, 13:22-14:35.
7. A series of parables, 15-17:10.
8. The coming of the kingdom, 17:20-18:8.
9. The Pharisee and the Publican, 18:9-14.
10. Jesus and children, 18:15-17.
11. The rich young ruler, 18:18-30.
12. Jesus foretells his death, 18:18-30.
13. Incidents at Jericho, 18:35-19:28.
14. The triumphal entry, 19:29-44.
15. Second cleansing of the Temple, 19:45-48.
16. Questions and controversies, 20:1-47.
17. Discourse concerning the destruction of Jerusalem, 21:5-38.
18. Conspiracy between the priests and Judas, 22:1-6.
19. The last supper, 22:7-30.
20. Christ's farewell discourses, 22:31-38.
21. Gethsemane, 22:39-46.
22. Betrayal and arrest, 22:47-53.
23. The trial, 22:54-23:25.
24. The crucifixion, 23:26-49.
25. The burial, 23:50-56.
26. The resurrection, 23:56-24:12.
27. The appearances, 24:13-53.

4. The Gospel According to John

(1) Authorship and Date. The book itself declares, of John, "the disciple whom Jesus loved" (21:20), that "This is the disciple who testifieth of these things, and wrote these things: and we know that his testimony is true" (21:24). The external evidence in favor of this authorship is good. Irenæus, writing about 180 A. D., bears witness to the fact that the Fourth Gospel was universally received in the churches as the work of John; and he also tells us of hearing Polycarp, who was born in 70 A. D. and was contemporary with John, when "he would describe his intercourse with John and the rest who had seen the Lord, and how he would relate his words," and how Polycarp had "received them from eyewitnesses of the life of the Word" (Logos). The internal evidence is also good as it shows that the author was a Palestinian Jew, intimate with Judea and Jerusalem and an eyewitness of events he is recording. Yet some scholars hold, on the ground of internal evidence, that the substance of the

Gospel is from John but that the actual writing was done by one of his disciples, perhaps John the Presbyter, an associate of John the Apostle in Ephesus. The trend of recent scholarship, however, is back to the Johannine authorship, and so competent a scholar as Dr. A. T. Robertson declares, "I pin my faith to the conviction that the Apostle John is identical with the Beloved Disciple mentioned in the Fourth Gospel as the author of the book."

The date of the Gospel, according to general agreement of scholars, falls near the end of the first century and may be about 100 A. D. Nearly all ancient tradition makes the death of John to have occurred at an advanced age in or near Ephesus at about this date.

(2) Purpose and Character. The purpose of this Gospel is clearly stated in 20: 31: "But these are written, that ye might believe that Jesus is the Christ, the Son of God; and that believing ye might have life through his name." The whole Gospel from the Prologue setting forth the eternal Sonship of Christ (1: 1-18) to its closing verse is concentrated on this point that Jesus is the Son of God through whose name we are saved by faith.

The outstanding characteristic of the Fourth Gospel is that it stands apart from the synoptics in contents and teaching and spirit. In general it describes the Judean ministry of Jesus in contrast with the synoptics, which are chiefly concerned with the Galilean ministry, and it is also contrasted with them in that it is the subjective while they are the objective gospel. Any Harmony of the Gospels will show that the Fourth Gospel coincides with the synoptics at comparatively few points, these with a single exception (feeding the five thousand) being events in the closing weeks of the life of Christ. On the other hand there are large portions of material, such as the discourses with Nicodemus and the Samaritan woman, that are found only in this Gospel.

John stands in a very different relation to Jesus, as compared with the other evangelists, in that he was the most intimate disciple and personal friend of the Master and was able to report and interpret his most spiritual and vital teaching and reflect his spirit most fully. The characteristic words of his Gospel are light, life, truth, and Spirit. The Logos or Word is the light that becomes the life of men, and eternal life in the Fourth Gospel very largely takes the place of the Kingdom of God in the synoptics. "God is spirit" (4:24), together with "God is light" and "God is love" of his First Epistle (1:5 and 4:24), is the sunlit summit of John's teaching.

A peculiarity of John's Gospel is that he stands so close to and is so intimate with Jesus as his interpreter that it is sometimes difficult to distinguish between what is the teaching of the Master and what is the comment and interpretation of the disciple. John is a philosopher and mystic and poet more than the practical Matthew and the objective Mark and the systematic Luke, so that his Gospel is in some degree tinctured and colored with his own subjective thought and spirit. The historical element is subordinated to the spiritual and the spiritual is deeply dyed with the mystical. For example, in the great discourse with Nicodemus it is not clear where Jesus leaves off and John begins. Was it Jesus that uttered the wonderful saying, "God so loved the world, that he gave his only begotten Son, that whosoever believeth in him should not perish, but have everlasting life" (3:16), or was John so caught up into the report and spirit of the Master's sublime eloquence that at this point his own soul took wings and was borne aloft to the height of this great utterance? At any rate, John takes us further into the heart of the mystic teaching of Jesus and immerses us more deeply in his spirit than do the synoptics.

The Fourth Gospel, being so much later than the synoptics, is largely supplementary to them and supplies the theological and philosophical and spiritual interpretation of Jesus that in some degree may be due to long-continued reflection and loving remembrance and deep meditation. It is therefore the most vital and precious of the Gospels and will ever nourish believers on the very Bread of life and reflect that Light that is the Life of the world.

(3) Contents. As already explained the contents of the Fourth Gospel come into contact with the synoptics at only a few points so that the list of its topics varies widely from that of the others; but we may fit them into our General Outline as follows:

THE PROLOGUE, 1:1–18

PART I: THE THIRTY SILENT YEARS, omitted.

PART II: THE PUBLIC MINISTRY.

I. FIRST YEAR: The Early Judean Ministry, 1:19–4:42.
    1. The ministry of John the Baptist, 1:19–34.
    2. The first disciples of Jesus, 1:35–51.
    3. First miracle, 2:1–11.
    4. First cleansing of the Temple, 2:13–22.
    5. Discourse with Nicodemus, 2:23–3:21.
    6. The coöperation of Jesus with John, 3:23–3:21.
    7. Discourse with the woman of Samaria, 4:26–42.

II. SECOND YEAR: The Galilean Ministry, 4:43–8:59.
    1. Departure from Judea and settlement in Galilee, 4:43–45.
    2. Healing of the Nobleman's son, 4:46–54.
    3. Visit to Jerusalem to the feast, 5.
    4. Feeding of the five thousand, 6:1–15.
    5. Jesus walking on the water, 6:16–21.
    6. Discourse on the bread of life, 6:22–71.

III. THIRD YEAR: The Later Judean Ministry, 7:1–21:25
    1. Jesus at the Feast of Tabernacles and his discourses, 7:1–8:59.
    2. Healing of the man born blind, 9.
    3. The Good Shepherd, 10:1–21.
    4. Jesus at the Feast of Dedication, 10:2–42.
    5. The raising of Lazarus, 11:1–46.
    6. Withdrawal to Ephraim, 11:47–14.
    7. Anointing of Jesus by Mary in Bethany, 11:55–12:11.
    8. The triumphal entry, 12:12–19.
    9. Incidents in Jerusalem, 12:20–50.
    10. The last supper, 13:7–30.
    11. Christ's farewell discourses, 13:31–17.
    12. Gethsemane, 18:1.
    13. Betrayal and arrest, 18:2–11.
    14. The trial, 18:12–19:16.
    15. The crucifixion, 19:17–37.
    16. The burial, 19:38–42.
    17. The resurrection, 20:1–18.
    18. The appearances, 20:19–21:25.

CHAPTER IV

THE ACTS OF THE APOSTLES AND THE EPISTLES OF PAUL

The Acts of the Apostles and the Epistles of Paul belong together and might be designated as The Life and Letters of Paul.

I. THE ACTS OF THE APOSTLES

(1) Authorship and Date. The opening sentence of the Acts, beginning, "The former treatise have I made, O Theophilus, of all that Jesus began both to do and teach," is plain evidence that Luke is the author of the Acts as of the Third Gospel, and this conclusion is confirmed by all the other evidence in the matter. The literary style of the two books in the construction of sentences and the use of peculiar words and phrases indicates identical authorship, and from the earliest times the two books have been accepted as the work of Luke.

We have already considered the question of its date and seen that in all probability Luke concluded the Acts before the death of Paul and that this places its date near 62 A. D.

(2) Purpose and Characteristics: As in his Gospel so in the Acts Luke indicates his purpose in his preface. He proposes to continue the narrative of "the former treatise," which contained "all that Jesus began both to do and to teach until the day in which he was taken up" (1:1-2) and to follow the fulfillment of the promise of Jesus to his disciples, "Ye shall be witnesses unto me both in Jerusalem, and in all Judea, and in Samaria, and unto the uttermost parts of the earth" (1:8).

The Acts is thus the continuation of Luke's Gospel, the second volume of a work of which the Gospel is the first.

It is to take up the story of the mission of Christ in the world at the point of his departure from it and carry it on in widening circles from Jerusalem through Judea and Samaria to the very ends of the earth. It is thus the Acts of the ascended and glorified Christ continuing his work from heaven, as the Gospels are the Acts of Jesus fulfilling his mission on earth; or it is the Acts of the Holy Spirit, "whom," Jesus promised, "the Father will send in my name" (John 14:26) to carry forward his work in the world; or it is the first history of the missionary church as it burst the narrow bounds of Judea and launched out upon the deep and set its sails for all continents and islands of the sea.

As it comes from the hand of Luke it is characterized by the same scholarly features that are found in his Gospel. It is systematic in its arrangement and evinces the same care in the selection of the materials and in the composition of the narrative. At points, even in minute matters, where it alludes to dates and names and facts in the Roman Empire, it is found to be correct. This has been proved to be the case in some matters in which it was long supposed to be in error.

Beginning at the point where Paul appears in the story as the chief character (chapter 9), the narrative drops out of view the work of the other Apostles and practically becomes the biography of Paul, with whom Luke traveled as a companion in some of his missionary journeys and work.

Viewed as a work of history the Acts has high merit and stands the test of our modern historians. Says Philip Schaff, one of our most eminent church historians: "Examine and compare the secular historians from Herodotus to Macaulay, and the church historians from Eusebius to Neander, and Luke need not fear a comparison. No history of thirty years has ever been written so truthful and impartial, so important and interesting, so healthy in spirit, so aggressive and yet so genial, so cheering and so inspiring, so replete with lessons of wisdom and encouragement for work in spreading the gospel of truth and peace, and yet withal so simple and modest, as the Acts of the Apostles. It is the best as well as the first manual of church history" (*History of the Christian Church,* Vol. 1, p. 739).

"On the whole," says Professor Kirsopp Lake, an extremely radical critic, "and considering the character of of the book, Acts is a first-rate historical document, and singularly easy to understand, so far as the mere enumeration of events is concerned" (*The Earlier Epistles of St. Paul,* p. 13).

The importance of the Acts as one of the early documents of Christianity is very great as it shows the fate of the gospel, its inherent power and persistence and expansion, after it was deprived of the personal presence of Christ and was left to make its own way in the world. It is an account of the most critical period and fateful crisis of Christianity when it faced the tremendous question of its relation to Judaism and was forced to determine whether it was to remain a Jewish sect or become a universal faith and world religion. The whole future of our Christian faith was then perilously trembling in the balance.

Luke gives us a vivid picture of this period as an eyewitness and shows us Christianity unloosing its swaddling clothes and freeing itself from Jewish strangulation and standing upon its own feet and setting forth on its world march. It is a magnificent spectacle we witness in these graphic pages and never can they lose their supreme interest for Christian readers. "Had it not come down to us," says Dean Farrar, "there would have been a blank in our knowledge which scarcely anything could have filled up. The origin of Christianity would have been an insoluble enigma."

And yet there are strange omissions and gaps in the book and at many points we wonder at the silence of the historian and wish he had told us more. We would like to have known more of the work and fate of the other Apostles, especially of Peter and John, and what became of Mary, the mother of our Lord. Epecially strange is the omission of any single allusion to any one of the Epistles of Paul, though Paul wrote some of them when Luke was with him. We are fortunate in having four Gospels that supplement one another, but we have only one history of this plastic and formative period of our Christian faith and organization of the Christian church. The silences of Scripture, however, may be as significant as its utterances.

(3) Contents. The history narrated in the Acts extends from the ascension of Jesus, A. D. 29, to near the death of Paul in Rome, a period of about thirty-three years. The contents of the Acts may be outlined as follows:

I. THE CHURCH AT JERUSALEM, 1-7.
   1. Events immediately following the ascension, 1.
   2. The day of Pentecost, 2.
   3. Preaching of the Apostles in Jerusalem, 3-4.
   4. The fate of Ananias and Sapphira, 5.
   5. Appointment of deacons and preaching of Stephen, 6.
   6. Martyrdom of Stephen, 7-8:4.

II. SPREAD OF THE GOSPEL TO SAMARIA AND GAZA, 8.
   1. Preaching of Philip in Samaria, 8:5-25.
   2. Philip at Gaza, 8:26-40.

III. SPREAD OF THE GOSPEL TO ANTIOCH AND EUROPE, 9-28.
   1. Conversion of Saul, 9:1-31.
   2. Work of Peter, 9:32-10:48.
   3. Council at Jerusalem over receiving Gentiles, 11:1-18.
   4. The gospel reaches Antioch, 11:19-30.
   5. Persecution in Jerusalem, 12.
   6. Paul's first missionary journey, 13-14.
   7. Council at Jerusalem over circumcision, 15-1:35.
   8. Paul's second missionary journey, 15:36-18:22.
   9. Paul's third missionary journey, 18:3-21:16.
   10. Paul arrested at Jerusalem, 21:17-23:32.
   11. Paul taken to Cæsarea, 23:33-26:32.
   12. The voyage to Rome and shipwreck, 27.
   13. Paul in Rome, 28.

II. THE EPISTLES OF PAUL

(1) Authorship. Of the thirteen Epistles ascribed to Paul, the following ten, Romans, I and II Corinthians, Galatians, Ephesians, Philippians, Colossians, I and II Thessalonians, and Philemon, are from his hand by clear internal and external evidence and by general agreement of scholars. They purport to be written by him and bear his impress in contents and knowledge and style. They fit into their proper places in Luke's narrative in the Acts, and we are as reasonably sure of Paul's authorship of these letters as we are that Cicero wrote those that bear his name.

In the case of I and II Timothy and Titus, called "Pastoral Epistles" because they give directions to these young ministers relating to their pastoral work, there is difficulty in fitting I Timothy and Titus into Luke's narrative of Paul's labors. In I Timothy and Titus Paul is away from Rome and leaves Timothy in Ephesus (1:3) and Titus in Crete (1:5), and it is difficult to find places for these events in the Acts. II Timothy, however, falls into place, for Paul is again in Rome awaiting execution.

This difficulty is largely cleared up by supposing that Paul was released from his first captivity in Rome and made a fourth missionary journey, during which he addressed I Timothy and Titus to these helpers and was then again arrested and was in Rome when he wrote II Timothy. Some scholars adopt this solution, and others suppose that some disciple of Paul who had some fragments of his letters put them into their present form after his death.

But there are serious difficulties in this latter view, and it seems better to take them as the letters of Paul and allow that there are incidental facts in the case unknown to us, which if they were known would clear the matter up. As to the vexed question why, if Paul made another missionary journey, Luke did not tell about it in the Acts, the answer would be the same as to why he did not tell about Paul's death. He told no more because he knew no more and he wrote the Acts before anything more had happened.

(2) Circumstances and Characteristics of the Epistles. We are not to suppose that these thirteen Epistles are all the letters Paul wrote. They are probably only a selection of his large correspondence which has been preserved and incorporated in the New Testament. Neither are we to suppose that Paul wrote these letters with any knowledge or thought that he was composing divinely inspired letters that would be thus preserved and read and studied through ages as Holy Scriptures. He wrote them as any one writes letters in his correspondence with friends, all unconsciously of the divine Providence that was guiding him and caring for these letters for our instruction and edification. Inspiration fulfils itself in many ways, and,

like the wind, the divine breath bloweth where and how it listeth.

They are all letters addressed to churches and individuals for practical purposes. Every one of them was occasioned by some special cause or condition that called for instruction or correction or advice from Paul. Their contents were thus adapted and addressed to local conditions and personal needs and are written in the free and direct and incidental method and style of personal correspondence. They almost wholly lack the structure and style of a systematic treatise, or of writings intended for general publication.

Yet they are none the less but rather all the more valuable on this account. They illustrate abstract principles in their concrete application, and this is one of the best ways of imparting such truth. They touch a large range and variety of topics both doctrinal and practical as they deal with the peculiar conditions of these first Christian churches while they were plastic and involved in all the difficulties and dangers, factions and corruptions of their day, when Christianity was new and had not yet developed forms and creeds and was especially subject to the environment of heathen customs and morals, temptations and persecutions. And all the way through Paul is the uncompromising defender and bold champion of the liberty of the gospel and the universality of the Christian faith against the claims and struggles of Judaism to constrict Christianity with its own bondage and doom it as a Jewish sect.

Paul was a born thinker and theologian and while dealing with these local and temporary conditions he was all unconsciously forging his own Christian ideas and experience into shape and use and working out the fundamental principles and doctrines of the new faith and thus laying the foundations of our Christian creeds and polities. Without imposing on us fixed and final forms he yet furnished us with the materials that are the substance of our formal faith today.

These letters are characterized by Paul's intellectual and emotional temper and spirit of independent thought and bold solution of problems and brave action. His pages are often so charged with thought and feeling that the words come tumbling from his pen in a tumultuous torrent, sometimes as broken or chaotic● sentences that defy the rules of grammar and give infinite trouble to the commentators. Yet Paul the philosopher and theologian was also Paul the mystic and poet and his imagination could utter winged words and soar into rhythmic melody and beauty that are the praise and the charm of the ages, such as the immortal prose-poem in I Cor. 13.

Paul was the first and greatest theologian of the Christian church. He forged the simple gospel into a logical system that roots it in the brain as well as in the heart; he put bones into its flesh and rocks under its flowers and fruits. Such a work was necessary to give system and stability to the gospel, without which "the sweet Galilean vision" might have melted into mist.

(3) Chronology of Paul's Life and Letters. In the Authorized Version the place of the writing of each of Paul's Epistles is appended to it, but these notations were added to the manuscripts by later hands and are omitted in the Revised Version as no part of the original text. As a matter of fact they are all wrong. But internal evidence indicates with a considerable degree of assurance the places of the writing of the Epistles with several exceptions.

The following outline of events and dates in the life of Paul will enable us to locate most of his letters. These dates are the ones adopted by Harnack and some other scholars, and while they are subject to more or less uncertainty and difference of view among scholars, yet they may be taken as approximating the truth.

Paul was converted within a year after the death and resurrection of Christ, and this gives us the year 30 A. D. as the base line from which to start. After spending three years in retirement, Paul went up to Jerusalem in 33 and then proceeded to his home city of Tarsus in Asia Minor, where he appears to have remained about ten years when he came to Antioch. He went up to Jerusalem with the famine relief fund (Acts 11:27-30), and the known year of this famine fixes this visit in 44. Counting back fourteen years, according to his statement in Gal. 2:1, gives 30 A. D.

as the year of Paul's conversion. His first missionary journey from Antioch through Cyprus into Asia Minor and back was in 45, and after his return to Antioch and before the council at Jerusalem of Acts 15 in 47 he probably wrote the Epistle to the Galatians. He set out on his second missionary journey in 47 and labored a year and a half in Corinth, 48, where he wrote I and II Thessalonians. He returned from Corinth by way of Jerusalem to Antioch, whence he started on the third missionary journey in 50 and spent three years in Ephesus where he wrote I Corinthians. Going by way of Macedonia, where he wrote II Corinthians, he went on to Corinth for a second visit where he wrote Romans, he again returned to Jerusalem, where he was arrested in 54, was held at Caesarea two years and arrived at Rome in 57, where he was in prison two years, 57-59, during which time he wrote Philippians, Ephesians, Colossians and Philemon. He was then probably released and made a fourth missionary journey, during which he wrote I Timothy and Titus. Arrested a second time, he was again imprisoned in Rome, when he wrote II Timothy, his last extant letter, and probably perished in the Neronian persecution in 64 A. D.

(4) Contents of the Epistles. As the Epistles usually do not follow any logical form, any analysis of their contents is more or less arbitrary, but their chief subjects and points can be stated. We shall follow the order in which they are found in the New Testament, which, as we have seen, is not the order in which they were written.

ROMANS

Paul wrote Romans as a letter to the church at Rome when he was at Corinth on his third missionary journey, as is indicated by his reference to Cenchrea (16:1), which was the seaport of that city. His thoughts had long been turning towards Rome as the metropolis and mighty hub of the Roman Empire and the world magnet which then attracted all eyes and to which all things in commerce and government and art and religion irresistibly gravitated. Already a Christian church existed at Rome composed of both Jews and Gentiles, and this Epistle was intended to prepare the way for his coming. Christianity had in the start and has ever since had an affinity for great cities and seized them as strategic centers, and Paul felt that his work would be incomplete until he had helped to establish the gospel in this central and supreme city in the world of his day.

The Epistle partakes of the characteristics of his mind and heart, logical in its arguments yet urgent and at times tortuous in its spirit and style and culminating in great practical applications. More than any other book in the Bible it approaches being a treatise on systematic theology and works out the great doctrines of God's sovereignty and grace. Its central word is righteousness, the righteousness of God as expressed in the redemption of the world. It will ever stand as Paul's masterpiece, and Coleridge declared it to be the "profoundest book in existence."

Its chief points are:

I. Salutation and plan, 1 : 1-15.
II. Doctrinal, 1 : 16-11.
    1. Righteousness based on faith, 1 : 16-8.
    2. Israel's rejection of God's righteousness, 9-11.
III. Hortatory applications. 12-15 : 13.
IV. Personal notes, 15 : 14-16.

I AND II CORINTHIANS

The First Epistle to the church at Corinth was written by Paul while he was in Ephesus on his third journey. He had founded the church at Corinth on his second journey, but much had happened in the several years of his absence and factions had arisen and moral laxness had developed and pagan customs had reasserted themselves. The general object of the first letter was to deal with these conditions and set them right.

Soon after sending the First Epistle he heard the good news that the evils at Corinth had been corrected and he then dispatched, from Macedonia whither he had gone (II Cor. 2 : 12-13), the Second Epistle in which he expresses his joy at the happy turn of affairs.

At this point we must consider the peculiar relations of First and Second Corinthians. We learn from 1 Cor. 5 :9 that Paul had written an earlier letter to the church at Corinth, which has been lost. In II Cor. 7 :8-9 we further discover that he had written still another letter to the Corinthians so severe in its condemnation that he was now sorry for it, and it is thought that this letter has also been lost. But chapters 10-13 of Second Corinthians are so sharp in their condemnation of Paul's opponents at Corinth that some scholars think that these chapters cannot belong to Second Corinthians, which was sent as a letter of thanksgiving and joy, and that they are the lost letter of condemnation, which Paul regretted, which has become bound up with the Second Epistle. This is only a conjecture, but it would explain the incongruity of the last four chapters of the Second Epistle with its main body and evident purpose and spirit. It would not be strange that manuscript letters should thus get joined together.

The chief points of I Corinthians are:

I. Salutation and thanksgiving, 1:1-9.
II. Rebukes, 1-6.
III. Answers to questions, 7-11.
IV. Spiritual gifts, 12-13.
V. The resurrection, 15.
VI. Personal matters, 16.

The chief points of II Corinthians are:

I. Introduction, 1:1-11.
II. Thankfulness in retrospect, 1:12-7.
III. The collection for the poor at Jerusalem, 8-9.
IV. Opponents at Corinth condemned, 10-13.

GALATIANS

The Epistle to the Galatians was addressed to "the churches of Galatia" (1:2), the churches in Asia Minor at Antioch in Pisidia, Iconium, Lystra and Derbe which Paul had founded on his first missionary journey (Acts 13-14:25). The occasion of the letter was the falling away of these churches from the liberty of the gospel into Judaism which caused Paul to "marvel that ye are so soon removed from him that called you into the grace of Christ unto another gospel" (1.6). Judaizing teachers, probably from Jerusalem, had come in among them and were telling the Gentile converts that they must be circumcised and obey the law of Moses, and some of them were on the point of accepting circumcision. This was all flat in the face of what Paul had taught them as to being free from the ceremonial law.

These Judaizers also attacked Paul himself, throwing doubt on the validity of his standing as an apostle. Paul defended himself against this charge by showing that he received the gospel, not from men, but by the revelation of Christ (1:11-12). He also tells in chapter 2 of a visit to Jerusalem in which he met with Peter and James and John where he stood for the "liberty which we have in Christ," and as a result of this private conference "the gospel of the uncircumcision was committed unto me, as the gospel of the circumcision was unto Peter" (1:7). Thus he stood on an equality with these apostles and the question of the liberty of the Gentile converts as being free from the ceremonial law was debated and settled.

If the time of this visit could be determined it would help to settle the time of the writing of this Epistle. There was a council held at Jerusalem to decide whether the Judaistic ceremonies were to be imposed on the Gentile converts, and a decree was issued to be delivered to these churches that they were not subject to the burdens of the Mosaic law (Acts 15). Does the visit of Gal. 2 refer to this council of Acts 15? It would seem that it cannot do so, for if it did we would expect to find Paul using this decree in his letter to the Galatians to sustain and prove his point as to their freedom from the law. But he is silent as to any such council and decree, and it is therefore held by many scholars that Gal. 2 refers to a visit to Jerusalem earlier than the council of Acts 15, possibly to the famine relief visit mentioned in Acts 11:30 or to some unmentioned visit. This view, which was held by Calvin, has the powerful support of Ramsay and other scholars.

If this was the case, then the Epistle to the Galatians was written between the return from the first missionary journey and the second journey, probably at Antioch. This view is confirmed by the fact that Paul did deliver the decree to the Galatian churches on his second journey (Acts 16:4), showing that he did not have this decree when he wrote his letter to them. This is at least a probable solution of this problem, but other scholars do not accept it and date the Epistle after the second journey, and some think it was probably written at Ephesus when Paul was there on his third journey.

If the Epistle was written at Antioch between the first and second visits to these churches, then Galatians is the earliest of the New Testament books, and with the first scratch of Paul's pen on the parchment of this Epistle inspiration, which had been hushed four hundred years since Malachi, broke its silence and the New Testament began to be written.

The main body of the Epistle is an impetuous and impassioned argument and plea against the bondage of the law which was being forced on the Gentile converts and for the liberty of believers in Christ. "O foolish Galatians, who hath bewitched you . . .? Having begun in the Spirit, are ye now made perfect by the flesh?" (3:1, 3). Paul felt that if these Galatian churches of his were led away into Judaism his work would be wrecked, and hence he fights as for the life of his children and for his own life in defending the liberty of the gospel and salvation by faith alone.

The main points of the letter are:

I. Introduction, 1:1-10.
II. Paul's defence of himself, 1:11-2:21.
III. Freedom from the law and salvation by faith, 3-5.
IV. Exhortations to the Christian life, 6.

EPHESIANS

Paul spent three years on his third missionary journey in Ephesus (Acts 19) and founded a church there. The letter to this church was writen at Rome, as were also Colossians, Philippians and Philemon, these four being known as "the Epistles of the imprisonment."

While it is said in 1:1 to be addressed to the saints "in Ephesus," yet these words are not in some of the earliest and best manuscripts. If the letter was specially addressed to this church it is strange that it contains no personal greetings, as Paul's letters nearly always do, and it is still stranger that he speaks as if their knowledge of his ministry were only hearsay (3:2-4) and of his knowledge of them as being of a similar character (1:15).

It is therefore thought that this Epistle was a general letter to be circulated among all the churches in the region of Ephesus and this would explain these characteristics.

It is a letter of general Christian doctrine and guidance

and comfort. No particular trouble has arisen to call for correction. The Judaistic controversy has been settled and the churches are in a state of normal peace and growth. Paul himself has quieted down and writes less impetuously and pugnaciously, and his style has grown calmer and smoother. He had won his case and established the gospel on the sure foundation of liberty and faith in Christ. This Epistle is not, therefore, a battle cry, as were his earlier letters, but moves in the serener region of faith and faithfulness and of growth in the knowledge and grace of Christ. The emancipator of Galatians has now become the spiritualizer of Ephesians.

Its main points may be outlined as follows:

 I. Salutation and thanksgiving, 1.
 II. The privileges and duties of the Christian life, 2.
 III. How Paul obtained his knowledge of the gospel and his prayer for his readers, 3.
 IV. Practical exhortations, 4-6.

PHILIPPIANS

The church at Philippi was the first Christian church in Europe and was founded by Paul on his second missionary journey after he had crossed at Troas from Asia to Europe (Acts 16:11-40).

The converts in this church were specially dear to Paul as he was to them. Knowing of his imprisonment in Rome they made up a contribution or donation which they sent to him by one of their members, Epaphroditus. This messenger fell ill in Rome and Paul nursed him through the disease and then sent him back to Philippi bearing this letter to his friends at that place (2:25-30). It is evident that Paul is in prison in Rome from various allusions in the letter, such as "the palace" or "prætorian guard" (1:13) and "Cæsar's household" (4:22). Though in prison yet he is expecting release (2:24), and this rather favors the view that he was released and engaged in further missionary labors and was then imprisoned a second time before his execution, thus leaving room for the pastoral Epistles, Titus, and I and II Timothy.

Paul writes to the Philippians to cheer them in view of their despondency over his imprisonment, to express his warm appreciation of their gift, to warn them against false teaching, and to counsel them to cultivate and exercise the Christian graces.

Its main topics are as follows:

- I.   Salutation and thanksgiving, 1:12-30.
- II. Statement as to Paul's condition, 1:12-30.
- III. Exhortations, 2:1-18.
- IV. Paul's plans for the future, 2:19-30.
- V.   Final exhortations, 4.

COLOSSIANS

The church at Colosse was not founded or ever visited by Paul, but may have been established by some of his converts from the city of Ephesus which lay to the west. Paul's Epistle to this church was written at Rome and was sent by Tychicus (4:7), who also carried the Epistle to the Ephesians (6:21). Onesimus was also along with Tychicus with his letter to Philemon (Col. 4:9).

Serious trouble was brewing in the Colossian church calling for a special letter from Paul in addition to the circular letter to the Ephesian and other churches. Judaizers were at work in this church (2:10-17), but along with these reversions to Mosaic ceremonies were mixed some elements of pagan philosophy, such as the worship of angels (2:8, 18) and other supernatural beings and also a tendency to extreme asceticism (2:20-23).

Paul meets these errors by emphasizing the liberty which is in Christ (2:16-17; 3:10-11) and especially by exalting Christ to equality with God (2:9) and showing that he is the head of the creation in whom all things consist or hold together (1:15-19). Thus Paul leaves no room for pagan powers as objects of worship and enthrones Christ in his immanent relation to the church and to the universe. In no other book of Scripture is the person of Christ so clearly set forth, and his divine rank and power more surely asserted and established.

The outline of the Epistle is as follows:

- I.   Salutation and thanksgiving, 1:1-15.
- II. The supremacy of Christ, 1:16-20.
- III. Warnings against false teachings, 2.
- IV. Exhortations, 3-4.

I and II THESSALONIANS

Thessalonica was the second city in Europe where Paul

founded a church (Acts 17:1-9). Here the Jews stirred up a tumult against him and he thought it advisable to leave, passing on to Berea and Athens and then to Corinth. He kept in communication with his friends at Thessalonica through Silas and Timothy (Acts 18:5) and heard of their steadfastness in the midst of continued persecution; and this good news moved him to write his first letter to them which is overflowing with thankfulness and joy at their Christian faithfulness so that from them ''sounded out the word of the Lord not only in Macedonia and Achaia, but also in every place your faith to Godward is spread abroad'' (1:8).

In the course of his letter he introduces a passage on the final coming of the Lord (4:13-18) in which he tells them that they are not to sorrow over their dead as those who have no hope, for they that sleep in Jesus will God bring with him and those who are alive at the coming of the Lord shall have no precedence over them which are already fallen asleep.

This passage, instead of comforting the Thessalonians, had the unexpected and unhappy effect of creating dissension and alarm, as the matter of the final coming of the Lord has so often done to this day. It was seized upon by some of the Thessalonians and made to mean that the coming of the Lord was already impending and might happen at any moment, and this was greatly exciting and dividing the church.

To correct this erroneous view Paul hastened to write his Second Epistle to the Thessalonians in which he expressly stated that ''that day shall not come'' until certain other events come to pass, and he mentions a falling away from the faith and the revelation of the ''man of sin'' (2:1-12), events which appear to be yet in the future.

This troublesome question and Paul's solution of it illustrates his skill in meeting emergencies and solving difficulties; and it also shows how the prevailing Jewish apocalyptic hope of the coming of the Lord in a cosmic catastrophe, that was attended with such alarm and practical evil consequences, was by him reduced to sanity and turned to orderly living. More and more in his Epistles the apocalyptic catastrophe kingdom becomes a spiritual reign of God in the hearts of believers which is to grow through the ages.

Thus early was Scripture misunderstood and turned to controversy and dissension and dangerous misinterpretation and perversion and uses, a fate that has attended it through all the Christian centuries and is still disturbing and dividing the church.

According to the scheme here adopted the two Epistles to the Thessalonians were the second and third letters written by Paul, Galatians being the first.

Outline of I Thessalonians:

    I.   Paul's thankfulness, 1.
    II.   Paul's defence of himself, 2-3.
    III. Exhortations, 4:1-12.
    IV. The coming of the Lord, 4:13-5:11.
    V.   Final Words, 5:12-28.

Outline of II Thessalonians:

    I.   Salutations and thanksgiving, 1.
    II.   The coming of the Lord, 2.
    III. Exhortations, 3.

I and II TIMOTHY

As we have already seen there is difficulty in inserting the Pastoral Epistles, I and II Timothy and Titus, in the narrative of Paul's life in the Acts, and therefore they can be best accounted for by supposing that Paul was released from his first imprisonment and did further missionary work, during which he wrote I Timothy and Titus, and that he was arrested and imprisoned a second time, during which he wrote II Timothy. Early tradition supports this view.

In I Timothy we learn that Paul had urged Timothy to remain in Ephesus when he himself went into Macedonia (1:3). Just where Paul was when he wrote the letter cannot be determined. He is chiefly concerned in his first letter to his disciple with two things: erroneous teaching and church government. The church at Ephesus, as was the case with all these early churches, was constantly exposed to false teachers (1:3), and their doctrines were generally some form of Judaism (1:4-8; 4:3) or of pagan philosophy (6:20). These converts, being mostly Gentiles, were greatly disturbed by claims that they must obey the Mosaic law; and that ancient world was rife with many religions and philosophies which were vain speculations as to strange forms of knowledge (Gnosticism) or as to the evil nature of the material world or as to the nature of angels and the spirit world. Paul is guarding Timothy and the church under his care against these dangers.

These early churches were also developing forms of organization or government with officers, such as elders and deacons. Paul did not himself institute any of these offices, but they grew up and were adopted as they were needed, as in the case of deacons in the church at Jerusalem (Acts 6:1-6). Paul, however, had much to say about the selection and character and conduct of these officers (3:1-13). Interspersed among these warnings and directions and other practical matters are many passages in which Paul rises to noble heights of doctrinal and spiritual eloquence, as in 6:15-16.

In II Timothy Paul is again in prison in Rome and under the very shadow of his execution. He is not now concerned with doctrinal errors and points of church polity but has passed into the state of mind in which he feels that his work is done and he is only waiting to be offered (4:6-8). His second letter therefore abounds in admonitions to Timothy to be faithful in doctrine and life (2:1-26), and he is anxious and urgent that his beloved disciple would hasten to come to him (4:9-15). The veteran soldier who has fought so many battles with unwearied energy and undaunted bravery is now spent and faint and longs for companionship and comfort. And yet his faith is undimmed and in the very presence of the tragic end his spirit rises to its noblest height of courage and eloquence in his final note of victory (4:7-8).

Outline of I Timothy:

I. Salutation, 1:1-2.
II. Personal exhortations to Timothy, 1:3-20.
III. Exhortations to prayer and as to women keeping silence in church, 2.
IV. Directions as to elders, deacons and widows, 3:1-16, 5:1-25.
V. Doctrinal injunctions, 4.
VI. Further exhortations, 6.

Outline of II Timothy:
   I.   Salutation, 1:1-2.
   II. Personal exhortations to Timothy, 1:3-4:8.
   III. Personal messages, 4:9-22.

TITUS

The Epistle to Titus closely parallels I Timothy in that the same doctrinal errors and problems of church government are dealt with in both letters. Paul had left Titus at Crete (1:5), just when cannot be determined, and now sends him instructions as to his work and duties among the churches on that island. False teaching by "vain talkers, specially they of the circumcision" (1:10), had appeared among these churches, and Titus was directed to "ordain elders in every city" (1:5), and specific directions were given him as to these officers. Thus the work of Timothy in Ephesus and the work of Titus in Crete are very similar, and hence the contents of the two letters, probably written near the same time, are similar in contents and teaching.

Outline of Titus:
   I.   Salutation, 1:1-4.
   II. Directions as to elders, 1:5-16.
   III. Admonitions as to the daily life of believers, 2-3:3.
   IV. Doctrinal instructions, 3:4-11.
   V.   Personal matters, 5:12-15.

PHILEMON

This letter is the gem among Paul's Epistles and is one of the most beautiful as well as one of the most profoundly significant things in the Bible. Onesimus was a slave who had probably robbed and then run away from his master, Philemon, in Colosse, and turned up in Rome, the whirlpool towards which all the flotsam and jetsam of the world then drifted. Here Paul found him and converted him and became dearly attached to him.

The problem now arose, What was to be done with the convert who was still the legal slave of his master? There was no hesitation on this point on the part of either Paul or Onesimus. Paul sent the slave back to his master with this little letter. He greets Philemon as "our dearly beloved brother" and thanks God for his Christian love and faith, appeals to him as "Paul the aged," for he was in prison for the last time, and beseeches him on behalf of "my son Onesimus whom I have begotten in my bonds," and begs his master to "receive him" "not now as a servant, but above a servant, a brother beloved." He offers to make good and pay out of his own pocket any loss which Philemon may have sustained through Onesimus, and reminds him how much he owes Paul and delicately hints at the emancipation of Onesimus, "knowing that thou wilt also do more than I say." Thus graciously did Paul negotiate this ticklish business with his friend Philemon and restore the slave to his master, but under new conditions in which the old relation of ownership was transformed and transfigured into Christian brotherhood.

Why did Paul not himself free the slave and demand his emancipation from the Christian master? Because the day for this had not yet come. Slavery was then so deeply rooted in law and custom and social ideas that it could not be suddenly eradicated by violent means. Only time could work such changes in the mental and moral climate of the world that this old evil could be abolished.

But Paul did breathe a spirit through this letter into this relation which in time was a silent but powerful influence in abolishing it. In fact this little letter put a charge of moral dynamite under the institution of slavery which did blow it out of the world; or it diffused through the atmosphere of civilization a spirit of humanity and brotherhood which in the course of the Christian centuries dissolved the fetters of slavery as the balmy breath of the spring melts the icy bonds of winter. Verily the hand of Paul in penning this brief letter reached through the ages and helped to write, along with the hand of Lincoln, the American Emancipation Proclamation.

Outline of Philemon:

   I. Salutation and thanksgiving, 1-7.
  II. Appeals to Philemon, 8-21.
 III. Personal matters, 22-25.

(5) Review of the Epistles. As we review the letters of Paul as a whole we see that they form his autobiography and reflect the many-sided, variously-colored aspects

of his life.   They are full of the city and market-place
and sea, of the Roman theater and games, of all the religious ideas and controversies of his day, and of all the
storm and stress of his picturesque career.   Hebrew religion and Greek thought and Roman life are interwoven
throughout their entire fabric.   They are Paul as painted
by himself, and no other life in the Roman Empire of his
day stands out in such intimate and lifelike portraiture
and realistic colors.

There is plainly in them a progression of ideas and
spirit.   In general this progress is from the outer to the
inner, from the objective and ceremonial to the subjective
and spiritual, from controversy to conciliation, from logic
to life, from the external apocalyptic kingdom in the
world to the inner reign of God in the heart, from theology to religion, from argument with others to meditation
in himself, from factionalism to fellowship, from tumult
to calm, from storm to serenity, and from passion to
peace.

The letters begin with the battle-cry and trumpet-blast
of Galatians and close with the quiet admonitions and
affectionate endearments of II Timothy.   At first Paul
is the aggressive emancipator as he stands up for his Gentile converts and dares to declare, ''There is no difference
between the Jew and the Greek''; then he is the conciliator
as he harmonizes parties and factions in his churches;
then in Romans he is the systematizer of doctrinal theology; in Ephesians he is a spiritualizer as he penetrates
and fills doctrine and church life with the vital breath of
the spirit; in Colossians he is a meditative and mystic
philosopher as he deeply reflects upon the cosmic Christ
as the immanent principle of the universe by whom all
things consist and reaches conclusions that are profoundly
akin to modern philosophical views of the universe; as a
mystic he loses himself in the life that is hid with Christ
in God; he is a philanthropist in Philemon in which he
writes only a few words that yet put dynamite under the
institution of slavery and helped to blow it out of the
world; finally he is ''Paul the aged'' writing farewell
words with a fettered and weary hand in which he declares that he is ready to be offered and is calmly waiting

for the sure stroke of a Roman sword. Thus the stream, that at first leaped forth as a raging mountain torrent and then ran a swift course, at length slowed down into a calm current and finally broadened out and silently mingled in the immeasurable sea.

There is one strange and startling omission in these letters: the life and teaching of Jesus. Not a parable or an utterance or a miracle or a deed of Jesus recorded in the Gospels, save the glorious exception of his resurrection, appears in the Epistles of Paul. He must have had knowledge of these things that are so precious to us, but he disregarded them as not pertaining to his purpose. The human Jesus becomes invisible in the life of the glorified Christ. It was the cross that absorbed the soul of Paul, and the risen Christ that filled the whole field of his vision. Hardly ever is Christ quoted, but his person is adored; his sayings are scarcely mentioned, but Christ himself is all in all.

It is because he is so many-sided that men of all theological views and emotional temperaments find support in Paul. Roman Catholic and Protestant, Calvinist and Arminian, conservative and liberal, theologian and mystic, philosopher and poet, all lay claim to Paul and can find in his letters apt texts to support their claims. Preacher and pioneer, orator and man of letters, logical thinker and mystical dreamer, a poet who could write a lovely lyric that is hardly surpassed in all literature and yet a man of practical action and daring adventure who could write down a catalogue of appalling hardships (II Cor. 11: 23-28), he poured his complex and rich nature and varied life into his Epistles so that they are among the most precious treasures of the New Testament and are the most valuable and vital letters in the literature of the world.

We conclude our review of Paul's Epistles with an evaluation of them by Professor Francis G. Peabody in his recent volume on *The Apostle Paul and the Modern World*, page 126: ''In short, the letters of Paul are the confessions of a great soul and the counsels of a great mind, revealing with the intimacy of passionate affection the hopes and fears, the ideas and ideals, which passing events conspired to suggest. Liberty, unity, spirituality, the bearing of each other's burdens, the supreme law of sacrificial love,—these essential graces of the Christian life, traced in a masterly fashion to the abiding influence of the grace of Jesus Christ, give to the letters of Paul their permanent place as guides of religious experience, and make them the most undisguised and the most inspiring chapters of spiritual autobiography in the history of literature.''

CHAPTER V

THE CATHOLIC EPISTLES AND REVELATION

The following seven Epistles, Hebrews, James, I and II Peter, I, II and III John and Jude, have from early times been designated "Catholic Epistles," probably because they are not addressed to particular churches but are letters for general circulation, and in this class we shall include Hebrews as being of the same nature.

These Epistles stand in contrast with Paul's letters in that they did not grow out of special conditions in particular churches or were not addressed to individuals, but dealt with general conditions of early Christian life. They put emphasis on conduct rather than on creed and are ethical rather than theological, although of course doctrine is interwoven with this ethical teaching as ethical teaching is interwoven with Paul's doctrinal Epistles.

HEBREWS

The Epistle to the Hebrews is unique among the books of the New Testament in several respects. It contains no internal indications of its authorship and of the time and place of its writing and of the location of the readers to whom it is addressed. While the Authorized Version calls it "The Epistle of Paul the Apostle to the Hebrews," yet the Revised Version designates it "The Epistle to the Hebrews," showing that the name of Paul is not found in the earliest manuscripts. These manuscripts have as a title simply the words "To Hebrews," and it is thought that these were supplied by a copyist.

As to authorship it is clearly not the work of Paul as the writer includes himself among those who received the gospel at second hand (2:3), whereas Paul emphatically claimed to have it by direct revelation (Gal. 1:12), and the whole method of reasoning and literary style are different from Paul's, and this internal evidence is strongly against his authorship. Other names that have been suggested for the honor, such as those of Barnabas and Apollos, are not supported by evidence.

Uncertain also is the location of the readers to whom it was addressed. The most probable and generally accepted supposition is that they were Jewish Christians in Rome; and the probable time of its origin is indicated by the fact that the Temple services apparently were still being observed (10:1-2), and this would place its writing before the destruction of the Temple in 70 A. D.

This Epistle is also unique in that it sets out to prove a definite proposition which is logically maintained from beginning to end. It comes nearer to being a systematic treatise than any other book in the Bible. Its proposition is that the Old Dispensation of the Mosaic Law is fulfilled and superceded by the New Dispensation of the Gospel. It announces its theme in the stately sentence with which it opens (1:1-4) in which it is declared that God, who had spoken in various times and ways to the fathers or prophets, has in these last days spoken unto us by his Son, who is the brightness of his glory and the express image of his person. Christ is thus at once set above Moses and above angels, and presently the cross is set above the altar, and this line of logic runs through the great argument as a musical theme recurs and rolls through a grand symphony.

It was therefore probably addressed to Jewish Christians who were called upon to make a great sacrifice and undergo a profound shock and change in passing from Moses to Christ, from Judaism, with all its sacred and patriotic roots and associations of a thousand years, to Christianity, and from the Temple, with its elaborate and gorgeous ceremonies, to the simple worship of a Christian church

The tendency was strong among these Jewish Christians to fall under the spell and back into the practice of Judaism, and to resist this tendency was the great battle of the early churches. Paul was a magnificent champion for freedom from Moses under the Gospel, and the unknown writer of Hebrews eloquently defended and contended for

42889

the same liberty. When it is considered how hard it is for people with long settled religious convictions to give up established and sacrosant orthodoxy for new forms of truth, we may appreciate the hard struggle it cost these Jewish Christians to make the transition from the old to the new. This Epistle is one of the historic landmarks of this change, an outstanding monument of this ancient battlefield.

The Epistle proceeds in logical order from its opening sentence from one telling point to another, and is written in a smooth and flowing and beautiful literary style. Interwoven with its logic at intervals are hortatory passages in which practical applications of its arguments are made. As we read it through we cannot but feel its charm as well as its logic, and some critics think it is the most beautiful book in the Bible.

Outline of Hebrews:

I. The finality of the Christian revelation, 1-4.
II. Christ as the true High Priest, 5-10.
III. Eulogy of Old Testament characters as illustrations of faith, 11.
IV. Practical applications and exhortations, 12-13.

JAMES

The contents of this general Epistle are moral teachings often expressed in aphoristic form after the manner of proverbs. At times it gives the impression of a string of pearls of wisdom with little inner connection, although the string itself is there as a common tie. There is a surprising lack of distinctive Christian doctrinal teaching, and Christ himself, although mentioned, remains in the background.

There is a contrast between faith and works running through the Epistle and coming out into special expression at particular points, notably in 2:14-26, and some have thought that the writer was opposing Paul's doctrine of salvation by faith and exalting works against faith. It is unnecessary, however, to put this interpretation upon the Epistle and it is plain enough that the writer is emphasizing the necessity of works as an expression of living faith and opposing a theoretical and unfruitful or dead faith.

Lincoln Christian College

As a homily or treatise on practical Christian ethics the Epistle was greatly needed among the early churches and it is needed not less today. It inculcates the doing of what we know and condemns profession without practice, creed without character and conduct, faith without works, and these are ever vital points in our Christian life. James in his Epistle supplements Paul in his letters, and the two together make the full-orbed Christian doctrine. Of course James also teaches the necessity of faith, and Paul teaches the necessity of works, but each puts special emphasis on the point he has in view, and the two are not antagonistic but complimentary and at the center are in harmony.

The author announces himself in the first verse as James, but there were many men of this name in apostolic times and in these early churches and so the name is indecisive as to the particular James. The traditional view has been that the writer was James the brother of the Lord and this remains a possibility. Yet there are difficulties that embarrass this view, such as that if the writer were the brother of the Lord would he not have said more about the Lord Jesus and his teaching and works? Many scholars hold that the author was some other James living at a later time and an unknown place. The authorship of the letter is of little importance: its contents remain the same on any theory of its authorship and are of permanent value.

Outline of James:
  I. Temptations, 1.
  II. Faults and failings, 2-4.
  III. Admonitions as to riches, patience, sickness and prayer, 5.

I and II PETER

I Peter declares itself to be a letter of the Apostle Peter written from "Babylon" (5:13) which is plainly Rome, to the "strangers scattered" through Asia Minor, or to the Jewish Christians in that region. It is written under impending "trial" (1:7; 4:12-19) which overshadows the pages of the letter like a storm cloud, and it is intended to strengthen believers in faith and godly living in those perilous times. It breathes Peter's spirit of deep conviction and urgency of action and recalls his speeches in the

Acts in its quotations from the prophets (1:16; 2:6).
Both the internal indications and the early external evidence strongly sustain the Petrine authorship.

As to its date, there is ancient evidence that Peter perished in the first Roman persecution of Christians under
Nero in 64 A. D., and if this is a true tradition this persecution would be the "trial" that was impending at the
time of the writing of this Epistle. The next persecution
was under Domitian about 90 A. D., and some date the
Epistle in this period.

II Peter also purports to be from the hand of Peter and
refers to I Peter (3:1), but it is so different in contents
and style that most scholars think it was written by a
later disciple of Peter and attributed to him after the
literary practice of the time. The Epistle deals with the
certainty of the Christian faith, with false teachers and
with the end of the world. It is notable as containing a
direct reference to Paul's Epistles (3:15-16) in which the
author found some things "hard to be understood." Commentators have had the same trouble with Paul to this
day.

Outline of I Peter:

    I.   Salutation and thanksgiving, 1:1–12.
   II.   Exhortations to holiness, 1:13-25.
 III.   Christ the chief corner stone, 2:1-10.
 IV.   Civil and domestic virtues, 2:1-10.
   V.   Coming trials, 4.
 VI.   Admonitions to elders and conclusions, 5.

Outline of II Peter:

    I.   Salutation, 1:1-4.
   II.   Christian graces enjoined, 1:5-15.
 III.   False teachers, 2.
 VI.   The end of the world, 3.

I, II and III JOHN

These three letters, two of them mere notes, are all
anonymous, but from early times they have been attributed
to the Apostle John, and there is much in their contents
and style that bears out this authorship. The writer evidently had personal knowledge of Christ (1:1), the literary style has close affinities with that of the Fourth Gospel, and the characteristic words of that Gospel, such as
life, light and truth, are also prominent in it. If the

author is John the apostle their date falls near the end of the first Christian century.

Their contents deal with existing conditions in the churches. The first Epistle glows with the love of God and it gives us two notable definitions of God: "God is light" (1:5) and "God is love" (4:8). The second letter is specially aimed at "deceivers" who denied that "Jesus Christ is come in the flesh," which denial was probably the ancient heresy that Jesus did not have a true human body but only a phantasm or appearance of one. The third brief letter condemns the self-assertion of one Diotrephes who was swollen with conceit and was troubling the church.

Outline of I John:
I. The incarnation of Christ and the duty of fellowship with him, 1.
II. Warnings against sin, 2.
III. The love of God and the duty it enjoins upon us, 3.
IV. On trying the spirits and living in the love of God, 4.
V. Faith in Christ and its fruits, 5.

Outline of II John:
I. Salutation, 1-3.
II. Exhortation to love, 4-6.
III. Warning against false teachers, 7-11.
IV. Conclusion, 12-13.

Outline of III John:
I. Salutation, 1.
II. Gaius congratulated on his faithfulness, 2-8.
III. The self-assertion of Diotrephes, 9-12.
IV. Conclusion, 13-14.

JUDE

This little letter is by "Jude, the servant of Jesus Christ, and brother of James," and from the earliest times the author has been identified with "Judas," one of the brothers of Jesus (Matt. 13:55). It is a general letter addressed to the "sanctified" or Christian believers. It warns against certain false teachers and urges faithfulness in Christian living. A comparison of verses 4-16 with II Peter 2 shows that the two passages are so closely alike that one or the other author has used the other, and the priority has by most scholars been accorded to Jude.

The letter is unique among the books of the New Testament in that it quotes from the Book of Enoch (14), one of the apocryphal books of the Jews, and probably also from the Assumption of Moses (9), another apocryphal book.

Outline of Jude:

I. Salutation, 1-36.
II. False teachers, 4-16.
III. Exhortations and doxology, 17-25.

REVELATION

The Book of Revelation belongs to the class of apocalyptic literature that abounded among the Jews during the period extending from 200 B. C. to 100 A. D. The word apocalypse means "unveiling" or "revelation" and such books were intended to reveal truth under symbolic forms which yet concealed it from hostile eyes. Two of these books are incorporated in the Bible, Daniel and Revelation, the one addressed to Jews under the terrible persecution of Antiochus Epiphanes, in the second century B. C., and the other to Christians under the Roman persecution of Domitian near the close of the first century A. D. The messages had to be conveyed in terms and figures that would not excite the intensified persecution of these enemies and yet would "unveil" the truth to persecuted believers; hence the apocalyptic form, a kind of literary camouflage with which the Jews were familiar and which would be plain to them.

This fact must be kept steadily in view in interpreting these books, or they will become a phantasmagoria in which the wildest vagaries will run riot. They have proven a mirage which has lured countless commentators into the pitfalls of fanciful interpretation. They have always been the "happy hunting grounds" of religious visionaries and fanatics.

When read in the light of this historical background Revelation ceases to be a hopeless enigma or tangle of puzzles and becomes reasonably clear in its meaning. It is true we are often mystified or in doubt as to the exact meaning of the highly figurative imagery employed, and yet the general purpose may be plain.

The author of the book is generally accepted to be the

same as the author of the Fourth Gospel, and its date is placed near the end of the first century A. D.

Outline of the Revelation:

I. Introduction, 1: 1-8.
II. Messages to the Seven Churches, 1: 9-3: 22.
III. Five visions, 4-16.
IV. The Fall of Rome, 17-18.
V. The Coming of Christ, 19.
VI. The Final Judgment, 20.
VII. The New Heaven and the New Earth, 21-22: 9.
VIII. Conclusion, 22: 10-21.

CHAPTER VI

THE CANON AND TRANSMISSION OF THE NEW TESTAMENT

There are now some general features or facts in connection with the New Testament that we may briefly consider.

1. THE CANON

The canon of the Scriptures means the rule of faith or the books that came to be included in the Bible as inspired or authoritative Scripture. The twenty-seven books in our New Testament are only a selection from a larger number of religious books produced in the first and second centuries by Jewish and Christian writers, and some of these extra-canonical books not only survive but are of value in the history of early Christianity.

Among these early Christian writings we may specially name the Epistle of Barnabas, the Shepherd of Hermas, the Second Epistle of Clement, and the Didache or Teaching of the Twelve Apostles. Some of these books were regarded and quoted as inspired and came near to being adopted into the canon, as is seen in the fact that some of them are found in early existing manuscripts of the New Testament.

The process of sifting out the writings regarded as genuinely inspired, however, began early in the second century and proceeded slowly and through much debate and difficulty and lingering doubt until it was finally settled in the fourth century. Early writers, Clement of Rome (95 A. D.), Ignatius (115 A. D.) and Polycarp (115 A. D.) began to quote or use words from some of our New Testament books. Justin Martyr (150 A. D.) was acquainted with the idea of a canon and "from his time onwards no one could doubt that the writings of the apostles were, for the church, the primary authority for the determination of apostolic doctrine.''

Justin Martyr's disciple, Tatian, composed a Diatessaron or Harmony of the Four Gospels, based exclusively on our canonical Gospels. At first the Christian converts and preachers appealed only to the Old Testament as Scripture, but presently in the second century they began to appeal to the Gospels and then to the Epistles as of equal authority with the Old Testament.

There was much difference of opinion about certain books. Opposition was strong against Hebrews, James, II Peter, II and III John and Revelation, and these were among the last to receive general acceptance. Divided opinion and debate continued through the second and third centuries, and it was not until the Synod of Carthage in 397, at which Augustine was present, that the canon of the New Testament as we now have it was finally settled. The Old Testament passed through the same process and a longer period of doubt and it was not finally decided by Jewish authorities until about 200 A. D.

The question is sometimes raised as to whether the canon is yet closed and as to whether we do not have the right to open it either to take from it or add to it. Luther proposed to exclude James and there are yet those who would exclude Esther and Ecclesiastes. No one, however, proposes to add any other book, and the question of excluding any book now in the canon is not seriously raised and is largely an academic one. The Roman Catholic Bible contains certain books in the Old Testament not found in the Protestant canon, but the New Testament canon is the same in all communions.

2. MANUSCRIPTS.

The New Testament at first was written by hand on parchment or vellum usually of calfskin or on papyrus rolls, and this process was slow and expensive and made copies of the Scriptures scarce and costly. No autograph copy of any New Testament writing survives, and the oldest existing manuscript of the Bible is the Codex Sinaiticus discovered in 1844 in a monastery at Mt. Sinai and now in the Imperial Library at Petrograd. It dates from the 4th century and originally contained the whole Bible, and it still has the New Testament complete. Still earlier fragments of the New Testament exist, but this is the oldest complete copy, and probably it is the most precious book or manuscript in the world. It has been published in fac simile and is thus open to the study of scholars.

There are altogether more than 1,800 manuscripts of parts or the whole of the New Testament in existence, and of these 5 date from the 4th century, 17 from the 5th century, 35 from the 6th century, and so on in increasing numbers to the 17th century. Of course the printing press finally put an end to making manuscript copies of the Scriptures. Many of these manuscripts are beautifully written and ornamented with color and gilt work, and some of them are costly and splendid works of art.

The comparing of these manuscripts, especially the early ones, has been carried on with immense labor and patience so as to derive and construct the most correct text. There are several hundred thousand variations among the manuscripts, but these are all relatively unimportant and most of them are quite trivial. The best text does not consist of any manuscript, but is the product of all of them as worked out by the science of textual criticism.

The early manuscripts not only have no chapter and verse divisions but usually have no punctuation marks and the words and letters run on without break. Our present New Testament chapters were introduced by Cardinal Caro in 1238 and the verse divisions were made by Robertus Stephanus in 1551.

3. TRANSLATIONS

The Bible early passed through translation into other languages, the Septuagint or Greek version of the Old Testament being begun in the third century, B. C. The New Testament was translated in the fourth century, A. D., into Latin, Syriac, Egyptian and Armenian. In time it was rendered into all modern languages and can now be read in whole or in part in no fewer than seven hundred and seventy different languages and dialects. Few are the human beings on the globe, among savage tribes or on lonely islands or far corners of the world, that cannot have at least some part of the New Testament in their own tongue.

The history of the English New Testament begins in the 8th century when the Venerable Bede, an eminent scholar and churchman, translated the first six chapters of John's Gospel into the vernacular, but unfortunately this has been lost. Portions of the Psalms were next translated, and in the 10th century the Gospels were put into Anglo-Saxon. Many translations of parts of the New Testament were made before the first complete rendering of the Bible into English appeared in the 14th century under the name of Wycliffe, though whether he did any part of the work or all of it was done by his followers is uncertain.

Succeeding versions now appeared, each one striving to improve on its predecessors, down to our day. The version of William Tyndale, "to whom," says Dr. Westcott, "it has been allowed more than to any other man to give its characteristic shape to the English Bible," appeared in 1525. Coverdale's Bible appeared in the same year, the Bishops' Bible in 1568, and the Roman Catholic Reims and Douai version in 1582. Our Authorized Version, undertaken under the auspices of King James I and hence called the King James' Version, was begun in 1604 and published in 1611. The Revised Version, the joint product of English and American scholars, was begun in 1870 and the New Testament was completed in 1881. The American Standard Revision, issued in 1895, incorporates the suggestions of the American Revisers which were not accepted by the British revisers.

Several translations into more modern English, aiming to give the meaning of the original in our everyday speech, have appeared, and the most scholarly and probably the best of these is *A New Translation* by Dr. James Moffatt. The reading of this translation gives one a strikingly fresh and vivid sense of the meaning of the book. Our English New Testament is thus the product of more than a thousand years of scholarship devoted to the best rendering of the inspired Word into our noble English speech. Each successive version was based upon all former versions, and the final product is the ripened result of the whole process and growth and enrichment of ten centuries of study and literary culture. Our English Bible is believed to be the best translation of the Scriptures ever made, retaining as few versions have succeeded in doing not only the meaning but the very spirit and flavor of the original.

Our New Testament brings to us "words that are spirit and life?" These words express the thoughts of the apostles and of Jesus himself and recreate them in our minds so as to beget in us the same spiritual ideas and states and experiences they had. The whole New Testament is thus passed into our spiritual blood and assimilated into our spirit and speech. The life of Jesus is lived over again for us from his birth through all its scenes and sayings to its glorious end. Again we hear the angels sing and go with the shepherds to Bethlehem, and again we walk the highways and byways of Palestine as they were pressed by his blessed feet, and we view his mighty works and hear his very words. We see him steeped in splendor on the mount of transfiguration, witness the tragedy of the cross, experience all the wonder and excitement of the resurrection morning and gaze after him as he ascends into heaven.

John diffuses his mystic Gospel in our hearts and unrolls his grand apocalyptic pictures in the gallery of our imagination. We go with Paul to Corinth and Rome and look over his shoulder as he composes a profound theological epistle or pens a brief note to a friend.

Our English New Testament thus enables us to live over again the lives and experiences of apostles and of Jesus and fashions us into their likeness. This book pours their blood into our veins. It crowds their consciousness into our minds, even the human consciousness of Jesus, and thus we live, and yet not we, but Christ liveth in us.

This is why we should ever study, mark and meditate upon it, and thus dissolve it in our hearts that it may reappear in the strength and fruitfulness, the beauty and the blessedness of our Christian life.

PART III

THE LIFE OF JESUS

CHAPTER I

INTRODUCTION

The central Fact of the New Testament is a supreme Person. Persons are the significant and dominant facts and forces of the world. Great men are the teachers and leaders of mankind, the creators of civilization, the prophets and apostles that dream dreams that shape the things that are yet to be. They are the path-breakers and road-builders of the world. They are the mountain ranges and peaks that lift the level of the ages and determine the directions of the winds and rivers and carve the continents of history.

History is largely the biographies of great men in whom were concentrated the ideas and energies that controlled countless multitudes of human beings through a long succession of generations. One masterful man with great creative idea and compelling will may mold millions and put a spell upon far centuries.

It is the power of personality that makes the great statesman, general, orator, thinker, writer, or leader in any field. It was by the impact of personality that Demosthenes spoke in Athens and his voice sent Asiatic hordes staggering back in confusion from the shores of Greece, Caesar mastered Rome, Napoleon dominated Europe, and Lincoln liberated a fettered race. What would the Hebrew people have been without Abraham, or the Israelites without Moses, or primitive Christianity without Paul, or the American colonies without Washington? Could fifteen or twenty of the topmost names be blotted from the roll of history in what a poor and pitiful world might we be living today?

On this principle, who can calculate the infinite loss and lowering of all the levels of the world were Christ stricken

115

from the calendar of the centuries! All the ancient world, as we have seen, was a background and preparation for his coming, all the preceding centuries gravitated and converged towards his birth, and all the succeeding Christian events have flowed from him as a stream from its fountain.

Christendom is Christ writ large. It dates its calendar from his advent and organizes itself around him as its center. The Christian centuries are his lengthened shadow. Our modern world bears his image and superscription.

It is sadly true that the image is yet dim and blurred and at points scarcely discernible, but it is slowly being stamped upon our civilization. There are yet deep shadows and frightful blots even on Christendom, but the light is appreciably dawning on a Christian day. More and more the world is weighing its worths in his balances, testing its principles by his teachings, and deciding its questions by his standards.

Christ stands in the New Testament as a dynamic Person who cannot be circumscribed within human limitations and explained in purely human terms. He is human yet also divine, exemplifying in the most perfect and beautiful ways our common humanity and yet overstepping all our human boundaries and manifesting himself as the Son of God and Saviour of the world.

We have traced the ancient background that prepared for his coming and examined the books that contain the records of his life and work, and now we shall look at him more directly and endeavor to construct a portrait out of these materials that we may hope will bring Christ somewhat nearer and make him more real to us.

Space will permit only an outline sketch that will present only the chief scenes and sayings in this wonderful life. An endeavor will be made, however, not to produce a narrative of bare facts, but to impart to the picture some color and charm that will make it an attractive reality and cause Jesus to stand before us as a living and present personality. Narrative and description will be accompanied and illuminated with some interpretation and application, and the selected scenes and sayings will follow and be fitted into the Outline of Events in the Life of Jesus already adopted in our treatment for the Gospels.

CHAPTER II

THE THIRTY SILENT YEARS

The first word in the life of Jesus is silence. All human life begins in the womb of secrecy and then emerges into the open and slowly proceeds through long preparation into full development and activity. The tree sinks itself deep into soil and rock, and all great souls hide their roots in solitude and silence and patiently grow in secret before they come forth strong and skilled to do their work.

This private preparation may be long compared with the period of public service. It may take the artist years to acquire the skill that can execute a masterpiece in a few days or weeks, as the meteor gathers momentum through millions of invisible miles for one swift flash of splendor. Jesus took thirty years of preparation for just three years of work. These silent years may seem a great price to pay for such a brief ministry, but it was because he took time in preparation and got so thoroughly ready that he could accomplish his mission in so short a period of activity.

1. THE GENEALOGY OF JESUS
John 1:1-4; Matthew 1:1-17; Luke 3:23-38

Biography begins before birth. Heredity runs its roots back through many generations and even the entire race, and a complete biography of any life would open in Eden. Every line of study leads to remote origins, and the supreme problem of philosophy is to get back to the First Cause. The Bible antedates all temporal origins in its sublime declaration, "In the beginning God created the heaven and the earth."

John opens his biography of Jesus in eternity. "In the beginning was the Word, and the Word was with God, and the Word was God." Jesus himself had an eternal con-

117

sciousness, declaring, "Before Abraham was, I am." This was the true origin of Christ, and here we must leave this mystery.

Matthew and Luke give the human genealogies of Jesus, Matthew beginning with Abraham and ending with Jesus, and Luke reversing this order starts with Jesus and runs back to Adam and up to God. The two lists are different and this has always given rise to much discussion and difference of view. Various theories have been advanced to explain this fact. The most generally accepted explanation is that Matthew gives the genealogy of Joseph, and Luke gives that of Mary. The question is a complicated one but it is not of great importance, and our space will not permit even an explanation of these theories. A compact and clear discussion of the problem will be found in Robertson's recent *Harmony of the Gospels,* pp. 255-262. —The important thing about these genealogies is that they show that Jesus was of true human descent with ancestral roots running back to Abraham and Adam and up to God. They are thus a suggested sketch of a complete human heredity rooted in our entire race. Jesus was bone of our bone and flesh of our flesh. He drew his blood out of the veins of humanity and had tiny drops that descended into him from the most ancient springs of our race, even from Adam himself.

This true human kinship was a necessary part of his equipment for his mission as the Saviour of the world. It enabled him to identify himself with us so as to know us and sympathize with us, and it enables us to know and enter into intimate fellowship with him. This humanity of Jesus does not exclude or obscure his divinity but is the human means by and in which the glory of his divine nature is manifested.

2. A HOLY MYSTERY REVEALED
Matthew 1:18-23; Luke 1:26-38

As the opening acts of a drama shift rapidly from point to point, so the early scenes of this story occur in quick succession at widely separated places. Angels seem to have been swiftly flitting up and down through Judea and Galilee, bearing messages to the chief characters in the opening scenes of redemption. The whole land was alive with the divine presence, and Jerusalem and Nazareth and Bethlehem were luminous points that attracted the celestial visitants.

Announcement was made in Jerusalem to Zacharias and Elizabeth of the coming birth of John the Baptist as the forerunner of Jesus, and the next announcement was made to the Virgin Mary. Nothing is known of her family, but no queen or empress born to royal power and splendor, no woman of genius crowned with fame, was ever so highly honored as this Jewish peasant girl. "Hail, thou that art highly favored, the Lord is with thee; blessed art thou among women" (Luke 1:28). She was picked out of the countless millions of her human kind for this transcendent distinction that has made her conspicuous through all succeeding ages.

This strange announcement troubled the simple wondering girl, and she cast about in her mind what this manner of salutation meant. Fear shadowed all these angelic announcements. The angel quieted the troubled maiden with the assurance that she had found favor with God. "And behold, thou shalt conceive in thy womb, and bring forth a son, and shalt call his name Jesus." The virgin was now thrown into a new and deeper perplexity. "How shall this be?" she exclaimed, "seeing I know not a man." Then the angel revealed the great mystery; "The Holy Ghost shall come upon thee, and the power of the Highest shall overshadow thee: therefore also that holy thing which shall be born of thee shall be called the Son of God."

This initial miracle of the gospel story is definitely declared in the Gospels and has on it inimitable marks of truth and none of the marks of fiction. It is a private fact, and Matthew tells it as it must have been known to and have come from Joseph, and Luke as it must have been known to Mary. It is told with matchless modesty and artlessness and the reader feels that it could not have been invented.

It is not an isolated and irrational wonder, but an harmonious and logical part of the system of redemption. It is congruous with the preëxistence of Jesus and with his incarnation of God and his sinless humanity. The Son of

God was separated from ordinary men both in his entrance into and in his exit from this world. We accept this holy mystery and believe that the birth of Jesus was unique and ushered a new Man, even the Son of God, into the world.

3. THE BIRTH IN BETHLEHEM
Matthew 1:24-25; Luke 2:1-7

Caesar Augustus, master of the world, probably between the months of December and March, 5-4, B. C., issued a decree that a census should be taken of the empire that he might know its resources and reap from it a rich harvest of taxes, a decree that set all the world in commotion.

In the town of Nazareth in the north of Palestine lived Joseph, a carpenter, and Mary, his espoused wife, who though a virgin was great with child, having been overshadowed by the Holy Spirit and the mystery revealed to her and her betrothed husband. They were both descended from the line of David, and therefore, in accordance with the law that they be enrolled at their ancestral seat, to Bethlehem they must go.

Bethlehem is six miles south of Jerusalem on the crown of a steep ledge of rock or spur of the mountain ridge, jutting out to the east from the central range. Up this rocky road climbed the humble carpenter and his wife and passed through the gate into the village. When they came to the inn, it was already crowded with visitors driven thither by the decree that had stirred all Palestine and started many families to their ancestral seats. In connection with such an inn, usually the central space of its square inclosure, but probably in this case a cave in the limestone rock, was a stable or place for the horses and camels and cattle of the guests. Among these Oriental people it was and is no uncommon thing for travelers to make a bed of straw and spend the night in this place.

In this stable, probably in the very cave over which now stands the Church of the Nativity, Mary and Joseph found lodging for the night. It was not a mark of incivility on the part of the inn or of poverty on their part for them to do this, and yet what a glory that inn missed by not having room for these visitors that night!

In that cave Mary brought forth her first-born son; and as there was no woman's hand there to minister for her, she herself wrapped the babe in swaddling clothes; and as there was no other cradle to receive it she laid the child in the trough from which the camels were fed.

This is all we know of what took place in that cave on that memorable night from which the Christian world now dates its calendar. The apocryphal Gospels, legends that afterwards grew up, fill the chamber with supernal light so that visitors had to shade their eyes from the splendor of the child; and the painters portray the holy child and mother with halos of glory around their heads. But all this is imagination and myth. Jesus was born as other children are born and looked just like a human child. No one seeing him could have guessed that a unique birth had brought a divine Man into the world.

No spectacular display attended his birth such as celebrated the birth of a Caesar. Jesus stole into the world quietly in human form and garb, and thereby he identified himself with our human kind so that he could knit himself into all our human needs and relations and truly be the Son of Man and Saviour of the world.

4. ANGELS AND SHEPHERDS. Luke 2: 8-20

The Christ-child was born, and now the problem was to get the wonderful news out into the world. An angel came from heaven to proclaim the epochal event to earth. Where shall he go and begin, what human ears shall first have the privilege of hearing the glad tidings? Let the angel go to Jerusalem, we would have said, and call upon the high priest and first take him into his confidence, and then let him go to the temple and stand amidst the splendors of that holy sanctuary and announce to the assembled priests and scribes that prophecy had been fulfilled and their long-expected Messiah had come. Shall not some respect be paid to official places and persons? Has not God ordained priests and presbyters through whom he dispenses his grace and administers his kingdom?

Yet history witnesses that at times few men stand in God's way more than ecclesiastics. They are rarely the men that earliest hear a new message; God must usually

tell it to some one else first.   One of the most startling
things in the Bible is the fact that the announcement of the
birth of Christ was made, not to priests, but to shepherds,
and the gospel was first preached, not in a temple or
church, but in a pasture field where there were more sheep
than men to hear.   What a rebuke is this to our ecclesiastical pretension and pride!   God can easily dispense with
us and may pass us by and speak to humbler souls.   The
great people up in the temple have no monopoly of his
grace and it may break out in some wholly unexpected
place.

On the night of the Nativity the shepherds were in the
field keeping watch over their flocks, for those faithfully
engaged in the lowliest duties may receive a splendid vis-
itation from heaven.   The skies were as serene and the
stars burned as calm as in all the past.   The shepherds
were as unconscious of any coming wonder as the sleeping
sheep that lay like drifted snow on the ridges.   Yet the
heavens were strained tense with expectation and were on
the point of being shattered into song.

Flocks of angels were flying downward from the stars,
and as their white wings struck earth's atmosphere they
kindled it into radiance with heavenly glory, and from the
gallery of the skies they chanted their song, accompanied,
as the poets and painters have imagined, with all the
golden harps and deep-toned organ pipes of the celestial
choir.

An angel voice sang the solo, ''Behold, I bring you good
tidings of great joy which shall be to all people: for there
is born to you this day in the city of David a Saviour,
which is Christ the Lord.   And this shall be a sign unto
you; Ye shall find the babe wrapped in swaddling clothes,
and lying in a manger.''   The solo was followed by the
chorus, ''Glory to God in the highest, and on earth peace,
good will among men.''

Glory to God and human good will are the keynotes of
this song.   They are the fundamental notes of the gospel
and are related as cause and effect.   Divine glory is the
sun shining in the heavens, and human good will is a garden and orchard all abloom with flowers and laden with
fruit.   As the glory of the sun is transformed into rosy

buds and sweet fruit, so is the glory of God transformed into human good will. These are the two sides of the same gospel, the two parts of the same song. They cannot be separated and must go together; in glorifying God we make peace among men, and in making peace among men we glorify God. This is the social gospel that will save the world.

Did these shepherds let the song vanish into the silence of oblivion with the last echo and fall back into the old dull routine? No, they did not let it lapse. "Let us now go," they said, "even unto Bethlehem, and see this thing which is come to pass, which the Lord hath made known unto us." They translated vision into action and presently were climbing the rocky slope to Bethlehem and "found both Mary and Joseph, and the babe lying in the manger."

"Lying in a manger"—so humble and lowly was the point at which the Son of God entered the world. He was not wrapped in a purple robe and laid on a downy couch but was born in a stable and shepherds were his first visitors. He came as one of the common people and to this day is their representative. No one can ever raise the level of society by winning over the rich and the great. Whoever would lift the world must get his lever under its foundation stones. Taking hold of the carved cornice will only tear the roof off, but raising the lowest stone will also push up the spire's gilded point.

5. WORSHIPPING WISE MEN. Matthew 2:1-12

The birth of Jesus created a new center for the world and set heaven and earth revolving around his cradle. All things began to gravitate towards him as by a new and more powerful attraction. Angels sang, shepherds wondered, a new star glittered upon the blazing curtain of the night, and wise men came from afar to worship him. These wise men were Persian priests, scholars, scientists, astrologers, students of the stars. Rumors of a coming King or Saviour were widespread in the ancient world and doubtless had reached these worshipers of the sun to whom the stars were embodiments of deity. They were obedient to the heavenly vision, and across long stretches

124   THE MAKING AND MEANING

of desert sand they came and appeared in Jerusalem with
their inquiry concerning the newborn King of the Jews.

They were therefore broad-minded men whose horizon
was wider than their own deserts, or they never would
have overleaped their national piety and patriotism and
prejudice into search and reverence for a Jewish King.
There was no war between the science and the theology of
these wise men. Their science did not kill their religion, and
their religion did not strangle their science.   The stars,
according to their simple-minded way of thinking, did not
crowd God out of his universe.   Knowledge and reverence
made one music in their hearts as both their science and
their faith grew from more to more.

In due time "they came into the house and saw the
young child with Mary his mother; and they fell down and
worshiped him; and opening their treasures they offered
unto him gifts, gold and frankincense and myrrh."   Is
there anything more beautiful in the Bible, or in all literature?   The imagination of painter or poet may well
kindle at the scene.   There are the wondering mother, the
worshiping wise men bowing down, the shining fragrant
gifts, and in the midst as the center and glory of it all the
young Child.   This Child, which even in its infancy sub-
ordinates mother and wise men and gold to itself, is indeed
a King.

These Persian scholars were forerunners of other wise
men going to Bethlehem. Through all the Christian centuries men of genius have been laying their most precious
gifts at the feet of Christ.   Columbus had no sooner set
foot on a new shore than he named it San Salvador, Holy
Saviour, and thus he laid his great discovery, America, at
the feet of Jesus.   Leonardo da Vinci swept the golden
goblets from the table of his "Last Supper" because he
feared their splendor would distract attention from and
dim the glory of the Master himself.   The hand that
rounded St. Peter's dome reared it in adoration of Christ,
and Raphael in painting the "Transfiguration" laid his
masterpiece at the feet of this Child.   Mozart there laid
his symphonies, and Beethoven the works of his colossal
genius.   Shakespeare, "with the best brain in six thousand years," who has poured the many-colored splendors

of his imagination over all our life, wrote in his will: "I commend my soul into the hands of God my Creator, hoping and absurdly believing, through the only merits of Jesus Christ my Saviour, to be made partaker of life everlasting." Tennyson begins his In Memoriam, in the judgment of many the superbest literary blossom of the nineteenth century, with the invocation, "Strong Son of God, Immortal Love." The gold of these wise men was only the first gleam of the shining heaps of wealth and of the most precious worths of the world that his followers are now piling on the altar of his service.

Every generation sends a more numerous company to Bethlehem. With every century worshipers arrive from more distant lands. From every quarter of the globe paths now run to the manger of this Child, worn deep by millions of feet. The nations are beginning to come. By and by these converging roads will be crowded and the ends of the earth will bring their gold and their most fragrant gifts and shall lay them at his feet.

To escape the murderous fury, born of fear of a rival, of Herod, who sent soldiers to thrust a sword through every cradle in Bethlehem, Mary and Joseph fled with the Child by way of Egypt and returned to Nazareth.

6. The Childhood at Nazareth
Matthew 2:23; Luke 2:39-52

Two or three brief descriptive verses and one anecdote tell us all we know of the childhood of Jesus. We would like to know more; for we are interested in the childhood of great men. We are curious to see whether the stamp of greatness was on them from the beginning, or whether at first they were indistinguishable from other children.

We wonder what may have been the boyhood of Jesus and long for a peep behind the veil. As usual the apocryphal gospels are most voluble where the inspired Gospels are most reticent. They fill the childhood of Jesus with marvels and miracles that are irrational and silly. The broad difference between the books that were put in and the books that were kept out of the New Testament is one of the wonders and proofs of inspiration.

But while the Gospels maintain an impressive silence, yet we know more than they tell us and have considerable general knowledge of the childhood of Jesus. We know that he was a true human child and grew up through the normal stages and experiences of our human life. He nestled and cooed and smiled in his mother's arms. His "baby hand was pressed against the circle of the breast," and he was lulled to sleep with a cradle song. He took his first tottering steps and invented his first childish words. He played in his father's carpenter shop and went to the village school. We know and use one of his school-books, for he studied the Old Testament in the synagogue which was the common school of the town, where attendance was compulsory. There were brothers in the home, and he grew up with them. He associated with the boys of Nazareth and played with them on the streets.

He must have walked the fields and climbed the hills around Nazareth and observed the beauty of flower and forest. From the hilltops he could see far and look down on the plain of Esdraelon, steeped in historic associations, and over to Carmel, and if he went far enough he could catch glimpses of snow-covered Hermon and sparkling Lake Galilee and the plunging, foaming Jordan and even of the blue Mediterranean.

He was a keen observer and a lover of nature and communed with it and saturated his soul with its mystic life. He did not for the first time observe the birds circling in the air and the loveliness of the lily when he used them as illustrations in his sermons, but all these nature references were reminiscences of his childhood life in Nazareth.

So also his knowledge of human nature that comes out so richly in his parables and teachings came out of his childhood knowledge, the unconscious education he picked up in the homes and streets of the village. He had seen his mother mixing dough or a neighboring woman sweeping her house in search of a lost coin before these incidents crept into his sermons as homely illustrations that made the truth picturesque and vivid.

In fact the whole childhood of Jesus was woven into his public ministry and can be read between the lines. His language was spun of the homely speech of rural life and all that he said and did ran back to the home and school and streets and hillsides of Nazareth.

We draw the line at any wrong act or thought. He was human, yet he was sinless. But he was not a grown-up boy, such as we used to find in the Sunday-school books, old beyond his years, morbidly self-conscious and unnaturally pious; but he was a genuine boy, artless, inquiring, spirited, with his whole nature in free and healthy play. The very charm of his boyhood lies in the fact that he was a boy and not something else.

The single recorded incident in the boyhood of Jesus is a "solitary floweret out of the wonderful enclosed garden of thirty years." It occurred when he was twelve years of age. This was a critical age and turning point in the life of the Jewish boy. At this age he was obliged to learn a trade for his own support; he began to wear the phylacteries; and he became "a son of the law" and was in some degree released from parental control. At this age the Jewish boy began to act upon his own responsibility and to take care of himself, and this fact throws light upon this incident.

Every year the parents of Jesus went to Jerusalem to the feast of the Passover, the great religious festival of the Jews, and on this occasion Jesus went with them. Probably for the first time he stepped out of the seclusion of Nazareth into the publicity of the metropolis, and it must have been with emotions of deep wonder and reverence that he entered the holy city and witnessed its scenes and shared in the services of the temple. He had a boy's interest and delight in the sights of the city, but the center of interest for him was his Father's house.

While at the feast the boy became separated from his parents, and they started home without him, supposing that he was in the caravan with friends—a not unlikely or unusual occurrence. On the third day, becoming anxious about him, they returned and found him in the temple in the midst of the rabbis, hearing them and asking them questions and displaying such wisdom that all were astonished.

This scene in the boyhood of Jesus has sometimes been

despoiled of its truth and beauty by making it out that he was instructing these rabbis and showing off his superior wisdom. On the contrary, he was hearing them and asking them questions; he was not instructor but scholar. Jesus never played the part of a smart boy but was modest and teachable and kept his place in the presence of superiors, and it was his rare spirit of wisdom and candor that elicited the admiration of those that heard him.

The parents were astonished—struck with admiration, as the strong Greek word means—at the scene. Parents are proverbially pleased with and proud of signs of promise in their children, and Mary and Joseph experienced this delight in a rare degree as the religious genius of Jesus began to flash out.

Yet there was also an ominous element in the situation which called forth from the anxious mother the chiding question, "Son, why hast thou thus dealt with us?" She realized that the lines of parental influence were slipping from her hands and that henceforth she could control her boy less and less and that he would act for himself more and more.

That was a painful moment for Mary, and it is a trying moment for every father and mother when they see their children beginning to separate themselves and assert their own individuality. But this is necessary and best for children. Ripened seeds must drop off the tree, or there could be no more trees.

Mary's question drew from Jesus his first recorded utterance: "How is it that ye sought me? wist ye not that I must be about my Father's business?" This reply is the kernel of this anecdote, the vital germ that kept it alive and caused it to blossom out in the gospel. Already Jesus was becoming aware of his divinity and his mission in the world. His life was now perfectly set to the music of the Father's will.

The parents of Jesus understood not this first recorded utterance—a sad commentary and mournful prophecy. How often has he been misunderstood and misrepresented so that his light has been turned to darkness? He came unto his own and his own received him not. And still the Christian world misunderstands him, and very imperfectly do the clearest Christian minds penetrate into the depth and power of his meaning. His simple words are larger than our largest thoughts of life and love.

7. The Carpenter. Mark 6:3

"Is not this the carpenter?" Yes, that is just who it was. The question was asked by his townsmen in derision and scorn as though it would place a stigma upon Jesus that would forever discredit him as a prophet, but the designation has ever since been worn by him as a mark of honor. Unconsciously they placed on his brow one of his brightest crowns.

It is a startling fact, which even after nineteen hundred years has not lost its wonder, that the Saviour of the world was a carpenter. This is not what the Jews expected, and it is not what we would have expected. They looked for a conquerer to break the power of Rome and possibly we would have looked for a great scholar or statesman, but God's ways are not as our ways and his Son came neither as the one nor as the other but as a carpenter.

This question is the only gleam of light we have from the life of Jesus from the twelfth to the thirtieth year of his age. Of this long period comprising more than half of his life not a word is recorded to tell us what he was doing except this word carpenter. But as an artist with a single sweep of his pencil or brush will sometimes draw the outline of his picture, so this word draws in outline the life of Jesus during this period. It sketches the life of one who did not separate himself from his fellowmen and from his home folk but knit himself into the humblest human relations. It shows us a common toiler working at an ordinary trade and living contentedly in honest poverty. There is color enough in this single word to paint a complete picture of Christ's early years. It is worth more than all the apocryphal gospels that are full of absurd stories of his youth. We may well be thankful for such a word.

The outstanding fact in these silent years of Jesus was that he was a producer; he was not an idle consumer but he added to the world's stock of goods. There were more and better houses in Nazareth or more ploughs and ox-yokes on the surrounding farms because he lived and toiled. We are sure that his trade was well learned and that everything that left his shop displayed the most thorough and finished workmanship. He who could build a star and sweep the orbit of a planet, whose hand had left its finishing touch on every grass-blade and dewdrop, could also lay off his angles and strike his circles true, and he would mortise timbers or shape ox-yokes so that they would render the best service and would last. His work never needed to be done over after him, he left no loose joints to be tightened up or rough places to be smoothed down. Every one knew that he could be trusted, and his work bore an unsurpassed reputation and commanded the highest prices.

All this was a true part of his ministry by which he helped to save the world from cold and hunger, and it was a fitting preparation for that spiritual carpentry by which he was to join humanity together and build a kingdom that would stand forever.

We need more of this spirit of faithful service in useful lines in these days when there is much slovenly work done in every trade and profession and so many are living in idleness and luxury on wealth that other hands have earned. Every one should be a productive worker by hand or head and thereby contribute to the wealth and welfare of the world. ''The thistle that grows in thy path,'' says Carlyle, ''dig it out, that a blade of grass, or a drop of nourishing milk, may grow there instead. The waste cotton-shrub, gather its waste white down, spin it, weave it: that in place of idle litter there may be folded webs, and the naked skin of man be covered.''

Paul commanded that ''if any would not work, neither should he eat'' (II Thess. 3:10), and the Saviour of the world, who ''goeth before'' us in all things, set us a noble and inspiring example at this point during these eighteen silent years.

CHAPTER III

FIRST YEAR: THE EARLY JUDEAN MINISTRY
YEAR OF OBSCURITY

The thirty years of preparation have done their work, and Jesus is now ready to step out into his public ministry. The first year was spent chiefly in Judea down in the Jordan valley and in and around Jerusalem with a visit to Galilee. It contained the striking opening events of the ministry and proceeded encouragingly though quietly so that it may be designated the year of obscurity. Dates cannot be definitely determined, but the probable dates are that the baptism of Jesus occurred in the fall of A. D. 26 and that the first year closed with his withdrawal from Judea for Galilee in December A. D. 27.

1. A GREAT REVIVAL MEETING
Matthew 3:1-12; Mark 1:1-8; Luke 3:1-20

A great revival meeting was going on down in the Jordan valley. The preacher was John the Baptist. Nothing had been heard of him for thirty years during which he was growing up in the hill country of Judea in that seclusion and silence in which all great things must grow. John was a Nazarite, we might call him a monk, a man who had withdrawn from human society and for years had lived a solitary life in the rocky regions around the Dead Sea.

What was the meaning of this strange life? It was a reaction against the formal hypocritical religion of his time. Religion among the Jews had gone to seed and husks. There was no sap in it, there were no green leaves and ripening fruit on it, but only empty pods. Jewish orthodoxy had thus become a huge heap of dry wood and straw: John the Baptist was the spark that set this tinder on fire; he was the Martin Luther of this reformation. Disgusted with Pharisaic hypocrisy he had turned from the Jewish church into the wilderness, not that he might have less religion, but more; that out there in the solitude far from men he might get close to God as did Moses in the mount.

At length, being filled with the Spirit, John suddenly emerged from obscurity and appeared on the banks of the Jordan where he began to preach. His striking personality, rough haircloth robe bound around his loins with a leather strap, uncut hair, flowing beard, and deep-set burning eye, suggested a prophet. The news reached Jerusalem that there was a prophet down at the Jordan, and the crowds went pouring down the steep rocky roads to hear him.

What was the secret of the preacher's power? Not his manner of dress and appearance. Eccentricities never made a Martin Luther or a John Knox. Long hair does not make a long head. John the Baptist was a sincere soul touched with the fire of God. He had gotten rid of empty forms and conventionalities and was speaking out his genuine beliefs and deep fiery emotions. Instead of mumbling traditional dogmas he spoke living truth from the heart to the heart. Such preaching created a tremendous sensation and drew people in great crowds.

The burning message of John was repentance as a preparation for the Messiah who was about to appear. The Greek word means "a change of mind," a mental act that reverses the mind and will from sin towards righteousness and God. It is thus in its root not an emotion but a volition which we can exercise and for which we are responsible. Such repentance prepares the way for Christ in the world and in our hearts and lives.

John also quoted Isaiah to prove his message had ancient authority and divine sanction. The truth he was preaching was not revolutionary but evolutionary. Isaiah was the original; John was the echo; Isaiah declared the message of repentance; John interpreted and applied it.

John also instituted the rite of baptism as an outer sign of this inner change of mind. The outer sign represents and confirms the inner act and roots it deeper in the soul and life. It is a public pledge that commits one to the new life and makes it easier to maintain one's loyalty to it.

2. THE BAPTISM OF JESUS
Matthew 3:13-17; Mark 1:9-11; Luke 3:21-22

At this point in the preaching of John Jesus appeared in his audience. Probably word of John's ministry had reached him in the seclusion of Nazareth and he knew that his hour was come. He offered himself for baptism, but John hesitated to administer the ordinance, saying, "I have need to be baptized of thee, and comest thou to me?" Jesus pressed the point, saying, "Suffer it to be so now: for thus it becometh us to fulfil all righteousness," and then John yielded and administered the rite.

There was some reason why Jesus submitted to this ordinance. It was not a fictitious performance done for mere show, but a genuine baptism. We must take this view of the whole life of Jesus. There was no acting or theatrical display in it, but everything was real, just what it purported to be. His growth in wisdom was a true process of education. His temptation was not a sham battle, but a veritable fight.

Baptism was a symbol of repentance and cleansing from sin, and in this sense Jesus did not need it and could not have accepted it, for he had no sins to repent of; but it was also a sign of entering the kingdom of God and a mark of consecration to his service, and in this sense Jesus could and did receive it. He himself first did what he asked others to do and wore this badge of loyalty to the kingdom of heaven.

This example of our Lord shows us the necessity of religious ordinances and the duty of observing them. Objections are made to religious rites as being unnecessary mechanical forms: only spirit is life. Undoubtedly the inner spirit is the life of religion, but can we have the inner life as fully and richly without the external form and means? The water is more important than the cup, but if we refuse the cup shall we get any water? We may have ordinances without religion, but not religion without ordinances. Dangerous as ordinances are, we must have them, and they that reject them cannot quote the example of the Lord Jesus Christ.

Jesus came up out of that baptismal water a new man into a new world. The heavens opened and the Holy Spirit descended upon him and filled him with all the fulness of God. Then came a voice from heaven, saying, ''Thou art my beloved Son, in whom I am well pleased.'' This probably marked the moment when Jesus became fully conscious of his divinity and Messiahship. Into the mystery of this moment we cannot enter and know not what glad recognition of the Father and what tremendous sense of responsibility and what mighty throb of joy he experienced in this epochal hour.

This great blessing came out of his obedience in receiving baptism. Jesus probably had no expectation of this gift when he offered himself for this ordinance. He was then simply doing his duty in fulfilling all righteousness. But he faithfully obeyed it, and, lo, this humble duty suddenly blossomed and bore this wondrous heavenly fruit! Had Jesus never gone down into that baptismal water, he never would have come up under an opened sky with the Holy Spirit streaming down upon him, and God never would have pronounced him his Son. We never can tell how near we are to unexpected and wonderful blessing when we are performing a duty, even the lowest and humblest.

3. The Temptation of Jesus
Matthew 4: 1-11; Mark 1: 12-13;   Luke 4: 1-13

Immediately after his baptism Jesus was led up into the wilderness to be tempted. Baptism and temptation are here crowded close together. Scarcely had the voice from heaven died away when a whisper was heard from hell. There are sudden and violent changes of weather in the spiritual world. The purest deed may be bordered with temptation; our finest moods may be marred by an evil suggestion. When God is especially close to us, Satan is nearby waiting for his chance. Out of the baptismal benediction of the Father, Jesus stepped into a desperate struggle with the devil.

Jesus was led up of the Spirit to be tempted. We are not to run into temptation of our own accord. We may not hunt the devil or go into his den ourselves. The path of duty as we are led of the Spirit will take us into temptation enough.

It was when Jesus was hungry and emaciated with forty days' fasting and was reduced to the lowest point of physical exhaustion that this temptation struck him. Satan did not assault him at his strongest moment but at his frailest hour when his vitality was at its lowest ebb. Satan knows a man's weakest time and waits for it. There are dangerous low tides in the strongest life, and the best man has his hours when he would not dare to meet the devil. These irresolute moments are often connected with bodily exhaustion and nervous depression, and we need to keep a constant grip on God that when we are weak we may be strong.

What was the state of mind of Jesus at this time and what was the meaning of this conflict? He had just come from his baptism which probably marked the moment when he became clearly conscious of his Messiahship and divinity and supernatural power. What would be the first, most natural, strongest and most deadly temptation in the possession of such power? To use it selfishly for personal ends. This is a temptation that always arises in connection with the sudden acquisition of power, such as great wealth or high office.

The question pressing on the mind of Jesus may have been, How would he use his divine power? For personal comfort and aggrandizement? or only in the service of God for the salvation of the world? Using his power in the first way would prostitute it to personal ambition and would prove his ruin, and using it the other way would lead by way of the cross to the fulfillment of his mission as the Saviour of the world. Satan saw this psychological moment and was there to try to push Jesus off the edge of this precipice into the bottomless pit.

The three temptations were all along this line of suggestion. To make bread out of stone was to do that which was harmless in itself and was only providing proper food for the body and so it came appareled in light as an innocent and reasonable and right thing to do. All sin practices this art of clothing itself in the garb of innocence so that hardly ever does a man do wrong until he has persuaded himself that the wrong is right. Yet this way of getting bread on the part of Jesus would have been to distrust and renounce his Father's providence in supplying his needs and to resort to his own power. Our senses and appetites are especially points of attack where temptation may assail us, sensuality is one of our commonest and most deadly sins, and at these points we need to be on our guard and keep on the whole armour of God.

Jesus saw through the false innocence of this proposal into its heart of disloyalty and disobedience and he struck it down with a sure stroke of the sword of the Spirit.

The second temptation to leap from the pinnacle of the temple was a proposal that Jesus should by this sensational act gain sudden popular applause and win quick support for his mission. It was a suggestion that he could fly from the appointed path of obedience and service off at any wild caprice and that God would keep him safe. The same temptation comes to us when we think to violate natural laws, as in some forms of faith cure, and expect God to keep us from harm. In such cases we want God to keep us, not in all his, but in all our ways. Jesus saw through this disloyal proposal and pierced it so that it lay slain at his feet.

The third temptation was an offer to Jesus by which he could win his kingdom in a moment by one little act and even get the world by a word. Perhaps the meaning of the suggestion that Jesus should worship Satan was that he was to resort to Satan's means, such as the sword and wealth and power, to establish his kingdom as other conquerors had done. Might not he also successfully do what Alexander and Caesar had done in their swift victorious campaigns and thus avoid the slow and tragic way of the cross?

The sword is Satan's own weapon and every night he sleeps on the pillows of power: why not put this quick instrument into the hands of Jesus? How strong is the temptation with us to take the short cut to our ends and to do the devil's bidding in using worldly means to reach worldly ambitions? We want the kingdom at a stroke and are in danger of selling our souls to get it.

Jesus felt the full force of this powerful temptation. He gazed upon the splendid prospect of that outspread world. He saw how short was the step that promised the kingdom. It was a perilous hour with him and his very mission as the Son of God trembled in the balance. Then turning in resistless might, he tore the mask from his tempter, revealed him in his hideous nakedness as Satan, bade him from his presence and declared his eternal allegiance and loyalty to God.

The Son of God was still untouched; not one fleck had spotted the immaculate whiteness of his soul. And the devil, foiled, defeated and crushed, fled and vanished into the infinite darkness whence he came.

We are to mark the means by which Jesus resisted these temptations: "It is written." "It is written." "It is written." The Word of God was his shield, and by it every flaming dart was quenched. He conquered by the ordinary means of grace. He did not call into action his divinity, but he bore this temptation in his humanity. He was tempted as we are, and he conquered as we may.

We need no new weapons to resist Satan, for still "it is written." The old Bible furnishes shields and swords to match all the temptations of modern life. The devil has invented no new weapon since the ones he used in the garden of Eden.

Yet Jesus did not conquer by merely quoting Scripture, for Satan quoted Scripture too. It was by his grip on the realities back of the written words that he won the victory. In proportion as we believe and feed upon these truths will they strengthen and inspire us and then when we resist the devil he will flee from us; and when he is gone, the angels of God will come.

4. How the Kingdom Started to Grow
John 1: 35-51

From his temptation in the wilderness Jesus came strong in spirit and wearing the victor's crown and returned to the Jordan where John was still preaching. On

seeing Jesus John exclaimed, "Behold the Lamb of God!"
and pointed his own disciples to the new Prophet. Here
was a preacher in the flood tide of his popularity and success turning his own disciples away from himself to another. John was now the central figure in all Judea and
all eyes were turned to him in expectation. It seemed
that a splendid crown was within his grasp. Why not announce himself as the Messiah? Yet he deliberately rejected it and placed it upon the brow of his rival. He appreciated the supreme and solitary greatness of Jesus and
cast his crown at his feet. "He must increase," he said,
"but I must decrease. He that cometh from above is
above all."

Two disciples turned from John and followed Jesus,
Andrew and John the son of Zebedee. To their inquiry,
"Master, where dwellest thou?" the answer of Jesus was,
"Come and see." From ten o'clock in the morning until
the evening shadows fell, Jesus and these two men engaged in earnest conversation concerning the Messiah and
his kingdom; and when they separated Jesus had bound
these first disciples to himself with cords of faith and
friendship that thereafter never broke.

There was no revival meeting or religious excitement in
connection with these conversions, but in the privacy and
quietness of a personal interview these men gave their
hearts to Christ. It is not necessary to engage in public
preaching and sway great audiences in order to save men;
a private word may be equally effective in drawing a soul
into the kingdom.

Jesus gained these two disciples himself, and now these
disciples started out to gain others. Andrew found Simon
his brother and brought him to Jesus. If John found his
brother James at the same time, the number of the disciples doubled the first day. Andrew, full of the joy of his
own discovery, hastened to his brother with the announcement, "We have found the Messiah!" That was glad
news to a Jew, and Andrew could not keep it to himself,
but immediately imparted it to his brother, "and he
brought him to Jesus."

Jesus found Andrew, Andrew found Simon: this is the
way the kingdom grows, each converted soul finding the

next one. Jesus began the process, and his own converts carried it on. Christians are Christ multiplied and continued. Andrew found his brother, and kinship and friendship are natural lines of connection along which the gospel still works. Ties of blood are powerful cords drawing others into the kingdom.

Jesus looked upon Simon with searching insight and said, "Thou art Simon the son of Jona: thou shalt be called Cephas, which is by interpretation, A stone." Peter means rock, and the new name described the new nature he was to receive through his fellowship with Jesus. Unstable and impulsive on the surface, there was yet lying deep in Peter a bed of rock that became a foundation of solid steadfastness in the kingdom of God. There are too many Christians of clay: Christ wants Christians of rock.

Andrew remained an obscure disciple, while Peter began to shine with brilliance and became conspicuous and forever famous, the one disciple revolving around the other as a mere satellite and known as "Simon Peter's brother." Yet it was the obscure brother that drew the more brilliant one within the attraction of the Sun of Righteousness and thus made him luminous. We may not be flaming apostles ourselves, but we may draw to Christ others who will be burning and shining lights.

On the next day Jesus started for Galilee, and presently he fell in with Philip and said unto him, "Follow me." Phillip joined the little company of disciples, and thus it grew even as it passed along the public road.

Again the process of one convert finding another started and "Philip findeth Nathanael, and saith unto him, we have found him, of whom Moses in the law, and the prophets did write, Jesus of Nazareth, the son of Joseph." This speech shows that Philip was a student of the Scriptures and knew what to look for in the Messiah and that he found these marks fulfilled in Jesus.

But this announcement that sprang from a heart of joy and full of good intention instantly struck a snag and stirred up prejudice in Nathanael's mind. "Can there any good thing come out of Nazareth?" He was from Cana (John 21:2), a neighboring village, and doubtless shared the prejudice that one town often entertains against another. So he met the gladdest announcement that could come to a Jew with a rebuff born of petty local jealousy and pride.

Prejudice in its myriad forms is still one of the greatest obstructions in the way of the gospel. Prejudice against Christian faith on account of its mysteries and difficulties, against the church on account of the inconsistencies of its members, many are the objections a prejudiced person can raise against the call of Christ, especially if secretly he does not want to follow him.

Had Philip undertaken to argue the point with Nathanael he might have gotten the worst of the argument; at least he would probably only have confirmed Nathanael in his prejudice. But his simple answer was, "Come and see." Nathanael acted on this reasonable proposal, and, after a brief interview with Jesus and a personal experience of his fellowship, he exclaimed, "Rabbi, thou art the Son of God; thou art the king of Israel." What no controversy could have done, simple seeing for himself did do.

This is still Christ's own proposal for the solution of all our doubts and difficulties. Fellowship and obedience are ever the way out of these into clearness and sureness of faith. Let us honestly go to Christ and try his doctrine and way of life, and we shall know that he is of God and accept him as our Lord and King.

Thus we see how the kingdom began to grow. It is instructive to study how Christ started his work. He did not begin and carry on his work, as we would have expected, with a great spectacular program and campaign. He did not go to Jerusalem, the civil and religious metropolis, and there build a great tabernacle seating five or ten thousand people and preach to packed audiences. On the contrary he went into the obscure parts of the country and engaged in his work quietly and privately, trying to keep down excitement and avoid crowds. Even when working miracles he endeavored to prevent their being blazed abroad as a means of creating wonder and drawing people through curiosity. He preferred to meet the people in small groups. It seemed that he would rather sit down and talk with one man than preach to five thousand.

It is true that he did at times attract great multitudes and preach in the open air. But it is remarkable that no conversion is recorded as having taken place under this public preaching. Jesus picked up most of his converts through private interviews. When he preached to a throng he might not get anybody, but when he talked with one he was sure of his man.

All growth takes place by gradual accretions. It is thus that Christ's kingdom grows. As the process of crystallization proceeds through a liquid atom by atom, as a tree grows cell by cell, so does the line of conversion move through the home and across the country and around the world. The method of Jesus is that of growth, first the blade, then the ear, after that the full corn in the ear; it is that of the leaven that spreads slowly through the whole mass. As Christ found Philip and Philip found Nathanael so are we to keep adding link to link in the lengthening chain of his kingdom until it binds his first with his final coming.

5. WATER TURNED INTO WINE. John 2:1-11

Arriving in Galilee, Jesus went with his disciples to the village of Cana, where a wedding was being celebrated and his mother was there. Possibly the wedding was the occasion of this visit, and it is deeply significant that he was present and participated in such a joyous ceremony. By this act he at once set himself in bold contrast with his forerunner, John the Baptist.

Jesus was not a recluse and an ascetic, separating himself from his human kind, but he was a man of the world, mingling freely in all its currents and sharing in its varied scenes and festivities. The Christian is not to keep himself out of the world, though he is to keep himself unspotted from the world. To be saved is not to be sad.

The joy of the occasion was suddenly halted: the wine failed. The wine of this world always does fail. Any joy that rests on a material basis is built on sand and cannot last. The mother of Jesus was quick to sense the situation and with delicate tact she said to him, "They have no wine." This gentle hint of the mother drew from the son a strange reply. While it contains no slightest discourtesy, yet it was an intimation to her that he must judge of the time and way of his own action and could not use his power at the suggestion of another. We must beware of the faintest suggestion in our prayers of dictating to God and must never try to hurry him up.

The mother, however, was satisfied with the answer, doubtless hearing between the words more than was said, and with beautiful trust directed the servants, "Whatsoever he saith unto you, do it." This is the bond that should bind us to Christ, and no surer ground of obedience and no finer fellowship can we find than simply to do what he bids us.

The moment for action came and at the command of Jesus the servants first filled with water the six large stone jars standing by and then drew out and bore to the ruler of the feast wine which he pronounced of the best quality. At some point in this process "the conscious water saw its God and blushed," the water reddened into wine. Into the inner mechanism of this miracle we cannot penetrate, but it is no more mysterious than the chemistry by which water is turned into wine inside the grape. Jesus did in a moment what the sun does in a month.

The miracles of Jesus were all acted parables, forms of the truth cast in the visible and vivid molds of concrete deeds. When the wine of this world fails and life looks dark, Jesus can work a transformation that will be as wine to our spirits. How often as we look out over the world and see its widespread misery and sorrow can we say of its millions, "They have no wine"? Somewhere there must be refreshment for its thirsting people, and the same hand that furnished the wine at that wedding in Cana can supply the spiritual wine of his wisdom and grace that is abundant and rich enough for all the world.

In giving us this blessing Jesus makes use of the means we have and gives us a part in the process. The servants filled the jar with water and drew out the wine. Had they put no water in, no wine would have come out. God has a part for us in all his dealings with us, and in all the blessings he gives us we are co-workers with him.

The wine proved to be of such good quality that the ruler exclaimed, "Thou hast kept the good wine until now." Christ always gives us the best he has. He offers us no cheap gifts, palms off on us no adulterated goods, but gives us the best his market affords, and his market is the universe. The devil gives his best wine first, but at last it biteth like a serpent; there is a snake in the bottom of his cup. The first end of sin is always pleasant: it is the last end that stings. The Christian life grows better and better and it will end with the wine of heaven.

In this beginning of his miracles Jesus "manifested forth his glory." Water changed into wine is a symbol of all his work. He transmutes sin into penitence, unbelief into faith, the vileness of wickedness into the beauty of holiness, and sinners into saints.

The chemist takes scum and dross and transforms them into exquisite perfume and the most beautiful colors. The artist takes coarse materials and transfigures them into masterpieces of painting, and the sculptor turns a block of stone into a white angel. The most brilliant diamond is only common coal transformed into a blazing jewel shooting vivid flashes of light.

All that Christ touches he transforms and transfigures. He brings the best possibilities out of men. Under his divine sunshine and quickening breath the wilderness shall rejoice and blossom as the rose and become a new Paradise of God.

6. FIRST CLEANSING OF THE TEMPLE. John 2:13-22.

Jesus sojourned for a few days in Capernaum and then returned to Judea and we next find him at the first Passover he attended in his ministry. Holy city as it was by calling and privilege, Jerusalem was no congenial place for Jesus.

We shall let the Italian novelist, Giovanni Papini, paint the picture for us in his *Life of Christ:* "Jerusalem like all capitals—great sewers to which flow the refuse, the outcasts, the rubbish of the nations—is inhabited by a mob of frivolous, elegant, idle, skeptical and indifferent people, by a ceremonious patrician class who have kept only the tradition of ritual and the sterile rancor of their decadence; by an aristocracy of property owners and speculators who belong to the herd of Mammon, and by a rebellious, restless, ignorant crowd, controlled only by the superstition of the Temple and the fear of the foreigner's sword. Jerusalem was not fit soil for the sowing of Jesus.''

When Jesus entered the sacred precincts of the temple, he found a terrible desecration of his Father's house. Immense numbers of animals were needed for the feast and offerings, and worshipers bought these in Jerusalem. There were also brokers for the exchange of the various kinds of foreign money into shekels for the temple offerings. All this business, attended as it was with gross evils, had invaded the temple court. The crowds and confusion, the cattle and merchandise and traffic, the clamorous hawking and haranguing of the noisy Oriental venders, the cheating and frauds, were a wicked and intolerable nuisance and desecration of the place of worship. The holy house of prayer had been turned into a den of thieves.

No associations that jar upon our sense of propriety and reverence should be allowed to invade and gather around our sanctuary. The church is exposed to the same evil in a more insidious and dangerous way through the intrusion of a worldly spirit into its worship and membership. When the selfishness and strife and unrighteousness of the world get into the church, it is no more a fit dwelling place for the Holy Spirit of Christ and there the Shekinah ceases to shine.

Jesus looked upon the shocking scene with painful aversion and holy indignation. He was a young man, an unknown Galilean, with no express authority to interfere, for the matter was under the supervision of the priests, but there are moments when petty points of order and mere technicalities must give way before some fundamental principle and mighty impulse of righteousness.

Jesus felt that this hour had come. The whole thing was broadly and glaringly illegal and should be ended at once. Picking up some cords and tying them together into a whip, he drove the animals out of the temple; then turning upon the money changers, he upset their tables, scattering their coins upon the marble pavement; lastly he ordered the dove dealers with their cages to leave, completing the work with the admonition, ''Make not my Father's house a house of merchandise.''

The sudden attack created consternation among the unholy traffickers, and the reform was accomplished in a moment. What was the explanation of this amazing act? Guilty consciences on the one side, and holy earnestness on the other. These noisy venders knew that they were desecrating the temple, and they quailed before and slunk away from the lofty personality of Jesus, "the starry light that shone in his eyes and the divine majesty that beamed from his features."

The incident shows the power of one brave man who is right against a multitude who are wrong. Jesus was not only gentle with divine tenderness, but he was also inflexible on every point of righteousness and out of him could flash divine wrath. He was no pure pacifist, but was a true soldier of God. In remembering that he is the Lamb, we should not forget that he is also the Lion.

This cleansing of the temple brought about the first clash of Jesus with the Jews and started the conflict that finally resulted in his death at their hands. As soon as they recovered from their astonishment at his temerity, they began to take note of this unknown reformer and demanded that he furnish them with a certificate of his authority in the form of a sign.

Jesus promptly answered, "Destroy this temple, and in three days I will raise it up." This enigmatical answer may have been accompanied with a gesture pointing to his body, but the Jews understood him to speak of the temple and they were still further astonished and indignant at his audacity. The temple stood as the very embodiment of their national religion and patriotism and pride, the holiest spot and structure on earth, and Jesus could not have made a more unpatriotic and unorthodox, radical and revolutionary utterance. But there are times when it is necessary to shock crass bigotry and corrupt ecclesiasticism with startling statements of truth. Such men as these Pharisees and scribes can feel only the thrust of a sword, and they have not yet all passed from us.

The answer of Jesus had primary reference to the temple of his body, and thus early did he plant the rock of his resurrection in his life-plan as a foundation stone; but it may also have had a further reference to the temple itself which he did sweep from that mountaintop as an exclusive place of worship when he taught that men should everywhere worship the Father in spirit and in truth. There mere place is unimportant.

The iron of this saying entered into the souls of these Jews, for they brought his declaration against him at his trial and coarsely flung it at him on the cross.

7. A DISTINGUISHED NIGHT VISITOR.   John 2 : 23-3 : 21

It is night and Jesus is closeted with one man. Two of our Lord's greatest discourses were delivered to single hearers, Nicodemus and the woman of Samaria, and with the great Preacher one soul was a great audience. This first recorded discourse of Jesus is compact with the great doctrine and duties of salvation, and his theology was complete from the beginning.

The inquirer who sought this interview is an interesting and attractive character. He was a Pharisee and a rabbi, a member of the Sanhedrin and a man of wealth. He was therefore a man of the highest religious orthodoxy, of unblemished reputation, of profound learning, of influential social position, and from every point of view one of the foremost men in Jerusalem.

Having seen the miracles of Jesus he came to him by night. The night visit has been used against him as implying timidity or something worse, but this is not a sure inference. There may have been good reasons why it was convenient for him to see Jesus at this hour, and yet it must be admitted that through his whole course Nicodemus at least displayed that discretion which is the better part of valor, and it was not until after the crucifixion that he came out boldly as a follower of the Nazarene. The remarkable thing, however, was that this prominent rabbi should visit the obscure Galilean, who had so fearlessly attacked existing institutions, at all.

Nicodemus opened the interview by paying a remarkable compliment to Jesus. He addressed him as rabbi and declared him to be a teacher come from God. This shows that he was already profoundly impressed with the mysterious young rabbi from the north. Doubtless his thought was that, as an orthodox Jew and conspicuous rabbi himself, he was entitled to a chief place in the kingdom Jesus was proclaiming and that all he had to do was to offer himself and be accepted.

And what a splendid convert and powerful accession to the cause of the lowly Nazarene he would have made? Would not an alliance with such an influential rabbi have in it the promise and potency of speedy success? The temptations of Jesus did not end in the wilderness, and it may be that this perilous thought pressed against his mind on this memorable night.

How did Jesus receive this distinguished visitor? With the bold and brusque declaration that he must be born again. He took no notice of his flattering compliment; he paid no deference to his orthodoxy and learning and social standing, and made no bid for his support. He no more relaxed the principles of his kingdom for this wealthy and powerful rabbi than he did for illiterate and profane fishermen. On the contrary he insisted on a new birth as a necessary condition of entering the kingdom of God and inflexibly applied this principle to Nicodemus himself. This eminent doctor of divinity stood high in the church, he was learned in the Scriptures, no stain was upon his professional robe, but he was not fit for the kingdom of God.

What chance was there for this young Galilean to make headway with his cause in the world when he started out by setting up such formidable conditions and boldly confronting if not affronting such a possible convert as Nicodemus with such terms? The splendid audacity of Jesus here flashes out. He was no time-server but set himself against all the currents of his age.

Nicodemus was puzzled, although he ought not to have been, for his Old Testament tells of a new heart and the rabbis had a saying that a convert is "like a child new-born." Yet Nicodemus did not know what Jesus was talking about and displayed surprising and lamentable ignorance, and there are still many surprising people in the church. Jesus explained the new birth as one of the spirit and brought it into line with the natural law that like must come from like, flesh from flesh, and spirit from spirit. Nicodemus was still perplexed, and Jesus expressed surprise that a master in Israel should not know these things.

Jesus proceeded to set forth his authority for his teaching. He was not a mere philosopher or theorist spinning out personal opinions and guesses at truth; neither was he teaching knowledge that he had gained at second hand; but "we speak," he declared, "that we do know and testify that we have seen." Jesus Christ knew what he was talking about, and on the subject of the kingdom of God he is ever the greatest expert and highest authority.

Presently Jesus was the only speaker. Nicodemus had become silent and sat as a rapt listener. Jesus rose to lofty and ever loftier heights. As he sat with this solitary hearer in the silence of the night he uttered some of his sublimest sayings. Presently he uttered that saying that is the richest and most splendid verse in the Bible: "For God so loved the world, that he gave his only begotten Son, that whosoever believeth in him should not perish, but have everlasting life." This sweeps the unbroken horizon of salvation. It mirrors the whole sky of redemption, thickest with stars. It gathers up all the notes of the gospel and strikes them in one rich massive chord. It is full of infinities and eternities. It is ineffably bright with divine love, and yet it is edged with divine wrath. Heaven is in it, and so is hell. Had we only this one utterance of Jesus and verse of the Bible it would have in it virtue to save the world.

Jesus ended the interview with the practical admonition, "He that doeth truth cometh to the light, that his deeds may be made manifest, that they are wrought in God." "He that doeth truth cometh to the light," said Jesus to the man that came to him by night, a possible hint that he should have come and that we all should come to him publicly in the day.

8. A Convert from Low Life. John 4: 4-26

At this point Herod threw John the Baptist into prison, and Jesus quietly withdrew from Judea and started for Galilee, not because he lacked courage but because he possessed prudence. His work was not yet done and the time for his final conflict had not yet come.

It was while he was on his way with his disciples up

through Samaria that he held another private interview and delivered another great discourse to an audience of one; this time with a woman. Nicodemus was a great and good man, but this was an obscure and disreputable woman. Christ was no respecter of persons, and any soul is worth trying to save and may prove a rough stone that is verily an uncut diamond.

One day at noon Jesus sat tired and thirsty on the stone curb of Jacob's well. A Samaritan woman came to draw water, and the well furnished the text and the woman the audience for one of Christ's greatest sermons. A well is one of the most useful and delightful things in the world. We look down into its cool mossy depths and see a pool of crystal water, the most beautiful liquid in the world, and that well is a center and source of blessing to all around it. With such a text in the hands of Jesus we may expect a discourse of extraordinary richness and power, for with him the simplest and most familiar thing became suggestive and eloquent of spiritual truth.

Jesus opened the conversation with delicate tact by asking the woman for a drink of water. The woman expressed surprise that a Jew would ask a favor of a Samaritan, for they were of different races and religious denominations, and narrow minds and bigoted sectarians think they should have no dealings with people from whom they differ. The woman's question opened a fine opportunity for a controversy, but Jesus passed it by in silence, for had he followed up her question he would simply have stirred up her race prejudice and partisan zeal, and the beginning of controversy is usually the end of edification. Jesus said nothing directly on the subject of their racial and religious separation, and yet he reached it indirectly and in the end closed up this gap.

Jesus answered the woman that if she knew the gift of God she would ask of him and receive living water. The woman, like Nicodemus, misunderstood him and supposed he was speaking of earthly water. She was surprised and perplexed that a travel-stained Jew, who had just himself asked for a drink, should have living water. He further explained his water as springing from a well within the heart as the water of eternal life.

Jesus had now reached the point where he could go no

further without making her conscious of her deepest need, and he suddenly thrust a sword into her heart exposing her guilty secret. Christ cannot go far with us until he touches some sore spot in our lives. The probe must precede the cure. Christ must know all about us in order to heal us, and our secret sins must be brought to light and be cleansed away before his spirit can dwell in us.

The conversation was now growing uncomfortably close and searching, and the woman may have thought it was time to change the subject; besides, she thought she saw a chance to have a fierce denominational dispute between the Samaritans and Jews decided. The burning point of this dispute was the place of worship and Jerusalem and Gerizim were crowned with rival temples, and altar flamed defiance at altar. The woman submitted to Jesus the question of which was the true place of worship and possibly waited for an answer that she hoped would give her own mountain a triumphant vindication.

What did Jesus answer? As he was himself a Jew, and all his patriotic and religious associations centered in Jerusalem, would he not now declare his own holy city to be the only true place of worship and brand the Samaritan temple as heretical and idolatrous? He did nothing of the kind, but gave an answer that was equally startling and disappointing, revolutionary and tragical to both Jews and Samaritans. "The hour cometh, when neither in this mountain, nor yet in Jerusalem, shall ye worship the Father." He delivered the grandest discourse ever uttered on the universality and spirituality of worship. He showed that worship is not a matter of mountains and temples, but of heart and spirit. He wiped Jerusalem off the map as an exclusive center of worship and set worship free and diffused it around the world as a universal privilege.

In this answer he refused to take either side of the denominational dispute and virtually swept both sides away with a broader principle. Jesus today is not interested in our little sectarian controversies and wants us to get away from them to great things and broader principles. If he were to deliver his decision upon many of these theological disputes, his judgment might bring disappointment and consternation to all sectarians. God is spirit, and place and technicality and form count for little with him. He looks at the worshiper, not at the place of worship. Worship is not like some rare plant that grows only on some solitary mountaintop, but it is like grass that grows all over the world. If we lift our eyes to the grand mountain of worship, we shall lose sight of the little divisive ravines that lie around our feet. Such worshipers the Father seeks.

The woman had now grown more modest and teachable and Jesus perceived that the moment for his self-revelation had come. She spoke of the coming of the Messiah, and with simple truth and dignity he said, "I that speak unto thee am he." This was Christ's first and clearest declaration of his Messiahship. There was no self-conscious vanity in this announcement, as it was the truth and it was needful that it should be known. It is not impertinence in the sun that it lets its light shine.

The woman went into the village proclaiming her Saviour: she had found her way from Jacob's well to the well of salvation; she went for the water of earth and found the water of heaven.

CHAPTER IV

SECOND YEAR: THE GALILEAN MINISTRY
THE YEAR OF POPULARITY

From Sychar Jesus with his disciples proceeded to Galilee where he carried on his Galilean ministry from December, 27, to December, 28, these years and months being only approximately correct but sufficiently near the truth for practical purposes.

It was the year of the increasing popularity of Jesus, for his teaching found a more congenial soil and a readier reception in the rural and industrial region of Galilee than among the aristocratic classes and the proud ecclesiastical hierarchy of Jerusalem.

On arriving in Galilee Jesus began "preaching the gospel of the kingdom of God, and saying, The time is fulfilled, and the kingdom of God is at hand: repent ye, and believe the gospel" (Mark 1:14-15). This was his first announcement of his mission and it continued to be his central message to the end. He came to establish "the kingdom of God," not a racial or national movement but a worldwide institution. The kingdom fills a large place in his teaching, the term occurring about one hundred and ten times in the Gospels, while the church is mentioned only twice.

The idea of the kingdom of God was familiar enough among the Jews, as it runs through the Old Testament, though in the days of Jesus it had become mixed and clouded with apocalyptic elements. The kingdom of God is the rule of God in the hearts of men. It has no geographical domain or boundaries and no physical equipment in the way of capitals and parliament and armies, its glory consists not in pageantry and pomp, and its weapons are not carnal, but it is a spiritual fabric and state that exists wherever and in whatever degree men love God and have the spirit of heaven.

The first step that Jesus urged men to take into the kingdom was, "Repent ye, and believe the gospel." "Change your mind," as the Greek word translated "repent" means, is what he commanded men to do, a rational and voluntary act which we can do. Such an act involves a sufficient reason as its motive, and this is found in "the gospel of the kingdom" which is good news great and joyful enough to convince and move the mind and heart with positive decision and earnest enthusiasm. The whole teaching of Jesus revolved around this worthy and weighty message and motive, and all the doctrines and deeds of his ministry run from this center as radii out to the full circumference of the Christian life and of the kingdom of God in the world.

After an incidental work of healing a nobleman's son at Cana (John 4:46-54), Jesus proceeded to Nazareth where he opened his public ministry in Galilee.

1. A Prophet Driven Out of His Own Town
Luke 4:16-30

Nazareth was a specially difficult place for Jesus to begin his ministry, his home town where he had lived for nearly thirty years and was familiarly known as the village carpenter. Only about a year before he had closed his shop and gone south into Judea, whence marvelous stories had presently floated back on the tide of returning pilgrims of his cleansing the temple and working miracles and appearing as the Messiah. His arrival in his own home would set all tongues gossiping and create a tremendous sensation in the sleepy old town.

He was to preach his first sermon in the village synagogue in which he had worshiped from childhood. The people had known him from boyhood and he knew them. As he stood before them he looked into the faces of his friends and neighbors, of his former companions, of his mother and brothers. We may suppose that he rose to preach with the usual diffidence and embarrassment of a young minister rising to preach his first sermon in his home church before his relatives and friends. Doubtless Mary had a mother's pride in her son. Jesus felt the delicacy and knew the danger of the situation, but he began his ministry at home, where every one's duty begins.

It is instructive to notice how Jesus spent this Sabbath day. "He entered, as his custom was, into the synagogue on the Sabbath day, and stood up for to read." He went to church according to his habit, not according to the weather or his wardrobe, but according to the calendar and the clock. There were doubtless things there that did not suit him. The preaching was unprofitable, intolerably dry and dreary, and the whole service was formal and lifeless and uncongenial to a true worshiper. The Jewish synagogue was a poor church, yet Jesus "entered as his custom was." He did not insist on having an ideal church or none. We should not be too sensitive and critical about the synagogue we attend. The preaching may not be to our taste and the prayer meeting seem hopelessly dull, but if on account of these things we stay away from church we cannot quote the example and sanction of Jesus Christ.

Jesus not only attended but he also took part in the service, not coming simply to receive from it but also to contribute to it and thereby add to its interest and profit. He chose his first text from the prophet Isaiah. Having read the passage (stopping the quotation at a significant point), he handed the roll of Scripture to the minister and sat down, according to the custom, to speak. All eyes were fixed upon him, and a breathless hush fell upon the congregation.

Only a single sentence of the sermon is recorded, its introductory words: "Today hath this scripture been fulfilled in your ears." This introduction is short and goes straight to the mark. It is not one of those long prosy introductions that give one a tired feeling before any point is reached, but it leaps right into the heart of the subject. It illuminates the text with a flash of light; it gives an ancient truth a modern application; and it puts Jesus himself in the focus of the Old Testament and converges all its rays on him as their burning center. We could wish that more of this sermon had been preserved, but we are fortunate in having its text, for it is one of the

richest Messianic passages in the Bible, striking all the
chords of Christ's ministry and full of the music of the
gospel.

How was the sermon received? "All bare him witness,
and wondered at the gracious words which proceeded out
of his mouth." This promises well for the congregation,
showing that it was an attentive audience, and a good sermon depends almost as much upon good hearing as upon
good preaching. Yet there is something suspicious in the
word "wondered." It suggests mere admiration for rhet-
oric and elocution, interest in the manner rather than the
matter of the sermon.

The next suspicious point in the reception of this sermon
is criticism of the preacher. They said, "Is not this Joseph's son?" Appreciation quickly turned to depreci-
ation. They began to judge the preacher by his parent-
age, they compared his profession of Messiahship with his
pedigree and said the two did not match. Because they
knew him so well as one of themselves, they thought he
could not amount to anything.

The next point in the reception of the sermon was the
demand for a miracle, that he would work wonders for
their gratification as he had done elsewhere. They wanted
to reduce him to the level of a sleight-of-hand performer.
Jesus proceeded to prove to them from their own Scriptures that if they did not receive the truth, God would
send it elsewhere.

This was too much for their bigotry and pride, and the
worshiping congregation suddenly became an infuriated
mob and hurried the preacher off to a cliff that they might
hurl him down to death. If we do not like the preaching,
let us fly mad at the preacher! If the divine message
strikes our pride, let us strike back at the human messenger. If we cannot throw him down a cliff, perhaps
we can throw him out of his pulpit; and if we cannot
break his head, we may at least break his heart.

Still the matter is not so easily ended. We may kill
the messenger, but we cannot kill the message. Truth is
immortal, and after we think we have slain it, it still lives
to confront us. Silencing man does not silence God. And
even the persecuted preacher shall not be forgotten of

heaven, for Jesus, protected by his own divine majesty from the murderous mob, "passing through the midst of them, went his way."

2. PREACHING AND FISHING AT LAKE GALILEE
Matthew 4:18-22; Mark 1:16-20; Luke 5:1-11

From Nazareth Jesus went to Capernaum which he now made his headquarters during his Galilean ministry. Although the people of his own town rejected him and tried to hurl him down a cliff, yet the people of the next town he entered were eager to receive him. A man may fail in one place and succeed in another.

Walking by the lakeside Jesus saw the two brothers, Peter and Andrew, and a little farther along the shore he found the other two brothers, James and John. He had received these four men down in Judea as his converts and followers, but now he gave them a formal call into his ministry, saying unto them, "Come ye after me, and I will make you to become fishers of men." These brothers thus transformed their business into Christ's business. The same powers and attainments of mind and body, knowledge of business, skill in the use of means, concentration and earnestness of purpose, that were used in the old service were now to be thrown into the new service. Jesus did not condemn their business, but he endorsed it and lifted it to a higher sphere; and he thus transmutes every calling.

And these first four disciples "straightway left their nets and followed him." They did not claim that business must be attended to first and religion afterward; they did not plead for delay and tell Jesus that, after the fishing season was over, he would hear from them; but straightway they followed. Faith instantly leaped into fact, conscience became conduct and love became life. It was the short sharp action of this "straightway" that saved these fishermen and at last made them such strong men.

And they "left their nets" behind when they followed Jesus. They were not so deeply enmeshed in those nets that they could not free themselves from them. They did not try to bring their boats into Christ's business. In entering the new life they cut loose from the old life. Too many Christians are still tangled up in their old fishing nets. Let us leave boats and nets behind. We cannot serve God and Mammon and in a profound sense must leave all to follow Christ.

A great crowd was soon gathered around Jesus and pressed upon him so that he extemporized a pulpit from a fishing boat lying near by, and from its deck faced a vast audience filling the amphitheater of the shore. The great Teacher knew how to adapt himself to every emergency. Doubtless his unconventionality shocked some of the Pharisees and high ritualists who thought his conducting a religious service in the open air from an ill-smelling fishing boat was coarse sacrilege. But Jesus was practicing the great truth he announced to the woman of Samaria that worship is not a matter of place and form but of the spirit and may be offered anywhere. The world is God's great temple and he may be worshiped on any shore or street. A camp meeting in a field or forest may burn with holy fire that may be lacking in a stately cathedral.

The sermon is not recorded, but at its close Jesus bade the disciples launch the boat out into the deep and let down the nets for a catch of fish. The Master thus combined fishing with preaching, business with religion. He was a practical man and knew how to build a house, handle a boat and catch fish. Yet he was as truly teaching spiritual truth when fishing as when preaching, for with him worship and work were fused into one life and made one music.

Peter interposed his doubt and objection, "Master, we have toiled all the night, and have taken nothing." This was as much as to say, "We old experienced fishermen have just tried that place and know there is nothing there." Peter thought he knew what he was talking about. He knew that lake, had been brought up on its blue waters, had fished it from shore to shore, knew all its deeps and shallows, and could tell just where and when to cast the nets. Jesus was a young man from back in the country who had had no experience on the lake. Is it any wonder that Peter put his judgment up against that of Jesus?

Certain it is that at times we are in this same blind and foolish state of mind.

We are close to Peter's thought when we think our place of work contains nothing of use and interest. We see others pulling up their big-bellied nets swollen with fish, but we think the waters under our boat are empty. We are sure we also would do splendidly if we were only somewhere else. So strong is this feeling in us at times that we are almost ready to put our opinions and experience up against the command of Christ and the providence of God!

Such was Peter's doubt; what, now, was his action? "Nevertheless, at thy word I will let down the net." This is a saving and beautiful "nevertheless." Peter was wrong in his thought, but he was grandly right in his action. His creed was faulty, but his deed was beautiful.

And what was the result when the nets were drawn up? Never had there been such a catch on that lake. It broke all records. Instantly all was intense excitement and activity in the boat. Another boat was called and both boats were loaded to the water's edge. If we will only fish our pool patiently, prayerfully, persistently, our nets may at length come up swollen with blessing so that there will not be room to receive it.

Jesus now turned the miracle into a parable. "Fear not," he said unto Peter; "from henceforth thou shalt catch men." The world is our sea, and the gospel is our net and line with which we are to catch men. Many of the arts of the fisherman apply to this work and we should study and practice them that we may use them skilfully and successfully.

Thus ended the first day's work on the shore of the lake that has been made forever memorable and blessed by the footprints of Jesus.

Clear silver water in a cup of gold,
It shines—his lake—the sea of Chinnereth,
The waves he loved, the waves that kissed his feet,
So many blessed days.

3. A Busy Day in Capernaum
Matthew 8:14-17; Mark 2:21-34; Luke 4:31-41

The choosing of the four disciples and the fishing on the

lake was followed by a busy Sabbath day in Capernaum in which we see Jesus at work.

Straightway he entered into the synagogue; in the morning he went to church. Jesus honored the synagogue as his Father's house and attended its service for worship. Though himself Lord of the sanctuary, yet he was also a worshiper in the sanctuary of the Lord. The church is the school of our higher life. Here we become conscious of our deepest needs; here sin is seen in its guilt and vileness and bondage, and holiness in its purity and beauty and blessedness; and here is revealed and offered to us the great gospel of mercy and love by which we are saved.

All the questions of life are illuminated in the house of God. We do not see any subject truly in all its connections and consequences until we see it in a religious light, from God's point of view. The church stands for our spiritual life, pointing its spire towards the sky, a finger feeling after the Infinite. But may we not be religious without the church? Jesus did not think so: "Straightway on the Sabbath day he entered into the synagogue." The church has its faults and failures, but it is still the divine means of our spiritual life and we should use it faithfully and seek to improve it.

And being in the synagogue Jesus taught. The synagogue service was social worship, like our prayer meeting, in which the people were free to take part. Jesus was not a mere passive listener, much less a critical faultfinder, but he expounded the Scripture and proclaimed the gospel of good news.

The people were astonished at his teaching, as well as they might be, for both matter and manner were a great and welcome change to them. They had been bored to death by the scribes. These fosilized ecclesiastics were droning away over hairsplitting questions of orthodoxy that were not of the least human interest or use and were repeating with interminable prolixity the traditional sayings of the rabbis. Across this dry parched wilderness of rabbinical lore came the simple charming teachings of Jesus like a refreshing breeze and shower of rain. The people knew what he was talking about and were surprised that it took hold of them with fascinating interest and power. Nothing else is so interesting as religion when it is properly presented, and it is by far the most popular subject in the world today.

The people were astonished at the teaching of Jesus, for he taught them as one that had authority and not as the scribes. The authority of Jesus consisted, not in any dogmatic claims and dictatorial air, but in his spirit of transparent self-evident truth, sincerity and earnestness. He spoke that he did know and testified that he had seen, and candid minds could not help but believe his witness. When one's religious faith is the very core of his heart, so that it is, in the words of Carlyle, "the thing a man does practically lay to heart and know for certain, concerning his vital relations to this mysterious Universe and his duty and destiny therein," he can teach in the church and out of it with authority and power.

The service was interrupted by a loud cry of pain and terror from a man in the congregation possessed of an unclean spirit. Jesus rebuked the evil spirit, saying, "Hold thy peace" (literally, "Be muzzled," a word for a beast), "and come out of him." Then the spirit, screaming and tearing the unhappy man with convulsions, came out and left the man calm and free. A murmur of excitement swept over the congregation as many exclaimed, "What is this? A new teaching! with authority he commandeth even unclean spirits, and they obey him." The Prince of Light has power over spirits of darkness and at his bidding every knee shall bow.

"A new teaching!" they exclaimed. Jesus Christ, then, was himself a teacher of new theology. He did not keep to the old paths of the scribes and Pharisees, but boldly struck out into new paths. He revised and rewrote the religious creeds of his day and started this process of ever bringing religion up to date down through the centuries. The fundamental principles of religion do not change, but our understanding and application of them do advance. The new astronomy interprets the same heavens as the old, but in a truer and more splendid way. It is the same old tree, but the blossoms are new every spring. It is the same gospel we preach from age to age, but its interpretation and application are ever new. Let us not be afraid of new theology if it is the old truth interpreted and applied with new power.

The gospel must be not only preached but also applied. We must get rid of the notion that merely sitting in a synagogue is religion. Worship must make war on wickedness. It is the business of the church and of Christians to cast out uncleanness and not to let any evil spirit alone.

What did Jesus do next on this Sabbath day? "And straightway, when they were come out of the synagogue, they came into the house of Simon and Andrew with James and John." And what did Jesus do there? Just the same kind of work he did in the synagogue: he healed Simon's wife's mother of a fever; he blessed that home.

We do not see much of the home life of Jesus; in truth, he had no home nor where to lay his head. But when we do find him in a home we always see it made better by his presence; a sin is forgiven, a dying child is healed, or comfort and cheer are given. If we get any good in the church, it ought to show itself speedily in the home. Some sick one should be ministered to with a kinder hand, more patience and gentleness should mark our behavior, beautiful courtesies should be more abundant, new Christian graces should bloom out in our lives. The home should be sweeter and brighter on Monday morning because we have worshiped in the church on the Sabbath day.

The day closed with a wonderful scene. The city gathered at the door as the evening shadows fell around the house, the sick were brought until they filled the street, and Jesus healed them. His mercy, that in the morning manifested itself in the synagogue and in the afternoon flowed into the home, in the evening overflowed into the street and filled the city. The stream of beneficence once started did not stay its flood until the whole city had been bathed in its healing tide. The love of God is expansive and has in it a wideness like the wideness of the sea. There is no danger of its ever running short, and it will reach the greatest sinner and the last lost child. Having worshiped God in the church, we should go everywhere, touching men with healing hands.

Such was this eventful Sabbath in the life of Jesus, and it is a pattern for our Sabbath days.

4. A MISSIONARY TOUR THROUGH GALILEE

Matt. 4:23; Mark 1:35-45; Luke 4:42-44; John 5:12-16

Jesus could not stand this incessant work and strenuous life without relief and rest, but he took his rest in a peculiar way. "And in the morning, rising up a great while before day, he ·went out into a solitary place, and there prayed." He sought change of scene by seeking solitude amidst the picturesque scenery of the lakeside that he might engage in meditation and prayer. He bathed his soul in nature and in God. Without this renewal of his own inner life by immersing his soul in silence and communion, his spiritual energies would have been exhausted and run dry. He must fill his own soul that he might fill others.

Meditation is necessary to mastery of life. We must live our lives inwardly in thought before we can live them outwardly in action. The architect thinks his building through from foundation to finish, he puts it all up in his brain before he puts it into stone and steel, and if we would be architects and artists in living we must take time to get ready, grow deep roots of wisdom and strength in meditation and prayer, and then we may throw our branches out and bear ripened fruit in the world.

In our hurried life we are in danger of losing this fine art and deep means of enrichment and of living a superficial feverish life in which we are always craving for a crowd and itching for a new thrill. Deep roots hidden in solitude and silence will cure us of this love of sensationalism with its high blood pressure and overweening worldliness and enable us to live a sane and strong and rich life. By soaking our souls in meditation and prayer we gather strength and wisdom to do the work and bear the burdens and fight the battles of life.

Presently the disciples found Jesus in his retreat and summoned him to service with the announcement, "All men seek for thee." Jesus was now supplying something for which the human heart hungered, and this announcement was prophetic of the great yearning of humanity by which it consciously or unconsciously seeks him.

However it would not do for Jesus to confine his ministry to one town, and so he proposed, "Let us go into the next towns, that I may preach there also: for therefore came I forth." This is the principle of home missions and foreign missions. Why did Jesus not just settle down and stay in Capernaum? That lake port and fishing town was not all converted to his gospel and cleansed and healed. He had scarcely touched the fringe of its disease and wickedness and there was there for him a lifetime of work. Why move on to "the next towns"?

This is precisely the argument of those who are opposed to home missions and especially to foreign missions. We have Christian work enough to do in our own town; let us save it before giving our time and money to save other towns; and besides, ought they not to look after themselves? Especially does this argument grow insistent and clamant when it comes to foreign missions and pour ridicule on the visionary scheme of sending missionaries to foreign lands when we have so much heathenism at home.

But we cannot completely evangelize one town before we go into the next towns because all towns are woven into one web in their interests and life, and the spiritual condition of one necessarily affects the condition of others. Even business understands this point and knows that one town cannot permanently prosper with other towns in financial depression, and one country cannot flourish on the poverty and ruin of other countries. If the people of one town resolved that they would completely evangelize their own town before they would help evangelize other towns, they would thereby doom themselves to remain spiritually crippled and withered; their very plan would be selfish and defeat itself. The last state of such a town would be worse than the first.

On the other hand, let a town begin to think of the welfare of "the next towns," and its own welfare will be promoted thereby; its unselfish spirit of helping other towns will invigorate itself and hasten its own evangelization. So also foreign missions react helpfully on home missions. The question is not only whether the heathen can be saved without us but also whether we can be saved without them.

So "Jesus preached throughout all Galilee," and thereby inaugurated the best policy of evangelizing even Capernaum and so must we, to have the gospel at home, go with it to all the ends of the earth.

We are given an instance of the work of Jesus on this tour. The case is that of one of the most dreadful maladies to which human flesh is heir. Leprosy is an intensely realistic and frightful symbol of sin, showing outwardly in rotting limbs what sin does inwardly in the soul. A poor fellow came to Jesus, exclaiming, "If thou wilt, thou canst make me clean," and a touch from the hand of Jesus gave the man blessed healing and relief. Only divine power could work such a cure, and the same power can cleanse us from all unrighteousness.

Jesus directed the cleansed leper to tell no man, but go and show himself to the priest, so as to get a certificate of his cured condition according to the law (Leviticus 13-14) and to offer the gift Moses commanded. Jesus obeyed the law in all points and therein set us an example.

5. STRANGE THINGS
Matthew 9:1-8; Mark 2:1-12; Luke 5:17-26

Jesus is back again in Capernaum and on this occasion was preaching in a house. The people crowded around it, blocking up the doors and the very street. The Pharisees and scribes were now beginning to have their suspicions aroused about the orthodoxy of Jesus and they sat around him cold and critical, watching their chance to entrap him.

Four men drew near, carrying on a bed a helpless paralytic whom they were bringing to the great Healer. When they drew near and found the way blocked up by the throng, they climbed up on the roof, tore a hole through the light thatch-work and let their man right down at the feet of the great Physician. Jesus forgave the paralytic his sin and sent him home carrying the very bed that had carried him.

The people dispersed, some criticising and others wondering, but all amazed, saying, "We have seen strange things today." What had they seen?

They had seen strange earnestness. The Pharisees and priests had become so conventionalized and cold in their religion that all the heat had been frozen out of them and they showed little warmth of human sympathy with their fellowmen in distress. The four men that came bringing their helpless friend on a bed and let him down through the roof must have seemed strangely undignified in their zeal to these high ecclesiastics.

The four friends, however, were not thinking of their own dignity, but of the helplessness of their neighbor and their consciousness was absorbed in him. As long as we are thinking of our own comfort and interest we are not likely to take much pains to help others, but when we become intensely conscious of their need we shall cast our own dignity to the winds.

Another strange thing seen on this occasion was a new method of religious work. The ordinary method of getting a man to a physician was to take him in through the door, but the extraordinary method followed on this occasion as to take him up on top of the house, tear a hole through the roof, and let him down. The people probably had never seen this done before, and the Pharisees and scribes, who were confined in their methods to a traditional ritual which could not be infringed upon or changed to meet any emergency, were shocked and scandalized at the irreverence of the method.

We should ever be ready and apt to adopt new methods in our church work and Christian service. We are in danger of becoming so wedded to the old ways that we think they cannot be changed without sacrilege. The history of the church is full of this spirit, and petty and ridiculous have been many little variations of old customs that have disturbed and even divided congregations and denominations. The old ways may have been good, but when a better way may be had we are to drop the old and use the new.

The simple principle to follow is that of highest efficiency. A new method is not to be adopted merely because it is new. If these four men could have got their friend in through the door, it would have been folly for them to have climbed up on the roof. We are never to tear the roof off simply for the sake of doing a strange thing. Ordinarily let us come in through the door, but when a man is to be healed, if needs be let us come down through the roof even though it creates a sensation and people say it is a strange thing.

A third strange thing the people saw that day was the discomfiture of the ecclesiastical authorities. The Pharisees and scribes were the doctors of divinity in the church. They represented authority and orthodoxy. Any departure from their traditions was a dangerous heresy to be put down. They challenged Jesus with the startling question, "Who is this that speaketh blasphemies? Who can forgive sin, but God alone?" Intense excitement swept through the crowd. The Pharisees had Jesus in a corner. He had been caught, so to speak, in the very act. The church now had him in its grip and was about to brand him as a blasphemer. His hour of judgment was come.

Sure enough it was come, for Jesus suddenly turned the tables on the Pharisees and threw them into confusion. As proof of his power over the man's sin he showed his power over his body, and at his command the paralytic got up and walked off. Then the people were amazed at the strange thing. They had been accustomed to seeing the Pharisees having everything their own way, with no one daring to utter a word of dissent. But here they were suddenly discomfited and discredited by this marvelous young Teacher. The church dignitaries had been contradicted and refuted, they had been shown up as standing in the very way of salvation, and the disclosure shocked the people as a strange thing.

The same strange thing has often happened and may easily happen again. We reverence the church as a source and means of truth and righteousness, and it is proper that we should. We expect the church to be right, and it generally is. But in its human administration and on particular points and occasions it may be wrong. It has sometimes stood in the way of truth and righteousness. Misguided ecclesiastics have often done this very thing. We are not, then, to worship the church or stand up for its infallibility, but we have a right to test its wisdom. The Word of God is our standard and Christ is our only Master. It would be a strange thing if the church were not sometimes wrong.

6. Jesus at the Pool of Bethesda. John 5.

The scene shifts from Galilee to Jerusalem where we find Jesus at "a feast," which, according to the view we have adopted, was probably a feast of Passover, the second which he attended during his ministry. These feasts were great attractions to all Jews, and Jesus felt this attraction, and these visits of his are the four chief milestones in his public life.

The pool of Bethesda was probably fed by a mineral spring possessed of curative virtue. By the side of this pool "lay a great multitude of impotent folk, of blind, halt, withered," a graphic and pitiful picture of the great world itself, which is a vast multitude containing every kind and degree of human misery and sorrow. But in the midst of this world there is a "Bethesda" or House of Mercy, where there is healing for all the diseases of sin. Out of this throng Jesus picked one crippled man and gave his attention to him.

This is an instance of that individual work in which Jesus mostly engaged and by which he achieved the best results. It is comparatively easy for us to look on the mass of impotent folk in the world with a considerable degree of compassion, but if we wish to do something practical we will have to pick out individual cases and help them. It is better to cure one crippled soul than simply to shed tears over a multitude.

Jesus approached this man with the inquiry, "Wilt thou be made whole?" Was not this a superfluous and even irritating question? What was the man lying there for, if not to be healed? Nevertheless the question was not superfluous but was just the one that needed to be pressed sharply into the man's consciousness and conscience. He had lain there so long and so helplessly that he had lost hope and had become reconciled to his helplessness. This is the fatality that falls on some people: they sink so deep into discouragement that they think there is no hope for them and refuse to do anything. The first thing that must happen to such people is some sharp question or experience that will arouse them out of their despair and drive them to do something.

The infirm man expressed this hopeless state of his mind

by explaining that here was no one to put him in the pool; "but while I am coming;" he said, "another steppeth down before me." How often does this very thing happen to us in this world? The reason why it is so hard for us to get some good things is that so many others are after the same things and crowd in ahead of us.

Jesus, however, overlooked all these difficulties and commanded the helpless man, "Rise, take up thy bed and walk." It was the very thing he could not do, and yet he was told to do it. God is often calling upon us to do what we think we cannot do, but his command is our warrant and urgent motive to try.

This command dispensed with the pool and came right to the point of immediate healing. Christ may dispense with the priest and church and all the human machinery of salvation and come right into the soul of the sinner himself. Yet the command gave the man himself something to do. "Rise, take up thy bed, and walk." Every word of the command is vibrant with a stirring call to action. Salvation is always an intensely active process on both the divine and the human side: neither God nor man can sit still while it is going on; both must rise up and be doing.

"And immediately the man was made whole, and took up his bed and walked." So quick and sure is deliverance from the bondage of sin when there is no lost motion between the divine command and human obedience.

"And on the same day was the Sabbath." What does this have to do with the matter? The Jews thought it had everything to do with it. The day made a great difference with the deed in their theology. And they had got things so turned around and upside down that they seemed to think that the better the day the worse the deed. "The Jews therefore said unto him that was cured, It is the Sabbath day, it is not lawful for thee to carry thy bed." They had so interpreted the law of the Sabbath (Exodus 23:12) and spun restrictions of their own devising around it that its blessing had become a curse. The extent to which they had carried these artificial distinctions and prohibitions was incredibly senseless and ridiculous.

This mind has not yet altogether disappeared from among religious men. Some appear to think that it is more important that creeds and canons should be meticulously kept than that souls should be saved. This healed man was guilty of the dreadful sin of carrying his bed on the Sabbath, and the Pharisees were hot after him. But if we have the word of Jesus for carrying our bed we need not care what canon we violate or what ecclesiastics say or think.

The healed man "wist not who it was" that had healed him. Many receive healing touches from the hand of Jesus who know him but dimly or not at all; for his healing virtue is diffused widely through Christian and even through heathen lands, and millions are better for his presence that know or acknowledge him not.

Jesus, however, found the man and followed up his healing: "Behold, thou art made whole: sin no more, lest a worse thing come unto thee." This implies that he had sinned and that this was the root of his infirmity. "The man departed, and told the Jews that it was Jesus, which had made him whole." As soon as he knew Jesus he confessed him, and this is ever the first duty of the forgiven and saved soul.

This work of healing precipitated the conflict between the Jews in Jerusalem and Jesus which henceforth grew in hostility until it reached its deadly end. Jesus proceeded to deliver a great discourse in which he set forth fundamental truth concerning his work and his relations to his Father and convicted the Jews of fatal unbelief.

7. The Choosing and the Mission of the Twelve Disciples

Matthew 10:24; Mark 3:13-19; Luke 6:12—19

On his return to Galilee from the feast at Jerusalem Jesus carried on his work, coming into conflict with the Pharisees over plucking grain in a wheatfield on the Sabbath (Matthew 12:1-8), healing the man with the withered hand in a synagogue (Matthew 12:9-14), and making a second preaching tour through Galilee (Matthew 12:15-21).

His work was now growing and spreading and the time had come to call men to enter into his companionship as disciples that they might be trained to carry on his work after he was gone. Spiritual ideas cannot go naked through the world but must be organized in an institution with leaders to serve as hands and feet, hearts and brains to perpetuate these ideas and ideals and give them concrete form and definite application. This principle is seen in all social organizations.

Jesus chose twelve men to enter his theological seminary to be under his personal instruction and inspiration and had this not been done his teachings might have floated off on the air and died away. The choice of these men was the beginning of the organized church with its officers and ordinances.

A list of the disciples is given and we scrutinize the names with interest. Some of these men had been called twice before (John 1 : 35-51; Matt. 4 : 1-22), but this is their final call. By arranging the names in groups of four each, it is easy to carry them in memory. Peter always comes first, and Judas last. There are two and possibly three pairs of brothers among them.

This is probably the most important list of names in the history of the world. These men were given a work to do compared with which winning battles and founding empires are of small consequence. They were to let loose a force that was to pervade all empires and shape all future ages.

Yet they were not great men, and there was not a man of genius among them. They were plain men unlearned in philosophy. Not one of them belonged to the priestly or professional class. None was of noble birth, but all were obscure and comparatively poor. At least four of them were fishermen and some of these were expert in profanity. One of them was a despised tax collector, and one was a zealot, a kind of anarchist of the day. One always has attached to his name the dark stigma, "which also betrayed him."

Jerusalem, the chosen city of God and proud university city and capital of the country, the metropolis where were the aristocracy and scholars and hierarchy and temple, was not permitted to put one name in this immortal list. Verily not many wise, not many noble, not many mighty, were called, but God chose the foolish to confound the wise, and the weak to confound the mighty.

Yet these men, so poorly gifted and unlearned and weak in themselves, could do mighty things and shake and reshape the world through Christ who strengthened them. The very simplicity of these men, unspoiled by human philosophy, made them unobstructed channels through which the grace of Christ could flow in the fullest measure.

The spirit of Jesus touched and transformed their souls with eternal issues and made them great. Often has God, in choosing men for great visions and victories, passed by the noble and rich and learned and found humble souls born in obscurity and breathed into them his Spirit and told them first the message he sent them to tell the world. The charcoal needs only a rearrangement of its atoms to become a diamond. The rough marble block needs only the sculptor's chisel to become an angel. The humblest men have in them divine possibilities. Any human soul needs only the transforming touch of Christ's spirit to become forever pure and beautiful.

These disciples were sent forth. They were with Jesus, not that they might stay with him, but that they might receive his gospel and then go from him, carrying the good news to others.

The next point in their equipment was their message. Jesus appointed them that "he might send them forth to preach, and to have power to heal sicknesses, and to cast forth devils." They were to preach the good news of the kingdom of God and their message was to be illustrated with works of healing. The gospel in their hands was not to be a mere theory but a practical power. Their mission was to be a march of mercy whose monuments would be healed men and saved souls. Part of this work has now been committed to physicians who are specially skilled in it, and the hospital is simply an annex of the church. This work of preaching and healing is now going on in our modern world on a wider scale than ever before, and the gospel is proving itself the power of God unto salvation.

The next point in their commission was the compensation. What salary were these disciples to receive? "Freely ye have received," said Jesus, "freely give." Receive no

money for God's grace, turn not the work of saving the lost
into an unholy traffic for gain. This admonition was specially needed for these disciples that were made of ordinary human nature and had among their number a Judas
Iscariot. But Jesus Christ did not come into the world
to make money either for himself or for his disciples, and
at the beginning he laid the axe at the root of this mercenary spirit. Few things are so ruinous to the ministry
as an instinct for money and the love of personal comfort, and any suspicion of self-interest puts a blight on
Christian service.

Yet because the disciples were to make no charge for the
grace of the gospel it did not follow that they were to
receive nothing for their support. They were to throw
themselves on the hospitality of the people, and Jesus also
laid it down as a fundamental principle that the laborer
is worthy of his hire.

Ministers dare not charge for the grace of God, but
they ought and must receive proper support while they
are administering it. Water is free as it falls out of the
clouds and gushes up in springs and flows in streams, but
it costs something to have it brought in pipes into our
homes. The gospel itself is free, but it costs money to
have it preached in our churches and sent out along missionary lines into the world.

8. THE SERMON ON THE MOUNT—THE BEATITUDES
Matthew 5:1-12; Luke 6:20-23.

The disciples having been chosen, the next step was to
deliver the constitution of the new kingdom and announce
its program. After a night spent in prayer, Jesus with
his disciples met a great multitude on one of the hills back
of Capernaum, and from that lofty pulpit he delivered this
sermon that has gone resounding through the ages, and
after nearly nineteen hundred years has lost none of its
sweetness and saving power. It is truly a mountain sermon, overtopping all human teachings and breathing the
air of heaven. It sets forth the spirit and the outcome of
the kingdom of God in holiness of heart and life, though
at this early stage it does not fully reveal the means by

which this is attained. The world has not yet caught up with its simplest requirements. Saturate society with its spirit and the world would be washed pure and the kingdom of God would be here. One day filled with it would be a bit of heaven.

The first word in this sermon is "blessed," and this is a word the world is eager to hear; but the second word is "poor," and this seems in flat contradiction with the first and is a word the world does not want to have mentioned. The theory of the world was and is that the blessed are the rich and satiated. But Jesus reversed this and declared that blessedness has its root in a sense of lack. Others had located it outside in worldly possessions and circumstances: he located it inside in the heart. The poor in spirit are those that realize their poverty of soul without righteousness and God; they do not measure their blessedness by outward wealth but by inward worth; they have that humble state of mind, conscious of its sin ànd need, that makes them receptive of spiritual blessings and brings them into fellowship with God.

The blessing pronounced upon such souls is that theirs is the kingdom of heaven. It is only into such souls that this kingdom can come; for by its very nature it is shut out of hearts full of self-satisfied pride. The kingdom of heaven is a present possession, bringing order into the soul, subjecting all its faculties to discipline and obedience, and filling it with heavenly riches. Such a kingdom within the soul is a blessing that includes all good things and abides amidst all the disorder and distress of this disjointed world.

The next beatitude is even more paradoxical to the worldly mind. "Blessed are they that mourn." This seems to shock the universal human heart, for in every breast it shrinks from sorrow; it finds its blessing in the wine of gladness and counts the day of mourning a blighted day. Yet there is a time to weep as well as a time to laugh, and mourning may be a bitter root that will bloom and grow into the fairest blossoms and the sweetest fruits. As long as there is unforgiven sin festering in the heart there is cause for mourning that may issue in purity and peace.

The mourning that springs from loss and sorrow, also may have in it a root of blessing. As pearls are the product of the sufferings of the shellfish, so the finest jewels of human character are crystallized out of the sorrows of the soul. "Had God not turned us in his hand and thrust our high hills low, we had not been this splendor and our wrong an everlasting music for the song of heaven."

"Blessed are they that mourn: for they shall be comforted." Jesus came to give this comfort. He picked his steps among the sinful and sorrowing, and to all such his words were a gracious balm and his touch was healing and life.

The third beatitude pronounces a blessing upon the meek. This also fell as a strange saying upon ancient ears, for in that age meekness was contemned as weakness, and might was worshiped as right. The Roman especially had small respect for a meek spirit and gloried in gleaming steel and martial might that could crush opposition and he trusted to his good short sword to cut his way to power and make him master of the world. But Jesus bravely stood up in that world bristling with spears and calmly said, "Blessed are the meek." This Teacher was not subject to the limitations of his age and did not simply repeat the opinions of his day, but he was a Teacher for all time and uttered eternal truths.

Meekness is humility, gentleness and patience of disposition. It is not puffed up with conceit and ambition and pride; and so it is not easily irritated and inflamed, offended and angered, and thus thrown into a fret of disappointment and a frenzy of passion. It keeps self-possessed and cool and concentrates all its powers into pure purposes. Such a state of soul is in itself an inner fountain ever springing up in rich blessings.

Not only was this beatitude strange, but the reason Jesus gave for it was stranger still: "for they shall inherit the earth." How can this be? would exclaim the Jewish patriot, looking for an armed and conquering Messiah; and with what scepticism and scorn would the Roman in his polished brass and glittering steel hear this prophecy? Yet the moral evolution of the world is more and more proving that meekness is might. War is disappearing be-

fore the peaceful march of industry, and the barbarity of
the battlefield will yet be vanquished by brotherhood. It
is not the most warlike nations today but the most peace-
loving that are inheriting the earth. Meekness is might
when it has just cause to fight, for then its strength is as
the strength of ten because its heart is pure.

The lowly Nazarene, who with legions of angels at his
command never harmed the hair of a human being and did
not even lift his hand in self-defence, was grandly right,
and in the heart of that warlike age here laid down the
foundation of ultimate statesmanship and national greatness as well as of individual blessing.

Other beatitudes step into this line and it grows most
paradoxical of all at its very end when persecution takes
its place in the procession and asks us to believe that
it brings a blessing.

These are the beatitudes of Jesus. They are a strange
contradiction to the maxims of this world, but they are
heavenly wisdom. They have rough shells without, but
they are full of sweet milk within. They are shunned by
the worldly mind that judges and is deceived by outward
appearances, but the spiritual mind that penetrates to their
core finds they are the eternal laws of blessedness.

9. THE SERMON ON THE MOUNT—THE LORD'S PRAYER

Matthew 6: 5-15

Jesus himself prayed, stood so close to God that he
could speak with him face to face, and therefore he could
teach others to pray. He was at his best, if we may so
speak, at this moment, and never from his lips issued
grander, sweeter music than in this immortal prayer.

Prayer, the highest and finest state of the soul, is attended with some of the deadliest dangers, as around snow-
capped, sky-bathed mountaintops sweep the fiercest storms.
One of these dangers is that of turning prayer into an actor's performance. The Jews observed stated hours of
prayer—morning, noon and evening—and these hypocrites
took care at such times to be caught at some public place,
such as a street corner, where they could strike an attitude of prayer and pose and perform before the crowd.

They would thus put on prayer as an actor's mask, and then with furtive glances slyly observe how their piety was impressing the public.

That kind of prayer did not cease to be performed when the last Pharisee with his broad phylacteries and public attitudinizing passed out of the world. It repeats itself in every prayer that is addressed to men rather than to God. "An eloquent prayer," of which we sometimes read, may not be a prayer at all, but only an eloquent performance.

Vain repetitions are another danger in prayer against which Jesus warned his hearers, and we need to take care that our prayers do not degenerate or crystallize into set forms which are only mechanical repetitions. There is no objection to set phrases and prescribed forms—they have their place and use—provided such forms are kept alive and meaningful with the devotional spirit.

The Lord of prayer now taught the people the prayer of the Lord. It is a model prayer of marvelous simplicity and comprehensiveness, helpfulness and beauty. The sentences are short and the words are the plain speech of the common people. There is not one theological word in it. The whole prayer contains only six petitions and can be slowly uttered in less than half a minute. How startling the contrast with many a prayer in the pulpit that may stretch its repetitious and wearisome length out to half an hour and even more. Yet this prayer sweeps heaven and earth in its range and grasp and leaves out no good thing. It contains the roots and germs of all worship and blessing.

Its first word strikes the keynote of Christian faith and theology. More than any other word the name Father tells us what God is, showering upon us the most charming memories and suggestions. It asserts his sovereignty and power and wisdom, and also his care and mercy and love.

"Hallowed be thy name," is the first petition. We might think we could have made a better start. Should not some pressing human need have been put in the conspicuous forefront of this prayer? But it begins with divine interests and looks straight away from human needs.

The prayer, however, begins at the right point. Right

relation with God is the central condition and foundation of all blessings. Reverence is the root of all virtues. Unless God be respected, the human soul has nothing to look up to, no ideal above it, no authority over it.

So the prayer begins and moves along these heavenly heights. "Thy kingdom come. Thy will be done in earth, as it is in heaven." Will the prayer never come down to our human needs and hear our human cries? It is the mountaintops, however, that keep the valleys green, and the sun shining above us that makes the earth blossom, and all our blessings come from above. The will of God is the supreme blessing for us. We sometimes think of his will as if it were a hard fate and heavy burden for us to bear, whereas it is the kindest and richest and most beautiful thing that can happen in the world and for the world. Nothing else could be half so welcome to us as the will of God if we only knew the depths and heights of blessing it contains and will bring.

The turning point of the prayer is at last reached. "Give us this day our daily bread." The prayer suddenly drops from the highest spiritual aspiration to the lowest physical need; in the midst of the holiest longings of the soul the human stomach has something to say. All the material conditions of life, bread, health, prosperity, are rightly the subject of prayer. Religion covers all life from top to bottom. Yet our requests for our material life should be kept within modest bounds for the necessities of life. Our daily bread, and not a year's supply or rich poundcake or an ample bank account, is all we are authorized to ask for.

"And forgive us our debts as we also forgive our debtors." Having descended and lightly touched our bodily needs, the prayer quickly bounds back into the spirit and rises to heavenly things. Forgiveness is a mutual blessing, and we cannot get what we do not give in the spiritual world. "And lead us not into temptation, but deliver us from evil." The great fear of the prayer is not poverty or suffering, but it shrinks from every slimy touch and stain. The prayer, as pieced out by later hands, goes up to God for its fitting conclusion and climax, for all things human must end in the kingdom and glory of God.

Such is the model prayer, short, simple, comprehensive,

laying hold of the greatest blessings and rifling heaven and earth for our enrichment. If we learn to pray after this manner, in its spirit, we shall know what things we ought to pray for, and whatsoever we ask shall be done unto us.

And such are samples of the Sermon on the Mount from whose slopes and summit have come down rivers of water for the blessing of the world. Of this water we should ever drink and live.

> Down from this Galilean mountaintop
> Rolled words that are eternal laws of life,
> More deeply grounded than its granite base;
> Flowed strains of sweetness that have power to set
> This inharmonious world in tune and cause
> Our jarring lives to grow to mellow music.

10.   JESUS HEALS A CENTURION'S SERVANT.
Matthew 8 : 5-13; Luke 7 : 10.

In this incident we have the first contact of Jesus with the Gentile world, and it was a prophetic foregleam of ages to come. While Jesus did shut himself up within a narrow Jewish field it was only that he might raise wheat to be sown broadly over the world.

Concerning this centurion nothing more is known that what is here recorded. He was a Roman officer in command of a hundred soldiers stationed at Capernaum, where, as in all the chief towns, the Romans kept a garrison. He had good points in his character. The first was his sympathetic regard for his servant. This servant was the centurion's slave, his personal property, and the Roman slave had no rights his master was bound to respect. Yet there were bright spots in the gloom, exceptional cases in which master and slave were bound together in the spirit of brotherhood, and such was the relation of this centurion and his slave.

The centurion was also a man of strong character. He had soldiers under him that would go and come at his bidding. He was also himself set under authority, so that he was not only able to command others but was also able to obey, which is often a harder thing to do. He had the power of self-control, which is the highest strength. He had also built a synagogue for the Jews, and this shows his liberal spirit both in religion and in financial giving.

So this centurion combined sympathy with strength, liberality in giving with firmness in exacting, power in commanding with self-control in obeying, and thus his character at many points is symmetrical and beautiful.

Yet this strong man, when his beloved servant fell sick, came to the end of his power and broke down. His love for his slave, his good will toward the Jews, the synagogue he had built, the soldiers under his command, none of these could help him in his hour of anxiety and trial. Sooner or later we all come to the point where all our resources fail us.

The centurion was helpless in himself, yet there was left one thing he could do, and he did it: he went to Jesus This was an act of courage. Jesus was not a popular prophet among many of the Jews, already he was under suspicion as a heretic and dangerous man. For this Roman officer to appeal to him was to expose himself to Jewish ridicule and scorn and possibly to charges of treason. Yet the soldier in him swept away all fear, and he boldly went to Jesus.

When he came to Jesus and received assurance that Jesus would go with him and heal his servant, the centurion said, "Lord, trouble not thyself; for I am not worthy that thou shouldest enter under my roof." It was not usual for a Roman officer to speak in this spirit: rather he was a proud man that spoke in imperious tones of superiority. But this centurion had a sense of humility which was a mark of loftier greatness. He concluded with a request that showed remarkable faith: "but say in a word, and my servant shall be healed."

Such faith drew from Jesus the wonderful testimony, "I have not found so great faith, no, not in Israel." This started him off on a train of reflection that many shall come from the east and the west and shall sit down with Abraham and Isaac and Jacob in the kingdom of heaven, but the sons of the kingdom shall be cast out: a revelation as by a flash of lightning that many who think they are in the kingdom and pride themselves on their superiority yet have no part in it. But there is also a bright ray of

hope in this revelation, for it shows many coming from
unexpected quarters into the kingdom. If church people
prove unfaithful and are shut out, many poor heathen
souls, true to their dim light, shall come in.

Jesus Christ had a large vision of his kingdom in the
world. He was no parochial teacher with little plans and
programs, but a kingdom-builder who looked through the
ages, threw wide open its doors to the people of every land
and saw them coming from every quarter of the horizon
and pouring into it. Our own eyes are now seeing the ful-
filment of this prophecy in many foreign lands.

Jesus bade the centurion to go home. "As thou hast
believed, so be it done unto thee. And his servant was
healed in the self-same hour." Faith is always the measure of our achievements. The great faith that sees a great
vision in any field, exploration, business, literature, is
matched and crowned with a correspondingly great victory. In the spiritual life it shall be done unto us according to our faith. Ask great things of God. "Open
thy mouth wide, and I will fill it" (Ps. 81:10).

11. How Jesus Dealt with John's Doubt.
Matthew 11 : 2-19; Luke 7 : 18-35.

John the Baptist had been in prison something like a
year in a lonely fortress down by the Dead Sea. Jesus
was up in Galilee, moving around among the villages with
a few disciples, preaching. John fell to musing on the
situation, and, as a result, a painful doubt began to grow
in his mind as to whether Jesus, whom he had himself introduced and vouched for as the Messiah, was indeed this
Prophet.

Several causes had produced this doubt. John was in
prison and had been there long enough to fall into a prison
mood. Hope does not burn brightly there. No wonder
that in that damp and dusky place the world looked dark
to John and that the checkered shadows on the stone walls
turned to ghostly spectres.

This was the state of things inside the prison: and what
was the state outside? Dark enough in itself to produce
doubt. Up in Jerusalem the Pharisees were strangling

the life out of religion with their bigotry and hypocrisy. Up in Galilee the court of Herod was living riotously and flaunting its scarlet sins shamelessly before the people. And what was Jesus doing about all this? Apparently nothing: only going around and preaching inoffensive little sermons in fishing towns and country villages. Where were the axe and the fan and fire of judgment that John himself had promised the Messiah would bring? They were not in evidence?

On the contrary Jesus had turned out to be patient, tolerant, mild, genial. He had abandoned Jerusalem and seemed unconcerned about Herod and his court; he had apparently forgotten his forerunner lying in the Black Tower down by the Dead Sea and was content to spend an easy life talking to insignificant fisher folk. A genial Christ was not what John wanted: that fiery prophet wanted a Christ that would come with axe and fire to chop things down and burn them up.

Under the convergence and pressure of all these facts John himself began to doubt the very Christ whom he had introduced with high hope and promise. That John doubted Jesus is the astonishing fact that stands out in this narrative, and it is an honest book that boldly writes this damaging fact down on its pages.

No thinking mind escapes these shadows of doubt. Good men in all ages, even prophets and apostles, have been enveloped in this darkness. The higher up one climbs in thought and even in saintly character, the more may doubt beat against him, as mountaintops are caught in storms that never sweep down upon the plains.

What, now, did John do with his doubt? He did not brood over it until it hatched out the serpents of unbelief and bitterness and hatred of all things good. He did not allow his doubt to destroy what faith he had in Jesus and sink into despair. The man who deals with his doubt in this way in doing an unfair thing and is driving his doubt straight into starless night.

John sent a committee of inquiry to Jesus, asking, "Art thou he that should come, or do we look for another?" He did not consult his disciples who were bringing various discouraging reports about Jesus; much less did he take counsel with the Pharisees, the enemies of Jesus, or with the Sadducees, the agnostics of the day; but he sent directly to Jesus and asked him for further light and gave him a further trial. This is the first course to pursue with our doubts. Doubt is a bad thing when it drives us away from Christ, but it is a good thing when it sends us to him for further facts and fuller truth and light and life.

How, now, did Jesus deal with John's doubt? He said unto John's messengers, "Go and shew John those things which ye do hear and see." This is a remarkable answer that blazes out upon the pages of the Gospel like a burst of light. It contains no harsh judgment upon John, or slightest trace of impatience with him for his doubt. Christ never dealt unkindly with any one for doubting him, and he will not be hard on us for our doubts if we will only bring them to him.

Go and tell John the facts, said Jesus. He did not send word to John that his doubts were damnable and that he should stop his thinking and hush them up. This has been a favorite way of dealing with doubt in some quarters. Some ecclesiastics from the Pharisees down to our day have been very much afraid of thinking on the part of the people and have tried to discourage and even suppress it. But this is not the spirit of the Bible which urges us to prove all things and try the very spirits whether they be of God. Jesus did not stop John's thinking, and mental death is not the cure for doubt to this day.

More remarkable still, Jesus did not undertake to do John's thinking for him. John's question was, "Art thou he that should come, or do we look for another?" Why did not Jesus answer with a plain and positive yes? Why not relieve John of all responsibility and perplexity in settling this question by settling it for him? Because this is not Christ's way and it is not God's way. It is a way that presents plausible pleas and attractions. It seems so plain and easy and conclusive, and it has often been tried. There are ecclesiastics who want to do all our religious thinking for us and kindly offer to relieve us of all trouble in the matter. Why not have the church fix and finish our creed down to the last letter and then simply accept it on its dogmatic authority? Because our minds will not let us and God does not want us to do this.

Christianity is not a superstition but a rational religion. God had not given us reasoning faculties and then stifled and stultified them by leaving them no room in which to work; on the contrary he is ever urging us on into a larger use of our reason. "Come now, and let us reason together, saith the Lord" (Isaiah 1:18).

So on this occasion Jesus said in effect to John's disciples, "Go and tell John the facts and let him draw his own conclusion; I will not answer this question for him dogmatically, but I will give him more facts and suggest to him a further line of thought and let him work out an answer to his own question." Jesus did not tell John to do less thinking, but he told him to do more thinking. Jesus is not afraid of reasoning in his disciples: he only wants them to reason enough and think their way through to right conclusions.

What were the facts Jesus submitted to John? "The blind receive their sight, and the lame walk, the lepers are cleansed, and the deaf hear, the dead are raised up, and the poor have the gospel preached unto them." These were not theological arguments but gracious works. They were self-certifying evidences.

There are other works being wrought in our day that come closer to our vision and experience. The character and deeds of Christ match and prove his divine claims. That white Life that grew up out of the hard barren soil of that selfish world must have had a divine root that was never born of earth. His magnificent march of mercy through the Christian centuries is a mighty fact. His sayings are self-evident truths, which are not dogmatic deliverances but spiritual laws that work in our lives as Newton's law of gravitation works in the skies. Thus Jesus boldly trusted this matter to John's judgment, and so does he trust us.

"And blessed is he, whosoever shall not be offended in me." With these words Jesus closed his answer to John. They imply that we must exercise some patience with Christ, that we cannot fully understand him, that after we have done our profoundest and most sympathetic

thinking towards him there will still be unexplored remainders and unsolved problems we cannot clear up, that
he is bordered with mystery that must ever transcend and
try our faith.   All our religious thinking is margined
and mingled with mystery.   It would be a superficial religion that we could fathom; it would be a poor and pitiful God that we could see through.   Some things in Christ
we must ever take by faith; some of his ways may ever
sorely perplex us.   But blessed is he that is not offended
on this account, but rather trusts and worships him the
more.

12. Jesus Teaching by Parables
Matthew 13:1-53; Mark 4:1-34; Luke 4:1-18

On the shore of Lake Galilee, standing on its sandy
beach and sitting on its grassy banks were an assembled
multitude, while from the pulpit of a fishing boat Jesus
delivered to them a series of seven parables.   It was the
first instance of his using this mode of teaching and seems
to have surprised the disciples so that they asked him
privately for an explanation.

A parable is a short story with a moral point, a picture
of the truth taught, a dramatized expression of doctrine.
An abstract statement of a truth is difficult to grasp and
is apt to be uninteresting.   Put the same truth in the
form of a story or illustration drawn from the familiar
things of life, and instantly it takes on form and color
and dramatic action and begins to attract attention.

Jesus was a master of illustration.   His parables are
pictures out of the daily experience of his hearers which
brought his teachings home to every one's business and
bosom.   He spoke to farmers of sowing and reaping, of
wheat and tares; to fishermen of casting nets and sorting
out fish and finding the pearl of great price.   The listless
housekeeper suddenly had her attention arrested by hearing mention of the leaven hid in the meal or of sweeping a
room in search of a lost coin; and the workman, weary
with his day's toil, stopped to hear of the laborers employed in the vineyard and of how they struck for higher
wages.   Jesus spoke in the language of daily life and

made religion as real and practical as farming and fishing. His sermons were picturesque and attractive and at times touched with humor; his hearers knew what he was talking about, and the common people heard him gladly.

The main object of the parable of the sower, which will be taken as an example of these parables, is to describe four classes of hearers with the view of persuading us to take heed how we hear.

First, are those that receive the seed of truth on the wayside. This is the path or road running through the grainfield which was traveled over so that it was kept beaten down bare and hard, and seeds falling on it were quickly picked up by greedy, watchful birds that were hovering about. Our hearts are thus traveled over and beaten down. Our sins trample over them with their hardening hoofs, the hurrying traffic of the world rolls over them its iron wheels, and what chance do seeds of truth falling on such hearts have to take root? The mind may listen, but quickly some worldly thought or desire comes in and snatches it away.

The second class of hearers receive the seed upon stony soil. This is only a thin layer of earth on an underlying sheet of rock, and the seeds falling on this warm soil quickly take root, but when the rootlets strike the layer of rock the plant all the more luxuriantly shoots up into stalk; but having no depth of earth, under a scorching sun it soon droops and withers. This represents a ready reception of truth that is only superficial and temporary. It may be due to an emotional nature that responds to every appeal as a leaf flutters before every breath of air. There are people that like to have their feelings touched and cry as easily as children, to whom tears may be a kind of luxury. But the excitement soon passes, the old temptations return, and such converts do not last and are soon ready for the next revival.

So runs the story. Other seeds are choked by thorns, and old habits constrict and strangle the seeds of the gospel. But good soil brings forth thirty and sixty and even a hundred fold. These are they of open mind and receptive heart who receive the truth with depth of conviction and fervency of faith and have staying power in the Christian life and bear the fruits of the Spirit.

The main point of the parable is the lesson that Jesus himself drew from it that we should take heed how we hear. Preaching is thought to be a difficult thing involving great responsibility, but hearing is generally supposed to be easy, involving little or no responsibility and no effort at all. But in fact hearing is in a sense as difficult and responsible work as preaching and teaching. There is plenty of poor preaching abroad in the land, but there is vastly more poor hearing; and no doubt one reason there is so much poor preaching up in the pulpit is that there is so much lamentably poor hearing down in the pews.

Good hearing implies preparation and a right state of mind, sympathetic attention to and concentration of thought upon the subject, and these are a difficult exercise of the mind. It makes some difference to the merchant how he hears the orders of his customers; or to the locomotive engineer how he reads the orders of the train dispatcher; or to the soldier how he hears the commands of his officer; or to a patient how he hears the directions of his physician; or to one asleep in a burning building how he hears the voice calling upon him to escape for his life. On the way we hear may depend life itself. Infinitely greater difference does it make how we hear the voice of the Lord Jesus calling upon us to repent and believe upon him and to do his will. On such hearing depend the issues of eternity.

These parables illustrate the whole manner of the teaching of Jesus as artless, simple, sincere, issuing as a living stream out of his own experience, appealing to the experience of his hearers, always bearing the accent of reality and throbbing with sympathy and earnestness. He taught with authority, not with the arbitrary authority of official station, but with that of inherent and self-evident truth. His words were their own witnesses and needed no official claim or station to confirm them.

Universality was stamped upon his teaching. His subjects, however personal and local, were yet universal in their range and application. The smallest matter in his hands became great. He kept clear of provincial and local affairs and dealt chiefly with the large and permanent interests of the human soul. The teachings of any ancient author, even the greatest, such as Plato and Cicero, are obsolete on many a page, because they have long since been left behind by the progress of human thought. Science has put them in a pitiable plight. But none of the teachings of Jesus is thus out of date and left behind. His words are ever abreast and in advance of the age; and still his sublime saying stands true, ''Heaven and earth shall pass away, but my words shall not pass away.''

13. A STORM ON LAKE GALILEE
Matthew 8: 23-27; Mark 4: 35-41; Luke 8: 22-25

At the close of the busy day of teaching, Jesus needed rest and he saw that the only way he could escape from the multitude and find retirement was to cross the lake to the other side. This lake, rimmed in with abrupt mountain walls cut deep with canyons, is subject to sudden and violent storms. The winds rush down the ravines and lash the placid sea into a boiling foaming mass of maddened water.

Such a storm fell upon the lake on this evening, and presently the boat containing Jesus and his disciples was being tossed about like a bit of wood on the angry waves.

The sea is a favorite symbol of life in all literatures. Its smooth surface and bright prospect and pleasant sailing and its changing moods and its storms and mystery and tragedy,—how these reflect our human experience. We might think that life in God's world would always be smooth and safe and pleasant, but he has not made it so. It has its broad bright expanse when heaven pours its splendor upon it and it seems like a sea of glass, and then its skies darken and break into a storm that sends all God's waves and billows over us.

Where was Jesus in this storm? ''In the hinder part of the ship, asleep on a pillow.'' It is a beautiful touch of the humanity of Jesus. Weary with the day's labor, in which he had expended his strength and imparted his soul to the multitude, spent in body and in mind, he lay

down in the arms of "nature's sweet restorer." He was
fatigued with toil, he had done nothing that day that
troubled his conscience, and he had committed himself
to his Father's care as he lay down in that boat, and these
are the secrets of sound sweet sleep at the close of any
day.

And what were the disciples doing in the storm? No
doubt they did their best to manage the boat. They were
fishermen and knew that lake and were expert in seamanship, many a storm had they weathered, and they knew
how to reef the sails and scud before the wind.

But this storm was too much for them. The waves
were beating into the boat and filling it with water, and
they thought they must have instant help or it would
soon be all over with them. At this point they awoke
Jesus and cried unto him, "Master, carest thou not that
we perish?" There is a note of impatience in their words,
and yet they appeal to Jesus, not as another boatman or
fellow man, but as Master and Lord. They knew that his
power underlay and overtopped that sea and storm and
could curb its wrath and put a hook in its mighty frothy
jaws and bring it low; and their faith in him, though at
times it wavered and was near to failing, now rose in its
strength and cast itself upon him.

We should trust in the Lord at all times, but especially
in the hour of darkness and storm. "Deep calleth unto
deep at the noise of thy waterspouts; all thy waves and
thy billows are gone over me. Yet the Lord will command his loving kindness in the daytime, and in the night
his song shall be with me, and my prayer unto the God of
my life."

This prayer was immediately answered. The sleeping
Christ awoke and arose and stood upon the deck of that
sinking ship, and with calm dignity and self-possession,
as of one who knew that he held that sea in the hollow of
his hand, he said, "Peace, be still!" The tempest-driven
waters fell flat and the holy calm of evening lay upon the
sea. What is this more than the mastery of mind over
matter? The human spirit can quiet down and control
the agitated human body even when it is in a paroxysm
of pain, and cannot the divine Spirit that pervades the

universe master it at every point and mold it to his purposes? One of the deepest facts of the universe is that
matter is servant of mind and may be only one mode of
its manifestation, and this miracle is an instance of this
fact.

What effect did this deliverance have upon the disciples?
"And they feared exceedingly, and said one to another,
What manner of man is this, that even the wind and
the sea obey him?" They had seen other exhibitions of
the miracle-working power of Jesus, but this so far surpassed all other wonders that they felt that they did
not know him and exclaimed, "What manner of man is
this!"

Yet the storm added nothing to Jesus, but only brought
out what was in him. An observer, noting the men in
that boat as it drew away from the shore that evening,
would not have discerned any marked difference in its
occupants. They were all plain men, wearing about the
same garb and belonging to the same class. But the storm
suddenly revealed a difference among them of immense
range and power and showed one of them to be divine
and made him master of the others and of the sea. Great
crises bring out what is in men. Lincoln did not seem to
differ greatly from other men until the Civil War came:
then his power came out and he stood master of the hour
and of the nation.

Jesus did not seem to many of his contemporaries to be
other than a common man and a deluded and dangerous
one at that. Yet the centuries have brought out the real
nature and rank and power of this Man and revealed him
as the Son of God and Saviour of the world.

Do we think that we fully know Jesus Christ? This is
the folly of our superficial knowledge and the blindness
of our conceit. We also need some outburst of his power
or extraordinary experience to shock us out of our self-
satisfied shallowness and give us a new vision of Christ.
Then we shall exclaim, "What manner of man is this!"
Even the centuries obey him and swing their orbits around
his cradle and date their calendar from his birth. Our
greatest safety and comfort and blessing consist in trust-
ing him in all the experiences and storms of life.

14. The Tragedy of the Black Tower
Matthew 14:1-12, Mark 6:14-29, Luke 9:7-9

Incidents following the storm on the lake were the healing of the Gadarene demoniac, the raising of the daughter of Jairus, the healing of two blind men, the second rejection at Nazareth, a third preaching tour through Galilee, the instructions to the Twelve, and then we come to the story of the death of John the Baptist.

As Jesus moved about from point to point in Galilee, the fame of his mighty works spread far and wide, and various theories were being offered to account for his wonderful doings, some saying he was Elijah and others that he was a prophet.

But Herod had a theory of his own which he could not keep from blurting out. "This is John the Baptist," he said, "he is risen from the dead." Sadducee and sceptic though he was, yet conscience overpowered his scepticism in the resurrection and he saw the murdered man alive. The sight of the holy prophet's blood dripping on the palace floor never could be banished from his mind and made him believe in a possibility which his creed denied.

The occurrence of this incident in the life of Jesus leads the writers of the synoptic Gospels to give an account of the imprisonment and death of John the Baptist which had occurred some time before. The tragedy occurred in Castle Machærus or the Black Tower, situated on a crag overlooking a deep mountain gorge nine miles east of the Dead Sea. Mineral springs were near by, and in the palace he had built there Herod spent a portion of each year. The prophet had been in prison about a year when, amidst the revelries of a royal feast, there was enacted this dark and revolting tragedy.

The crime had its roots in causes far back, and there was a woman in the case. Herod Antipas had inherited and developed many of the traits of his father, Herod the Great, that monster of iniquity. He lured away Herodias, the wife of Philip, Herod's elder brother, who was an ambitious, fascinating and unprincipled woman. He already had a wife and she had a husband, but these were slight obstructions in the way of such people, and the unholy union was formed. Fawning courtiers flattered the guilty pair, but when John the Baptist got a chance at them he did not mince his words. "It is not lawful for thee to have her," he said. He shot a flash of lightning into Herod's guilt; he put his finger on the burning point of his sin and made him writhe under its touch.

From this hour the prophet's doom was sealed. The fury of an enraged woman that had the heart of a tigress was let loose against him. She would have killed him outright, but was restrained by Herod. He was afraid to go so far, but sent and seized John and hurried him off to the Black Tower and thrust him into its dungeon dug deep in the rock. Herod would not stand such preaching and made way with the preacher.

The scene is now set in the Castle Machærus and we look in upon revelry and dancing. Herod's birthday was being celebrated with a great social function. It was the society event of the season, and the lords of the court, the officers of the army, and the wealth and fashion and beauty of Galilee were present. The Castle gleamed with lights and strains of minstrelsy floated out upon the air.

But there was one unhappy woman there that night. In the midst of the revelry Herodias was rankling with revenge and her brain was busy with plots and plans. At such a feast it was customary to introduce a professional dancing girl to entertain the guests, and this dance was immoral in character and pleased the spectators in proportion as it passed the borders of modesty.

On this occasion Herodias introduced as the dancer Salome, her own daughter by a former marriage. It was a shame for a mother to prostitute her daughter to this end, but this was a link in her cunning plot and it worked like a charm. The dancer caught the fancy of Herod who, infatuated with the girl, offered her whatsoever she might wish, even to the half of his kingdom. The daughter withdrew to consult her mother. The tigress was lying in wait in her lair outside the dance hall and her hour was come.

Beneath the marble floor of the palace, right under her feet, chained to a rock was John the Baptist, the hated preacher who had dared to cross her path. All that scene of revelry and splendor could not give her satisfaction while this object of her fury was alive. "What shall I ask?" was the daughter's question. The answer was ready on the very tip of the mother's tongue. Without the waste of a word she hissed, "The head of John the Baptist."

The daughter was of the same cold and cruel blood as her mother and carried the request to the king. He was shocked at the dreadful idea, but he was now afloat on the swift-rushing current of his sin. Instantly a soldier was dispatched to execute the order. Suddenly the door of the cell creaked on its hinges and the officer stood in the gloom, peering around for the prisoner, all unexpectant of his fate. One strong sure stroke of his keen sword and the deed was done. The head was placed on a charger and brought dripping up into the palace before the horrified guests and handed to the daughter and from the daughter it passed to the mother. Her revenge was complete: the hated preacher's voice was silenced.

But was that the end of the tragedy of the Black Tower? No, it was only the beginning. Afterwards Herod believed the murdered man was alive and was terrified. Not all the multitudinous seas could wash the stain of the prophet's blood out of the consciences of the guilty pair. Presently the scheming Herodias got Herod into trouble at Rome, and he was banished into France and then into Spain, where they both died in exile. They went down to their dishonored graves stung with disgrace and fear and have been pilloried before all the ages for their crime. Once more it was terribly confirmed that the wages of sin is death.

Thus John the Baptist went to his cross before his Master. "And when his disciples heard of it, they came and took up his corpse, and laid it in a tomb."

15. FIVE THOUSAND FED
Matthew 14:13-23; Mark 6:30-46; Luke 9:10-17; John 6:1-15

After the execution of John the Baptist, Jesus with his

disciples crossed Lake Galilee to the northeastern shore
for safety and rest. No sooner had he started than the
people followed after him in boats and around the shore
so that presently a great multitude was gathered before
them. That was the end of his rest, and the work of
teaching and healing began.

Evening drew on and a difficulty loomed up. What was
to be done with all these people? Jesus intimated that
they must be fed. The perplexed disciples took stock of
their provisions and put their heads together and were
at their wits' end. Already the sun was dropping behind
the western hills and the chill of evening was in the air.
Something must be done quickly; what could it be? They
thought of the multitudes; they thought of their few
loaves and fishes; they thought of everything, except
Christ. It does not seem to have occurred to them that
he could help them out of their difficulty. Sometimes in
our perplexities we think of everything—except God.

At last they hit upon a way out of their trouble and
came to Jesus with their plan. "Send the multitude away,
that they may go into the villages, and buy themselves
victuals." Send them away! How natural the suggestion, how easy the solution, what a quick riddance of the
burden. We must not, however, be too hard on these
disciples, as we would probably have thought of the same
thing and their plan seems to be only common sense. But
nothing can make bigger blunders than common sense
when it forgets God.

This thought may get into our theology and church life.
A church that makes itself exclusive and welcomes people
of a certain class and gives the cold shoulder to others, a
silk-robed, kid-gloved Christianity that separates itself
from the common crowd, is saying in tones that are not
misunderstood, Send them away. The anti-missionary
spirit that says, We have heathen enough at home, is saying to the heathen abroad, Send them away. When in any
way we have made sure of our own basket of provisions
and are not willing to share it with others, but look with
indifference on their hunger, we are bidding them to take
themselves off and buy bread for themselves.

"Send them away," said the disciples. "They need not

depart," instantly said Jesus. Any plan that would send people away from Jesus Christ is no part of his gospel. Here is the contrast between the disciples and the Master: the one short of means, narrow and selfish and wanting to send people away; and the other full of resources, broad and sympathetic and having abundance and welcome for all.

When asked what they had, Andrew, who seldom had anything to say, ventured the remark, "There is a lad here, which hath five barley loaves, and two small fishes: but what are they among so many?" Evidently Andrew did not think much of this boy with his pitifully few loaves and "small fishes" and thought they were hardly worth mentioning. This is what Moses thought of his power of speech when God commanded him to go and speak to Pharaoh. "O Lord," he said in effect, "I can't speak: send Aaron." Yet Moses spoke great thundering words that shook Egypt, but who can quote anything that Aaron ever said? This is what we often think when we are called to do a work. With our few means and narrow opportunities we have no chance! Give us large means and big opportunities and see what we will do.

What did Jesus say? "Bring them hither to me." The Master was not alarmed at the smallness of the means. What the disciples despised he took and with them wrought astonishing results. It is not the means, but the power behind the means that does the work. Give Samson only the jawbone of an ass and with it he will slay a thousand Philistines. Give David only a smooth stone out of a brook and with it he will bring tumbling down huge blustering Goliath who had defied the whole army of Israel. Give the chemist only scum and dross and out of it he will extract exquisite perfumes and the most beautiful colors. Give the poet the rudest pen and with it he will write musical lines and fairy visions. There are undreamed-of possibilities in us and in the means in our hands if we will only develop them.

Jesus now had the multitudes sit down on the green grass in ranks of hundreds and fifties. What was this? Business efficiency, order and organization, division of labor. We must cut up our work and apportion it out so that each one will have a definite part, and the work can then be done without confusion and overlapping and waste.

The bread was then passed, and "they all did eat and were filled." When the multitude saw these few loaves started out, perhaps those around the distant edges of the crowd thought and feared that the bread would never reach them. But nearer and nearer it came, the mysterious supply never running short, until the last rank was reached and the last child was fed. Let us never fear that the mercy and resources of God will ever fail.

"Gather up the fragments that remain," said Jesus, "that nothing be lost." And they gathered up of these fragments twelve baskets. Was not this strange frugality on the part of him who could create such abundance? But unbounded resources and the largest liberality may be closely connected with the strictest economy. The Hand that could create a hundred loaves did not disdain to pick up a crumb.

God with all his infinitude of resources never wastes anything, or lets any fragment fall useless and forgotten out of his hand. Wasting fragments has ruined many a business, and by-products are often a source of large profits. Waste no fragments of time or bread or opportunities of doing good, but gather them up and keep them for the hour of need and service.

16. JESUS BREAKS WITH THE PHARISEES
Matthew 15:1-20; Mark 7:1-23

"Why do thy disciples transgress the tradition of the elders? for they wash not their hands when they eat bread?" The question thus put to Jesus by the Pharisees and scribes does not seem to raise any vital point or portend any serious consequences; yet it is the spark of fire that kindled into a white heat the whole issue between him and them; it is the gleam of the dagger with which they meant to pierce his heart. Here Jesus breaks with the Pharisees and this point marks the beginning of the end.

The washing of the hands, to which the Pharisees referred in their question, was not the ordinary cleansing of the hands, but a ceremonial requirement of the most complicated kind. Before eating, the hands had to be washed by an elaborate process involving many precise ways of holding them and pouring water on them and letting it drain and drip off, which had to be most carefully and rigidly observed. There were twenty-six rules for this rite in the morning alone, and to violate or neglect them was declared to be a sin as bad as adultery or murder and worthy of death!

It is easy to see what would become of the spirit of religion when caught in such a system: it would be constricted and strangled to death. The outer material form gradually buried and crushed the inner spiritual reality. More and more care and importance were attached to mechanical acts and less and less to spiritual states.

Not only so, but the mechanical form came to be used as a deliberate means to kill off spiritual life and as a mask to hide all manner of wickedness. While the Pharisees were so punctilious and ostentatious in observing their own traditional inventions and were ready to persecute even unto death any one who dared to neglect them, they were robbing widows, refusing to support their parents and reveling in all manner of iniquity. They were like sepulchres, outwardly white but inwardly full of dead men's bones. This has ever been the tendency of ceremonial religion.

What did Jesus say in answer to this apparently innocent question as to the practice of his disciples? It seemed to be only a trivial point of personal habit, but he discerned its true import and far-reaching consequences. It was a critical moment with him; he stood facing a temptation as perilous as that which assailed him in the wilderness. His kingdom was at stake, and he faced the Pharisees as boldly as he had faced the devil. "And he answered and said unto them, Why do ye also transgress the commandment of God because of your tradition?" He then charged them with having set aside and violated one of the Ten Commandments of Moses, even the one bidding them to honor father and mother, with their cunning devices, again denounced them for having "made void the Word of God because of your tradition," and quoted Isaiah against them.

Then calling the multitude he cried out, as if to all the world, "Hear, and understand: not that which goeth into the mouth defileth a man; but that which cometh out of the mouth, this defileth a man." Not that which is outside a man and passes into his body can do him any spiritual harm, but that which is inside and comes out of his heart. Thus Jesus boldly broke with the Pharisees and trampled upon their human traditions. He would have none of their petty rules and regulations as a necessary condition of living a religious life.

It is true that he observed and instituted simple ordinances himself, but these were only means to an end and not the end itself. His kingdom did not consist in meat and drink, ordinances and ceremonies, images and incense and all the gorgeous spectacle of the stately temple or cathedral, but in righteousness and peace, a pure heart and a right life.

The answer he gave that day was a turning point in his career. It shattered the whole Pharisaic system and made him a terrible heretic. From that hour he was a doomed man in the eyes of these ecclesiastical authorities. So deeply were they wounded, so open was their resentment, that the alarmed disciples said to Jesus, "Knowest thou that the Pharisees were offended, after they heard this saying?" Well did Jesus know this and know the price he would have to pay, but he calmly answered, "Every plant which my heavenly Father hath not planted, shall be rooted up." He was teaching, not simply for that time, but for all time, and he foresaw the final victory.

Tradition has its place in religion, as in all things else. It stores up the accumulated experience and wisdom of the past and hands it down to us as our precious inheritance. The race would never get forward if every generation had to begin at the beginning. The Bible itself is simply so much tradition: it is the religious experience of the chosen people as recorded and interpreted for us by prophets and apostles. As such it is of immense value to us, saving us from fighting our way up out of barbarism and heathenism and planting our feet on the summits of Christian truth and attainment won by illuminated and holy men. Jesus himself used tradition. He did not cast away all that had been done by Moses and Isaiah and begin anew, but he adopted and adapted their materials; he introduced his religion, not by revolution, but by evolution.

Nevertheless, tradition has its limits and dangers. It is to be used as so much valuable material for building, but not as a fixed and finished structure. It furnishes us with seeds and roots, but these are not to be kept from sprouting: they are to be made to grow into their proper flower and fruit. When tradition is used as a bond to bind our brains and constrict our hearts, when it becomes an artificial system of human invention and not a vital breath of the Spirit, then we are to break through it and trample upon it that we may win our way to our liberty and our right to grow. Tradition, however ancient and sacred, must always be tested by living truth and experience.

This break with the Pharisees marks the practical close of the ministry of Jesus in Galilee. He now withdrew into the region of Tyre and Sidon and returned through Decapolis to Galilee, where he fed the four thousand and had some further relations with the Pharisees and Sadducees, but the year of popularity was now ending and was soon to enter upon the year of opposition.

17. THE INTERVIEW AT CAESAREA PHILIPPI
Matthew 16:13-20; Mark 8:27-30; Luke 9:18-22

Jesus with his disciples now went north to Caesarea Philippi with the object of having a close private interview with them and making a momentous revelation to them.

When they were far from the busy scene in which they had been moving, Jesus put to them the question, "Who do men say that I am?" This question is still throbbing in the heart of our civilization. First asked by an obscure Galilean in that far-off solitude, it has come thundering down the ages and is the mightiest question in the world today.

Ideas determine life and in the long run rule the world. What men think is the inner force that shapes what they are and do. The theories that are generally held with reference to industry, wealth, government, art, morals and religion, mold human society into all its forms, as the hidden life of a tree fashions every leaf and bud. What men think of Christ is the master force of the world and more than anything else shapes its life.

The disciples gave the various answers men were giving. The answers differed, but they all agreed that Jesus was an extraordinary person, at least a prophet, a mysterious personality containing an element of the supernatural. Men are still giving various answers, but they all take high ground as to his character and work. The answer that Jesus was a myth, or a dupe, or an imposter is no longer tolerated. Even the greatest sceptics see something in this man that they cannot explain on ordinary principles and they pay tributes to him that fall little short of divinity.

Renan, sceptic as to the supernatural, ends his *Life of Jesus* with these words: ''Whatever may be the surprises of the future, Jesus will never be surpassed. His worship will grow young without ceasing; his legend will call forth tears without end; his sufferings will melt the noblest hearts; all ages will proclaim that, among the sons of men, there is is none born greater than Jesus.'' Charles Lamb once said to a company of friends: ''If Shakespeare should enter the room we should all rise; if Jesus Christ should enter, every one would kneel.''

Jesus now turned the general question into the sharp personal inquiry, ''But who say ye that I am?'' Important as is the general question, far more important to each one is this individual inquiry. No one can escape its keen personal point. A neutral attitude is impossible. Whatever we do is a decision; and nothing else goes so deep down and so far out into our lives as who we say Jesus is.

''Thou art the Christ, the Son of the living God,'' exclaimed the impulsive Peter. For once Peter was grandly right. He hit the truth at the center. His great confession exalts Christ as the Son of the living God, lifting him above humanity and crowning him with divinity.

The great confession was instantly capped with a great blessing. ''Blessed art thou, Simon Bar-jona.'' Faith on the Son of God is the root of all spiritual blessing, and every duty instantly brings its own reward. The next blessing for Peter was that he should be a foundation stone

in Christ's church: "Thou art Peter, and upon this rock
I will build my church; and the gates of hell shall not prevail against it." There is a play upon the words in the
Greek which may be brought out by translating: "Thou
art rock, and upon this Rock I will build my church."

Few passages of Scripture have been the subject of so
much controversy. The two main interpretations are, first,
that the rock on which Christ will build his church is Peter
himself, and, second, that this rock is the faith he has just
confessed. The two views may be combined into the view
that it is Peter as making this confession that is the foundation rock of the church. The Rock of Ages and chief
corner stone on which the church is built is Christ himself,
but on this Rock is laid the foundation of apostles and
prophets (Eph. 2:20). All believers are built into Christ's
spiritual house as living stones (I Pet. 2:5) and are thus a
foundation for those that come after them and build on
them.

And now across the path of the disciples for the first
time fell the fateful shadow of the cross. From that time
began Jesus to part the veil of the future before them and
show them things to come. He saw his path running
straight up to Jerusalem into the murderous hatred of the
priests and Pharisees; beyond their hatred he saw the terrible cross standing with its arms outstretched waiting to
clasp and crush him in an agony of death in their bloody
embrace; and beyond the cross he saw the power and
splendor of the resurrection morning. Jesus had spared
his disciples this painful disclosure until they were able to
bear it, and God often hides things from us in mercy and
reveals them to us only when we are ready for them and
can stand the strain.

Impetuous Peter could not endure this disclosure and
broke out in the exclamation, "Be it far from thee, Lord:
this shall not be unto thee." This was just like Peter, unloosing his self-restraint and speaking unwisely with his
tongue. The plan of redemption unfolded by Jesus and
running back through eternity, was not to Peter's liking
and he proposed to stop it! How true is this to Peter's
short-sighted vision and impulsive nature.

But Jesus made short work with Peter's presumption.

He unmasked him as an agent of Satan and bade him from
his presence; he showed him up as a stumbling-block in
the way; and he exposed the root of his folly in a worldly
mind. Never had such withering words from the lips of
the Master fallen upon poor Peter; but he richly deserved
the reproof. This is what comes of our attempting to
hinder God's ways and to put finishing touches on his
plan. We frequently slide down into worldly views and
utter foolish speeches.

Jesus was not to be turned aside from his duty and his
cross by any such suggestion. He had set his face steadfastly towards Jerusalem and thither would he go. The
way of Christ is not the way of the world. "Then said
Jesus unto his disciples, If any man will come after me,
let him deny himself, and take up his cross, and follow
me."

18. THE TRANSFIGURATION
Matthew 18: 1-13; Mark 9: 2-13; Luke 9: 28-36

It is significant that in all the three Gospels in which it
is recorded the transfiguration, which probably occurred
on or near Mount Hermon, is closely connected with the
announcement that Jesus had just made of his coming
crucifixion. This unexpected and startling revelation must
have shrouded the disciples in deep gloom: it seemed the
utter disappointment and destruction of all their hopes.
They needed a glimpse of the divinity that was hidden in
Jesus and of the glory that lay beyond the cross to disperse the darkness and sustain and inspire them. Possibly
also Jesus himself, as he drew near to his passion, needed
a fresh assurance of the Father's presence and love.

The transfiguration met this need for both disciple and
Master. It was a revelation of power that the cross could
not crush. It shot its splendor through the gloom and
kindled despondent faith and hope into new strength and
joy.

The transfiguration is a mountain scene and ranks with
Sinai and Calvary among the loftiest summits of sacred
story. Jesus with Peter and James and John, his most intimate and trusted disciples, climbed the mountain slope to

a place of prayer. It was night, and Jesus engaged in communion with the Father.

Presently the disciples were aware that a mysterious change was being wrought in the dim and dusky figure of the Master. His face began to shine and his clothing to emit gleams and sparkles of light. The strange luminosity grew into effulgence until his countenance was radiant and his raiment dazzling white. His whole person seemed steeped in splendor, a glory from within was streaming through the veil of his flesh.

There is a mystery here whose border we may not cross. There were divine possibilities in Jesus of which this transfiguration gives us a glimpse and hint. It would seem that his divinity was hidden by the veil of his humanity and that for a moment its glory was kindled and burned through.

In a weaker degree Moses was transfigured when, after his forty days of communion with God on Sinai, his face shone; and they that looked on Stephen at his trial "saw his face as it had been the face of an angel." Thus even the human spirit, when intensely kindled, shines through the flesh and in a degree transfigures it. Of Daniel Webster it is recorded that, for several hours after he had delivered his great oration at Bunker Hill, his face wore an indescribably grand expression that awed those who came into his presence. Character carves the countenance. Sydney Smith said of Francis Horner that the Ten Commandments were written on his face. "Human physiognomy," says Victor Hugo, "is formed by the conscience and the life, and is the result of a multitude of mysterious excavations." Some people have become so sanctified by the Holy Spirit that they wear a heavenly aspect and are verily transfigured into the likeness of Christ.

It was as he prayed that Jesus was transfigured, and it was after forty days of communion with Jehovah that the face of Moses shone. Prayer kindles the soul into intense consciousness of God, and it is then that the glory of holiness shines through.

Two visitors from the heavenly world now appeared upon the scene, Moses and Elijah, themselves shining with glory, and talked with Jesus. Few facts in the gospel story are so deeply and richly significant. Moses, representing the law, and Elijah, representing the prophets, are here associated with Jesus, the Messiah whom they foretold and prepared the way for, thus binding the Old and the New Dispensations together into unity. Redemption is the same through all ages and forms one plan.

Immortality is here brought to light. These are travelers returned from the other world, clothed in the same bodies transfigured with light prophetic of the resurrection body. They were in the possession of the same faculties and speech that they had in this world so that death and heaven do not change the essential constitution and individuality of the soul. They talked with Jesus about "his decease which he should accomplish at Jerusalem" so that redemption is still the subject of interest in heaven and its point of intensest glory is the Lamb slain from the foundation of the world. If heavenly inhabitants are so interested in this redeeming love, they must find it a subject of greater glory than all the starry spaces and splendors through which they may pass, and there is no greater and worthier subject that can engage our minds.

As the visitors were departing Peter spoke up in a bewildered state of mind and proposed to build three tabernacles that they might remain on that mountaintop. It was good to be there, but that was no place to stay. Religious rapture should not become a luxury that we wish to enjoy and that causes us to forget the great world below lying in sin and sorrow and needing our help and healing.

A cloud now overshadowed them and a voice came out of the cloud, saying, "This is my beloved Son: hear him." The cloud was a symbol of God's presence, but one that hid him from view: the voice was the voice of God, setting his seal on his Son. The cloud concealed and the voice revealed. The cloud shut the mystery and splendor of the Father's face out of sight, but the voice brought him near and declared his will. It is the glory of God to conceal a thing. He always hides from us much that we could not bear, but lets us know enough to have a clear path for our feet.

The voice died away in the silence, the cloud melted into the invisible, and Jesus was found alone. The transfiguration glory had vanished from his person and he was his ordinary self. The vision splendid had faded into the light of common day. Intense ecstatic experiences cannot last. Nerves would snap and the brain break down. We cannot always live on the mountaintop.

They went down from the height to the plain below to heal an epileptic boy. Jesus transmuted that great white splendor on the mountaintop into a shining stream of mercy to heal sick and troubled people and to irrigate the wilderness of the world and make it rejoice and blossom of rose. Splendid visions and fine emotions are vain unless they are carried down to the plain and transmuted into sympathy and service.

The disciples held their peace and told no man. They did not boast of their experience and blab it out. Some things we should not tell. Let us climb the mount of prayer and communion until we are transfigured before God: then let us come down into the world and say nothing about it, but get to work and heal some troubled soul.

> The mount for vision; but below
> The paths of daily duty go,
> And nobler life therein shall own
> The pattern on the mountain shown.

CHAPTER V

THIRD YEAR: THE LATER JUDEAN MINISTRY
THE YEAR OF OPPOSITION

The transfiguration may be taken as marking the end of the Galilean ministry. Although he did some further work there, yet his ministry around the Galilean lake was now practically closed. So quickly had the promising popularity of the opening and middle course of his career in Galilee subsided into suspicion and growing hostility. The end was now looming into view and could no longer be postponed. Jesus steadfastly set his face towards Jerusalem, and neither the mistaken opposition of friends, as of Peter at Caesarca Philippi, nor the growing opposition of avowed enemies, could deter or delay his proceeding along the road of duty towards his fate on the cross.

1. THE MAN BORN BLIND. John 9.

Passing by many incidents that happened on the way on the final journey of Jesus to Jerusalem, we again find him in the capital city. He attended the Feast of Tabernacles, which was the national thanksgiving week of the Jews and was celebrated in October, and a little later occurred the incident we shall now consider. He was now under strict surveillance, and the Pharisees were keeping close watch on his doings. The healing of a blind man precipitated the conflict and hurried the course of affairs towards the fatal end.

As Jesus passed by this man blind from birth the disciples were moved to ask him, "Master, who did sin, this man, or his parents, that he was born blind?" The pitiful sight of this man only suggested to them a cool, critical, cruel, theological question: not, How can we get this man out of his blindness? but, How did he get in? They were

only curious to know how the trouble began; not, how it
might be ended. Not only so, but they went the length of
fastening on the unfortunate man a cruel suspicion; and
if they could not charge it to him, then they would unload
it on his parents. This is not altogether ancient history.
We may do this very thing. It is always easier to be critical than correct.

Jesus answered, "Neither hath this man sinned, nor his
parents: but that the works of God should be manifest in
him." All misfortunes cannot be connected with personal
guilt. The Book of Job disposed of that theory. Jesus did
not stop to inquire and did not care how the man got into
trouble: his only concern was to get him out.

Here is another contrast between the disciples and the
Master. In the presence of pitiful human affliction they
could only think of a curious theological question, he was
filled with practical compassion; they were concerned only
with how the trouble began, he was concerned only with
how it might be ended; they were disposed to add to the
poor man's misfortune the further charge of personal fault,
he was disposed to take both misfortune and fault away.
They coldly speculated, he acted. The poor man's extremity was his opportunity.

In the presence of the world's blindness and sin and sorrow, let us not coolly speculate as to causes and attribute
misfortunes to other people's fault, but touch blind eyes
with healing hands and put our shoulders under others'
burdens.

Action immediately followed. Means were used. Even
in his miracles Jesus kept near to nature, and the natural
and supernatural may be closer together than we think.
In using salve of clay on the eyes of this blind man the
great Physician honored the medical art. The "faith cure"
undivorced from any means receives little sanction from
this act. Salvation itself is not a magical process, but definite means are used and it follows a line of strict causa-
tion. "Sanctify them through thy truth: thy word is
truth."

The blind man himself was given a part in the healing. "Go, wash in the pool of Siloam." Jesus gave efficiency to the means, but the man himself had to use them.

Had he refused or neglected to do this, his eyes would never have been opened. Divine sovereignty and human agency must work together at every point.

"He went his way therefore, and washed, and came seeing." A new world opened before his wondering eyes, at first dimly and then in increasing clearness. The valley of the Kedron rolled below him in a flood of color, the temple flashed its golden roof above him, the sky was painful splendor, the way back was a path of beauty, and he saw the face of Jesus. And when Jesus opens our spiritual eyes we behold wondrous things and there is a new glory on the very grass.

The return of the blind beggar restored to sight created a sensation among the neighbors. There was a commotion among them as they disputed as to his very identity, but he said, "I am he." And it took bravery to do this as it instantly drew upon him the persecution of the Jews who now had no toleration for the unpopular Nazarene or for any one that acknowledged any relation with him.

Pressed still further and more hostilely on the point the restored man gave utterance to the most direct and powerful evidence of faith any soul can have: "Whether he be a sinner or no, I know not; one thing I know, that whereas I was blind, now I see." What a good creed is this utterance! It is short, has but one article, comes to the point and rests on the rock of experience. Standing on this fact we can defy all opposition and doubt.

At this point the Pharisees appear on the scene, and from this moment they plague and pester the man with all kinds of questions to catch him in a trap. They first seize on the fact that the alleged deed was done on the Sabbath day, and that was condemnation enough for them. Others of their number, however, took a different point of view, and when they were in danger of falling out among themselves they adopted another line of attack, saying, "We know that God spake unto Moses: as for this fellow, we know whence he is."

The man now grew exceedingly bold and delivered to them a logical lecture on theology, concluding with the unanswerable declaration, "If this man were not of God, he could do nothing." Is not this the strongest evidence of the divinity and saving work of Christ to this day?

This reply enraged the proud Pharisees beyond all self-control and they retorted, "Thou wast altogether born in sin, and dost thou teach us?" Their pride could do not more than explode in these words and this act that really only exposed their furious impotence.

The closing scene is a beautiful one. Jesus found the man and inquired of him, "Dost thou believe on the Son of God?" The man answered, "Who is he, Lord, that I might believe on him?" Jesus was quick with the full revelation, "Thou hast both seen him, and it is he that talketh with thee." Was it not to a disreputable Samaritan woman that Jesus first revealed himself as the Messiah? Did not the angels first announce the good news of the Saviour's birth to shepherds? Verily not many wise and mighty are chosen to hear the best news of God, but humble souls who have not been spoiled with their own conceit and pride. Then came the confession, "Lord, I believe. And he worshiped him."

2. MARY AND MARTHA
Matthew 26: 6-13; Mark 14: 3-9; Luke 10: 38-42; John 12:1-11

After the break with the Pharisees in Jerusalem over the healing of the man born blind Jesus passed the rest of his ministry outside the city and chiefly across the Jordan in the region of Perea. During this last winter of his life, 28-29 A. D., many important incidents occurred and discourses were uttered, such as the bringing of the children to Jesus (Matthew 18:1-14), the sending forth of the seventy disciples (Luke 10:1-24), the healing of blind Bartimaeus (Mark 10:46-52), the conversion of Zacchaeus the tax collector (Luke 10:1-10), the rejection of the rich young ruler (Luke 18:18-23), the cleansing of ten lepers (Luke 17:11-19), the raising of Lazarus (John 11:1-46), and the great parables of the Good Samaritan, the Prodigal Son, and the Rich Man and Lazarus. We can only take a look into the home of Mary and Martha.

We here (Luke 10: 38-42) find Jesus paying his first

recorded visit to that house in Bethany which, more than any other place during the last year of his ministry, was home to him. Here he found rest and hospitality and friendship, and here he spoke words that still relate to vital points in our homes. Jesus during his ministry had no home of his own, but he gladly entered into homes and irradiated them by his presence and exhibited behavior as perfect in form as it was beautiful in spirit, and he is now making all homes better.

Two sisters were in this home whose contrasted temperaments complicated their domestic relations and who represent different types of human personalities and of Christian character and service.

Mary was the passive sister who sat at Jesus' feet, a rapt listener to his wonderful words. She is a type of a meditative person who draws apart at times from busy activities for reading, meditation and communion, sitting at the feet of great teachers, thinkers, poets, prophets, and entering into the secret place of prayer.

Martha was the active sister, who when Jesus appeared as a guest forthwith set about preparing a meal, and there was a clatter of dishes out in the kitchen, and a rushing around and a general air of haste and confusion in the house. She is a type of an active and practical person, overloaded with work, always busy to the point of distraction, buried in the kitchen or office and seldom rising into the higher calmer region of the spirit, superabundant in labors, but deficient in meditation.

These two sisters misunderstood each other and came near to clashing in the very presence of Jesus. And these two types may easily misunderstand and criticize and berate each other. The pushing hustler may have small respect for the quiet thinker who seems to do nothing but sit and read and meditate, and the thinker may underrate the practical worker as a shallow and sordid person and fail to appreciate his real worth in the world.

We should know that it takes all kinds of people to make a world, different types and temperaments to blend their varying individualities into a stronger and richer unity, and this should make us broad and sympathetic in judging one another. We have these different tem-

peraments in the home and church and community and
we should learn to understand and adjust ourselves to
one another and live and work together in mutual harmony.

The scene now shifts to Simon's house and we find
Jesus a guest at this table. Mary also was present, and
she did a characteristic thing on this occasion. Brooding
over the mystery of the impending death of Jesus she
brought an alabaster jar of spikenard, and, snapping off
the slender neck, poured the costly fragrant ointment on
the Master, anointing his person and filling all the room
with the perfume. It was a beautiful Oriental expression of devotion and love.

A strange thing now occurred. Some of the disciples
saw Mary's act with surprise and indignation, and whis-
perings began to pass around among them and these found
outspoken expression from Judas, ''Why was this waste
of ointment made? For it might have been sold for more
than three hundred pence, and have been given to the
poor?'' These rough fishermen did not appreciate Mary's
fine act. They were square-headed, hard-fisted, practical
men used to counting pence, and had no sentiment
in them. They thought that she had wasted her costly
ointment and had nothing to show for it, whereas it might
have been sold for hard cash with which she could have
done much practical good and had something to spare for
herself. If Mary loved Jesus, why did she not simply
tell him so and save her ointment?

This pence view of things is still common enough
among us. There are people who look on all things in
this light. They measure everything in feet and pounds,
and especially in dollars and cents. They call for statistics and refuse to believe in anything that cannot be
put down in a column of figures. They come into a church
and ask for the number of converts and baptisms and fig
ure out how much they cost apiece and make comparisons
with other churches and ministers to see who are saving
or getting the most people at the least expense. Like
Gradgrind they believe in ''facts, Sir, hard facts.''

Now the money view of things often has its time and
place and then may be decisive. Statistics have their use

and must often be compiled and consulted. There is much expenditure of money that is waste and worse and ought to be stopped. But there is saving that is loss, and there is apparent waste that is wealth. The money view may be a money vice, and in some cases statistics can tell us everything except the truth.

The finest things in the world cannot be measured and bought or sold. We can compute the size and weight of the earth, but not the value of the sunset and the blue sky. We can weigh the newborn baby in the scales, but not the mother's love for her child. Character cannot be measured with a tapeline or sold by the pound. Love cannot be bought or sold in the market, any more than can sunbeams or bits of gorgeously colored clouds. We have slipped far away from the spiritual into the material when we begin to talk of pence in connection with devotion and love. Affection, heart, spirit, are not in the same class with money and cannot be compared with mountains of gold.

There was one person present on this occasion that deeply appreciated Mary's act: Jesus. "Let her alone," he said to these cold critical disciples; "why trouble ye her? she hath wrought a good work on me. . . . She hath done what she could." No grander eulogy was ever pronounced on man or woman. It is the brightest crown that can be placed on any human brow and is a more imperishable monument than marble shaft or tablet of brass. Yet Mary had done no great thing as men count greatness. She was not that finest idol of the world, a woman of genius. She had not written a great book, or charmed the world with her song. She had no wealth or influential family connections. She was only a plain home-keeping woman, not to be distinguished outwardly from countless others. And she simply broke a jar of ointment on Jesus as the expression of her devotion to him. But her fine act greatly pleased and deeply touched Jesus and cheered his heart.

This beautiful deed that men so criticized and scorned has spread its fragrance through the whole world, and it is literally fulfilled that wherever the gospel is preached Mary receives her memorial of honor.

3. THE TRIUMPHAL ENTRY
Matthew 21:1-11; Mark 11:1-11; Luke 19:29-44;
John 12:12-19

We have reached passion week and enter upon the final
scenes. So important and precious are its events that
nearly one-third of the Four Gospels and nearly one-sev-
enth of the entire New Testament is devoted to this one
week.

On the morning of Palm Sunday there was a stir in
Bethany and along the road leading to Jerusalem. It
was understood that Jesus was to enter the city that day.
Arrangements were completed, and in due time the procession started. Jesus rode on an ass, the humblest of
animals, and the disciples carpeted the dusty roadway
with greenery and their own many-colored garments,
while their hosannas rang out over the hills. The procession would not have compared with the triumphal entry
of a returning Roman conqueror, but it meant more for
the world.

As the procession reached the summit of the Mount of
Olives, the holy city broke upon the view. It is an impressive spectacle even at this day, but then it was one
of the wonders of the world. The city sat like a jeweled
crown on the brow of Mount Zion. In the foreground
rose the marble walls of the temple of stainless whiteness,
crowned with its flashing gilded roof; in the background
stretched the streets and squares of the city, and over
it all lay the spell of a thousand years of patriotic and
sacred associations.

When he saw the city, "Jesus wept." What a strange,
incredible, unaccountable interruption of these festivities
of the hour! How the disciples must have been amazed
at his tears. Only twice is it recorded of Jesus that he
wept: at the grave of Lazarus and on this occasion. In
the former instance, as the word means, he shed silent
tears; but on this occasion, as the word means, he wept
aloud, he broke down and sobbed like a child. A child
cries at a touch, a woman's tears lie near the surface, but
a man's tears are buried deep and it requires some over-
mastering emotion to unseal and break up their fountain.

And these tears of Jesus grow all the stranger when we consider the circumstances of the hour. It was the springtime and a mass of fresh colors lay palpitating on the landscape, the air was balmy with the fragrant breath of spring, and over it all was the splendor of a Syrian sky. Did not Jesus appreciate nature, and how could he weep in the midst of so much beauty? Jerusalem also was the chosen city of God, the holiest city on earth, dear to the heart of Jesus himself by every patriotic and sacred tie. Let him go and weep great hot tears over apostate Samaria or pagan Rome, but will he not lift his hands in blessing and his face beam with benediction over Jerusalem? It was also the hour of his triumphal entry into Jerusalem in recognition of his rights as king: shall he not share in the festivities and joy of the celebration? But when he saw the city he "wept over it." Again we wonder at these strange tears.

Why did Jesus weep over Jerusalem? First, because of the sinfulness of the city. Any city is a pool of iniquity and wickedness with depths of degradation that sink into hell, and if we could only see deep enough we would weep over it. Jesus saw to the bottom of that city of a million people, and the sight drew tears from his eyes.

He also wept over Jerusalem because it had rejected him. What is the deepest sin of any city? Not its social vice, for this may be a sin of frailty, but guiltier are its spiritual sins of pride and selfishness and hardness of heart. Jerusalem was chosen of God that it might prepare the way for and receive the Messiah, and now it was casting him off and getting ready to crucify him, and this was the iron that most cruelly entered the soul of Jesus.

He also wept over the city because he saw its coming doom. There it sat on its hill all unconscious of impending judgment, and yet Jesus saw the Roman legions gathering around it and shutting it in and sweeping in slaughter through its streets and leaving it a smoking heap of ashes and broken stones, and the prospect caused him to sob like a child.

Deepest of all Jesus wept over Jerusalem because he

loved it. It was dear to him and often would he have gathered its children in his arms, but they would not. This is the deepest root of God's sorrow over the world: he loves it and so loved it as to give his only Son for it.

Having wept over the city, what did Jesus now do? Did he simply spill his tears on the ground and pass on unconcerned? No, he turned his weeping into working, his tears into toil, his sympathy into service, and his sorrow into a great salvation. Some people like to indulge in sad emotions as a kind of sentimental luxury and even like to cry provided it does not cost them anything. But such superficial emotionalism is weakening and may wither the heart into dust. Emotion is good only as it imparts motion to the will and moves it to practical worthy action.

Jesus, having wept over Jerusalem, went over into that city and up into its temple and drove out the thieves and robbers and faced and condemned with splendid bravery and scorn the principal offenders, the doctors of divinity and chief men of the city: he cleaned up that town, and then he paid the price as he laid down his life outside the city wall for the redemption of that city and of all the cities of the world. In vain do we weep over our city unless we also are willing to pay the price of its redemption in service and sacrifice that may cost us dearly and even life itself.

But what came of this triumphal entry with all its pomp and pageantry and promise of a royal coronation? Was Jesus crowned on this day? No, nothing came of it. Having condemned the priests, Jesus "left them and went forth out of the city." The great day was over and nothing had resulted from it: Jesus was not yet king.

And never will he be king by such means. Doubtless the disciples had had high expectations and thought that the processions and banners and shouts would surely carry Jesus to his throne and themselves into the chief offices. Deep and tragical must have been their disillusionment, as ours will be if we put our trust in such means. But Jesus himself entertained no such dreams and experienced no disappointment, for he knew that the kingdom of God cometh not with observation.

4. Certain Greeks

John 12: 20-36

On Monday and Tuesday following the triumphal entry Jesus went into the city from Bethany, teaching and healing, while the Pharisees and scribes were endeavoring to entrap him and plotting how they might compass his death.

"Certain Greeks" came up to worship at this feast. These were not Hellenistic Jews, or Jews from Greek countries speaking the Greek language, but genuine Greeks who were converts in some degree to Jewish faith and worship. They heard of Jesus and wished to know more about him. They therefore found Philip, whose Greek name betrayed his Grecian affinity, and made to him their request: "Sir, we would see Jesus."

Philip seems to have realized that this apparently ordinary request was fraught with more than ordinary significance, and so he first reported it to Andrew, another disciple with a Greek name. These two disciples went to Jesus and reported to him this request for a personal interview.

So far this incident suggests nothing extraordinary. People were frequently seeking interviews with Jesus, and these Greeks were only two or three people more. What significance attaches to this fact, why report so trivial an incident? But trivial incidents may be the germs of tremendous consequences, as the first acorn contained all the oaks in the world. The moment this request was reported to Jesus it produced upon him an extraordinary effect. Hardly any other incident in his whole ministry affected him so profoundly as this. Instantly he exclaimed, "The hour is come that the Son of man should be glorified."

What bearing has this on the request of the Greeks, what is the psychology of this strange answer? These Greeks were suggestive. To the common mind they would have been only a few strange-looking foreigners, but to the prophetic imagination of Jesus they were radiant with significance and opened a wonderful vision of glory. These Greeks were Gentiles, heathen from the great world outside the chosen people. They represented the pagan world at its best, its most brilliant and cultured race.

What were these Greeks but the forerunners of a great multitude that would come to Christ out of that world from the east and from the west and from the north and from the south, the first fruits of a vast harvest that was to be gathered out of every land and clime? A single drop of rain that comes splashing down on the hot dusty earth may seem altogether trivial in itself, but it derives immense significance from the fact that it is the first drop of a copious shower that will saturate the thirsty ground and gladden every living thing. The first tiny green blade that pushes up through the clods of the wheat-fields rejoices the heart of the farmer because he sees it is the pioneer of a million other blades that will shoot up through the pores of that field and presently cover it with golden grain. A few things are not few when they are the forerunners of many things.

Jesus rejoiced in these inquiring Greeks because he saw that they were the budding prophecy that pledged him the heathen for his inheritance and the uttermost parts of the earth for his possession. With prophetic vision he saw himself in possession of this inheritance and out of his exultant consciousness he exclaimed, "The hour is come that the Son of man should be glorified." We need such faith that in small seeds we may see the promise and potency of great harvests.

Suddenly this joyous consciousness of Jesus changed and swept into a shadow. The painful thought came to him that except a grain of wheat fall into the ground and die, it abideth alone; but if it die, it beareth much fruit. He saw the cost of the great victory which had just filled him with a sense of triumph.

How was he to gain the world? He knew that he was already rejected by the Jews. Might he not now go with these inquiring Greeks out into the Gentile world and try his fortunes there? Might not the intellectual Greeks, so reasonable and so religious, give him a readier reception? Might not his journey through pagan lands be a march of triumph that would bring the nations into his kingdom?

Did any such perilous thought beat against his mind and

heart at this hour? Did Satan again offer him all the kingdoms of this world if he would forsake the way of the cross? The devil in the temptation in the wilderness only left him "for a season," and has he here returned? When he goes away he is always ready to come back.

Certain it is that Jesus cast any such alluring vision down, as he did on the mountain. He clearly foresaw that not by thus saving his life could he save the world, but only by losing it could he reach his kingdom. The grain of wheat with all its wealth of nourishment and golden beauty must be buried in a grave and perish that it may shoot up into a green stalk and blossom and multiply itself a hundred fold. Nature is full of such sacrifice. Life always costs life. The weak must suffer for the strong, and the good for the bad.

This principle reaches intense expression in our human world. This is the meaning of motherhood. The parent must sacrifice for the child, and one generation for the next. Our liberties are the costly victories of many battlefields. All our inherited blessings are the transmuted blood of countless ancestors who suffered and died for us. If no more grains fell into the ground and perished there would be no more sheaves of wheat; and if there were no more lives laid down for others in this world there would be no more harvests of human welfare.

This principle reaches incomparably its highest expression in the cross of Christ. Had Jesus forsaken the cross and gone with these Greeks in the hope of winning the world without sacrifice, we would never have heard his name. That grain of wheat would have been saved, but it would have remained alone and never would have sent a harvest down to us. But because Jesus fell from his cross into his grave, his Life is now springing up in our life and is everywhere enriching the world.

5. The Lord's Supper

Matthew 26:17-36; Mark 14:22-26; Luke 22:7-30; John 13:1-30; I Cor. 11:23-26

Wednesday of passion week Jesus remained in Bethany in seclusion and rest. It was the lull before the storm.

He knew that his hour was now come. Calmly he rested and gathered strength for the supreme trial. On Thursday afternoon the preparation for the Passover was made, and in the evening, which according to the Jewish reckoning was the beginning of Friday, the Passover was eaten and the Lord's supper was instituted.

As they were eating the disciples were startled by the sudden declaration of Jesus, "Verily I say unto you, One of you shall betray me." This unexpected announcement filled the disciples with alarm. Such baseness excited their horror. Could it be possible there was such treachery lurking amongst them? And they began to say, one by one, "Is it I?"

This was a better question than, "Is it you?" There are hidden possibilities in us of which we may be seldom or never conscious, and we should be more concerned in finding out our own sin than that of others. The disciples wanted to know the guilty one, but Jesus left the point uncertain that all might be warned.

Then Jesus uttered a deep mystery of divine providence. "The Son of man goeth, even as it is written of him: but woe unto that man through whom the Son of man is betrayed!" Divine sovereignty and human responsibility are here strangely interlinked. Jesus "was delivered up to die by the determinate counsel and foreknowledge of God," and yet man is held responsible for his death. God's plan is wide enough to include our most wicked acts, and yet it leaves our free agency and responsibility untouched. He permits but does not cause our evil deeds.

"And as they were eating, Jesus took bread." The Lord's Supper was not an abrupt creation, but a further evolution. The new ordinance grew out of the old and was the fulfillment and perfect blossom of the past. Jesus came not to destroy but to fulfill, and Christianity is not a new faith but the final outgrowth and fruitage of the old faith.

The few words instituting this ordinance are among the most precious in the Gospels and in all the literature of the world: "And as they were eating, he took bread, and when he had blessed, he brake it, and gave to them, and said, Take ye: this is my body. And he took the cup, and when he had given thanks, he gave it to them: and they all drank of it.   And he said unto them, this is the blood of the covenant, which is shed for many.''

Man cannot live by the bread of earth alone: the soul has its deeper hunger and must have proper bread or die. Christ is the bread of life that cometh down from heaven, and this bread and this cup ever symbolize to the believer his body broken and his blood shed as his sacrifice for our redemption.

The outward emblems are simple and unadorned, but the inner meaning is deep and rich.   The significance of any sign is not to be measured by the nature of the sign itself.   The flag of our country is only so much colored silk or cheap muslin, and yet what a mighty meaning does it carry wherever it floats, representing the law and order, the power and majesty, the history and glory of a great nation.   A little lock of hair carefully preserved may seem to the undiscerning eye of a stranger of slight significance, but to the bereaved mother it suggests thoughts and memories that are too deep for tears.   So this bread and cup may seem common and meaningless to the world, but to believers through all the ages they have been and are precious beyond any other symbol in the world.

''This do,'' said Jesus to his disciples, ''in remembrance of me.''   Why did Jesus want to be remembered?   Partly for his own sake.   He had a human craving for such remembrance and the thought that he would be forgotten and his very name be lost in oblivion would have been painful to him.   Immortality is wrapped up in this deep yearning of the heart: we cannot believe that we are only creatures of an hour and will quickly pass into the night of forgotten names.   Jesus craves this remembrance and as long as this bread and cup pass from hand to hand among his followers, he will have this reward and be satisfied.

Jesus also wanted us to remember him for our own sakes. Memory is one of the ties that bind us to him, a vital artery through which his teachings and influence and life pass into us and become incorporated in our life.   This commemoration is one of the means by which at intervals we are brought into close and tender fellowship with him and renew our pledge of loyalty to him, and it could not pass out of our lives without serious spiritual loss to our souls. If ever Christ is forgotten in this world, Christianity will wither and be blown away and itself be forgotten.

The ordinance also has in it a gleam of prophecy. It looks back upon the past in remembrance, but it also looks forward into the future "till he come" in that day when, as he promised, "I drink it new with you in my Father's kingdom." It thus links Christ's first with his final coming. How slender and frail seems the thread of continuity and yet how long it has lasted. How perishable are the elements and yet how imperishable the memorial! It is one of the oldest things in the world and will yet outlast all the fabrics of human hands. Men make every effort to perpetuate their name in the world: they write books or paint pictures, or they rear marble shafts or pile up vast pyramids of stone. But the books are soon forgotten, the marble soon crumbles into dust, and the huge pyramid disappears or its very meaning is lost in oblivion.

This bread and cup is the only material monument Jesus Christ left to his memory. It seems frailer than a thread, and yet it has survived without a break through all the revolutions of nineteen centuries, outlasting cities and empires. It must have in it some substance and vitality that the world will not let die. It has deep rich roots, but it has not yet come to its perfect blossom and ripe fruit.

"And when they had sung a hymn, they went out to the Mount of Olives." Having instituted and partaken of such an ordinance it was fitting that they should sing. Right under the shadow of the cross, Jesus planted a song blossom. He opened the service of his Supper by giving thanks and closed it with a song. Always he could find something to be thankful for and to sing about; in his darkest hour he was full of thanksgiving and praise. He lived with God "who giveth songs in the night" (Job 35:10).

He joined in this hymn and then went straight to his agony and trial and passion. If we are united in fellowship with him, we can sing hymns of faith and praise and then go out to do our work or out into the night to bear our cross.

6. GETHSEMANE

Matthew 26:36-46; Mark 14:32-42; Luke 22:39-46; John 18:1

After the closing hymn of the Lord's Supper, Jesus and his eleven disciples, Judas having left the Twelve to carry out his traitorous plot, went out of the city near the hour of midnight across the Kedron to the garden of Gethsemane on the western slope of the Mount of Olives. This Garden of Sorrow is the real battlefield of the cross. Gethsemane won the victory of Calvary. Out of this hour of agony and prayer Jesus emerged calm and strong for the final hour. We must win our battles before we come to them in secret prayer and gathered strength.

At the entrance of the garden Jesus left eight of his disciples and with the other three went on deeper into the shadows to engage in prayer. Prayer was the preparation for his passion. He wanted to see full and clear the light of his Father's face before he stepped into the final darkness. He sought to harmonize his will into perfect unison with the Father's will: he knew he could then bear the cross.

"And he taketh with him Peter and James and John." The three witnesses of the transfiguration were also witnesses of the agony in the garden. They saw Jesus on the mountaintop steeped in splendor and they saw him in the dusk of the garden bowed under bloody sweat and sorrow; by such scenes were they fitted to be witnesses for him.

Why did Jesus, leaving the other disciples behind, take these three with him? Partly as an inner guard against interruption, but mainly for the sympathy and support of their presence. They were the close circle of disciples that understood him best and trusted him most. It was a beautiful but pathetic exhibition of the humanity of Jesus that in his hour of trial he wanted his dearest friends near by. Their simple presence helped to support and comfort him; their shoulders were under his burden; he was so much stronger by reason of their added strength. Solitary suffering is doubly hard to bear, and sympathy is a wonderful power to lighten a burden.

When Jesus with his three disciples was buried deep in the seclusion and shadows of the garden a mysterious dread as the horror of a great darkness came upon him. He was "in an agony" and "began to be sore amazed and to be very heavy and saith unto them, My soul is exceeding sorrowful unto death." We cannot enter in the secret of this anguish, for it involves roots and relations that stretch infinitely beyond our understanding and experience; it is a burden and a weight of mystery of which we can only touch the edge. Its deepest meaning was that "the Lord had laid on him the iniquity of us all." This was the agony that forced from the sensitive quivering nerves of Jesus great drops of blood and a pitiful cry of sorrow out of his heart. This was the unspeakable cost of our redemption.

Out of this garden floated one of the most wonderful prayers in the Word of God; out of this darkness and agony came strong trust and sweet submission. "Abba, Father": "Abba," the Aramaic word for Father, is one of the very few literal words of Jesus that have come down to us, so that in this word we hear the very sound of his voice. "All things are possible unto thee": this is the strong ground of confidence prayer first stands upon. "Take away this cup from me": what a pathetic cry is this, how human it is. The cup of the cross was now becoming so bitter that Jesus instinctively prayed that it might pass from his lips. The humanity of the Son of God is here laid bare down to its shrinking quivering nerves. "Nevertheless, not my will, but thine, be done": this was the strong sure check that Jesus put upon his own will, the invulnerable safeguard he threw around himself against unholy desires and ignorant petitions, the mighty rock on which he kneeled. "Thy will be done," is a petition that should condition all our prayers.

Three times Jesus returned to his disciples, whom he had asked to keep vigil with him, and found them sleeping. They were in some degree blameworthy and Jesus singled out Peter for a gentle rebuke. At his third return he said in calm tones, "The hour is come." The victory was won. Through prayer his will had been wrought into absolute unquestioning obedience to the will of the Father, the peace of God was upon him, the strength of God was in him, and he was now ready to be offered.

"Rise up," he said: "let us go; lo, he that betrayeth me is at hand." Even while he spoke the multitude led by Judas appeared at the gate, and Jesus calmly went out to meet them. "Whom seek ye?" he asked of them. "Jesus of Nazareth," they answered, to which he replied, "I am he."

At this word the soldiers and priests and Pharisees and also Judas and the rabble "went backward, and fell to the ground." Was there ever a more striking instance of unconscious obeisance, a truer witness to the grandeur and majesty of the personality of Jesus? Let the letters stand out in living light in this record that his enemies, Judas the traitor, bitter priests, proud Pharisees and even stolid Roman soldiers, at his presence went backward and fell to the ground.

No doubt conscience made cowards of them all, and the unexpected and startling appearance of Jesus at the gate of the garden in his calmness and bravery precipitated this sense of guilt and helped to cast them prostrate before him. But his personality must have shone out of his appearance in impressive power. The starry radiance of his eyes, the lofty majesty stamped upon his countenance, the transparent truth and purity and peace of his soul, the calmness and poise of his bearing, all combined into a total personality that put a subtle and irresistible spell upon all those that came into his presence.

Judas betrayed his Master to his enemies with a traitorous kiss, and "so the band and the chief captain, and the officers of the Jews, seized Jesus and bound him."

7. THE TRIAL

Matthew 26 : 57—27 : 31; Mark 14 : 53—15 : 20; Luke 22 : 54—23 : 25; John 18 : 12—19 : 16

The trial of Jesus is a complicated story that falls into six parts: three ecclesiastical and three civil. He was first taken before Annas, the father-in-law of Caiaphas the high priest, then before the high priest and the Sanhe-

drin in an irreguar hearing at night, and again before
Caiaphas and the Sanhedrin in a regular trial in the morning.

He was then taken before Pilate, as the Sanhedrin
could not finally pass sentence of death. Pilate, after
hearing the case, sent it to Herod, tetrarch of Galilee,
then present in the city, on the ground that Jesus was
a Galilean. Herod returned the case to Pilate, who then
passed the final sentence of death.

Pilate was the Roman governor of Judea with his
capital at Cæsarea down on the Mediterranean, but with
his residence during the feasts up at Jerusalem, probably in Herod's palace. He was unscrupulous and corrupt, tyrannical and cruel, and exasperated the Jews into
fanatical rebellion by repeated acts of sacrilege and violence.

The most momentous event of his governorship, though
perhaps to him one of the most trivial, was this trial.
He doubtless looked on Jesus as a contemptible Jew, possessed of a harmless delusion, yet had it not been for
his accidental association with that Jew we never would
have heard of Pilate. He stepped into the presence of
Jesus, as a mote floats into a sunbeam, and in that light
stands revealed forever. He showed some disposition to
deal fairly with his prisoner and made some feeble attempts to release him, but in the end he played the part
of an unjust judge and a coward, and "Suffered under
Pontius Pilate" is the indelible stigma that has been
affixed to his name.

When the Jews brought Jesus in the gray light of the
morning to Pilate's judgment hall, they would not enter
lest they should be defiled: for men may be intensely
religious at one point while engaged in the deepest wickedness at another; especially may they be punctilious in
the observance of petty matters of ceremony while dis-
regarding and trampling upon moral principles.

Pilate inquired what accusation they brought against
the man, and their indefinite and evasive answer was,
"If this man were not an evil doer, we should not have
delivered him up unto thee." The charge on which they
had condemned him before their own court was blasphemy,

but they knew this would have no meaning and force with Pilate and therefore did not mention it, but hoped that he would blindly condemn the prisoner at their instigation.

But this was not in accordance with Pilate's Roman ideas of legal procedure; and, as they made no definite charges, he attempted to throw the case back into their hands by telling them to take the prisoner and judge him according to their own law. This was Pilate's first device to shift his own responsibility and get rid of Christ; and from this point on it is pitiful to see him tossed about in his indecision and cowardice, impaled now on one and now on another horn of the case, vainly trying to escape and yet mercilessly driven on by the murderous mob to a fatal decision.

Pilate now saw that he must look into the case and took Jesus back into the palace for a private interview. The Jews by this time had presented charges to the effect that Jesus was perverting the nation, forbidding to pay taxes to Cæsar and declaring himself a king—charges that were false, but that they knew would be effective with Pilate.

Pilate began the interview by inquiring into this point. "Art thou the king of the Jews?" "Sayest thou this thing of thyself, or did others tell it thee concerning me?" was the searching question with which Jesus replied. "Am I a Jew?" contemptuously answered Pilate. "Art thou a king then?" persisted the Roman governor, who asked the question with a supercilious air.

The prisoner did not look like a king as he stood there, a despised Galilean, humbly clad, so pale-faced and wan, with his visage cut deep and marred with lines of sorrow. He did not look like a king and nobody thought Jesus was a King that day—except himself.

Pilate appeared before the people and declared, "I find no fault in this man." This, then, was the outcome of his investigation. This was the verdict this governor and judge, trained in Roman law, pronounced upon Jesus. High above the blasphemous charges and clamor of the fanatical priests and people rang, and still rings across all these centuries, the judicial voice of Pilate, "Behold, I, having examined him before you, found no fault in this man.''

We might now expect some just and noble action from this Roman judge. Having become convinced of the innocence of the strange prisoner, will he not vindicate him? What says the record? ''I will therefore chastise him, and release him.'' What an illogical and impotent conclusion was this for a Roman judge! Pilate did not have the courage of his convictions and stood timid and cringing before the fanatical crowd.

The shifty Pilate now tried another device. He proposed to observe the custom of releasing a prisoner at the feast. In the prison near by lay Barabbas, a notorious robber. For a moment the fierce light of this trial falls on him. Pilate now thought he saw his chance. So he put the question, ''Whom will ye that I release unto you? Barabbas, or Jesus which is called Christ?'' Instantly the mob yelled back at him, ''Away with this man, and release unto us Barabbas.''

This is what comes of putting Jesus to vote: the majority is against him. As between Barabbas and Jesus it is a question whether Barabbas will not still get the most votes. We need only scratch our own Christian skin to find barbarous blood, and the beast in us still yells for Barabbas and not for Jesus.

Pilate is now about to seal his own doom. Before doing this he tried to exonerate himself by a vain and foolish devise. He took water and in the presence of the multitude washed his hands, saying, ''I am innocent of the blood of this righteous man: see ye to it.'' Yet by the very terms of his declaration his hands were dripping with the blood of the righteous Man whom he was sending to death, and not all the multitudinous seas could wash them clean. The people shouted back, ''His blood be on us, and on our children''—an ominous prophecy that is being fulfilled to this day.

''And Pilate gave sentence that it should be as they required.'' So ended the trial of Jesus. Yet the case was not closed when Pilate delivered him to be crucified. This trial is still open, and every one must record his verdict.

8. The Crucifixion

Matthew 27:32-56; Mark 15:21-41; Luke 23:26-49; John 19:16-37

From Pilate's judgment hall Jesus was led away to the place of crucifixion. He was forced to carry his own cross, but on the way an African Jew was compelled to share the burden. A company of women followed him, bewailing his fate, but Jesus bade them weep, not for him, but for themselves. In all that throng he was the one man that did not need to weep.

At last the procession reached the place outside the city wall on the north where the great tragedy was enacted. The name of the place was Golgotha in Hebrew, Calvary in Latin. The name, meaning a skull, was probably given to a small knoll in the shape of a skull and it was a significant place for man's redemption.

How eloquent of death is a skull! The delicate organs of sight and sound that were so expressive are utterly gone, leaving only dark caverns staring blankly around; and the great golden bowl of the brain, once the seat of intelligence and affection and will, is empty forever.

So is man in his sin. It was fitting, then, that the cross should be lifted at Golgotha, the place of a skull, for it was to bear the guilt of sin and undo all its work. On that cross were to be nailed all the wounds and woes that have reduced man to a skull, and from it were to issue such virtue and power as would restore his shattered faculties and make him once more a living soul.

The soldiers that led Jesus to the place of execution promptly dispatched the business. The victim was first stripped quite naked and scourged with whips, into which had been woven bits of iron, until his flesh was all lacerated and bleeding. He was then laid upon the cross, two beams of wood nailed together crosswise, his arms stretched out upon the cross beam, and large iron spikes were ruthlessly driven through hands and feet into the solid wood behind.

The cross, bearing its victim, was then raised upright and dropped into the hole dug for it with a violent jolt. Hanging on four great wounds, naked under a blazing

sun, torn and bleeding, with wounds inflaming, fiery thirst
raging, every nerve quivering and writhing with pain,
the sufferer endured the mortal agony for one, two, or
even three days, before death mercifully put an end to
the scene. And through it all the soldiers and rabble
mocked and jeered and tormented the wretched creature,
even spitting upon him and brutally striking him as they
passed by.

This is what they did when "they crucified him." There
by the holy city at the place of a skull, surrounded by
enemies, cruelly tormented, with only a few women and
a single disciple looking on from a distance in silent sympathy, Jesus hung upon the cross. All the horror of this
death burst upon him in flames of agony so fierce and
terrible that in a few hours his life was consumed. Yet
no spot of guilt was upon him, no secret fault was in him,
but he was laying down his life for the life of the world.

The soldiers in charge of the crucifixion received the
garments of Jesus as their perquisites. Wholly unconscious that they were fulfilling ancient Jewish prophecy
(Ps. 22 : 18), they divided the outer garments into four
parts, one for each soldier; and then, rattling dice in
their brass helmets, they gambled for the inner garment
which was woven without seam. Thus unwittingly do
men even in their deepest wickedness fulfill far-off divine
purposes.

How little these soldiers realized the overshadowing significance of that death while they were noisily busy getting a few shreds of this world's goods? Is it not even
so today? How much of our bartering and living is but
blatant worldliness and selfishness in the presence of
Christ? Let the shadow of that cross on Calvary ever
fall upon our lives to quiet and restrain them into holy
praise and high endeavor.

A furious mob raged like an angry sea around the
cross. There were the preachers and elders of the church,
Pharisees in their ostentatious piety, Sadducees in their
silken robes, Roman soldiers in their scarlet cloaks, coarse
people drawn by low curiosity, and the basest dregs of
the city. These kept up a constant uproar of jeers and
taunts and insults and violence against Jesus. And in

the midst of it all what was he doing? Praying, "Father, forgive them; for they know not what they do": the sublimest prayer in the Bible and in all the literature of the world.

A few of the taunts of that ungodly crowd were caught up into the Gospels and have come down to us. Like everything that was said in derision against Jesus, they add to his honor and are so many crowns unwittingly placed upon his head. "He saved others," they jeeringly cried; "himself he cannot save." No grander eulogy could be pronounced even upon the Son of God. Unconsciously they placed upon his brow his brightest crown. He had "saved others," as many could have then testified, and as millions have testified since. But "himself he could not save," for he could have done this only at the cost of his devotion to the Father and of his love to the world. No imagination could picture the consequences if on that eventful day Jesus had saved himself.

On the top of the cross over the head of Jesus was a board whitened with gypsum, bearing in black letters the inscription, THIS IS THE KING OF THE JEWS. Pilate wrote the inscription, doubtless as a deadly insult to the Jews, but he wrote better than he knew. It was written in three languages: in the official Latin, the current Greek, and the vernacular Aramaic—a fact that may explain the variations in its forms in the Gospels. Everyone present could understand one or another of these languages. The gospel is for all men of every race and tongue and nation, and it must be put into all languages that all may hear it and none may miss its good news.

The Latin was representative of power in the ancient world, the Greek of culture, and the Aramaic of the common people; and Christ is still king over all: he is mighty to rule the strong, he has truth for the intellectual, and everywhere the common people hear him gladly.

Passing by the deeply significant incident of the two thieves, we come to the final scene. It was now three o'clock in the afternoon and life was about spent. Human nerves could endure the strain of suffering no more. The last thread was about to snap. With a great cry of mortal agony Jesus commended his spirit to his Father, his head fell forward, and he was still. Life had fled and he was dead. With wicked hands they had crucified him.

Only in the presence of this cross can we know man: how deep is his sin and how immeasurable is his worth. Only in the presence of this cross can we know God: how inexorable is his justice and how infinite is his love. The love of God in Christ, the worth of man, the sinfulness of earth and the holiness of heaven, all these were gloriously manifested when, on that green hill far away, the dear Lord was crucified.

9. The Resurrection

Matthew 28 : 1-10; Mark 16 : 1-11; Luke 23 : 56—24 : 12;
John 20 : 1-8; 1 Cor. 15; Gal. 1 : 18-20

After the crucifixion the body of Jesus was prepared for burial by Joseph of Arimathea and Nicodemus and laid in a new sepulchre hewn in the rock, and the grave was closed with a great stone and sealed. There it lay indistinguishable from the dead of earth through Friday night, Saturday and Sunday morning. But there was a difference in that grave, and in the morning of the third day an event occurred that has transformed all succeeding centuries.

The morning opened with the faithful women, who were last at the cross, first at the tomb. What were they doing? They had bought spices and had brought them to anoint the body of Jesus. This loving act has immense value as showing the state of mind of these women and all the disciples after the crucifixion. They believed that Jesus was dead and had no hope or thought of his resurrection. They were utterly bewildered, scattered and crushed and supposed that all was over. They were in no condition of mind, then, to invent or imagine a resurrection, and any theory of fraud or of hallucination or vision on the part of the disciples is a psychological impossibility. This is incidental and undesigned but strong confirmation of its reality that meets us on the threshold of this event.

On their way to the tomb the women had wondered how the stone that closed it could be removed, but when they reached it they found it rolled away, yet they "found not the body of the Lord Jesus." An angel announced to them the great news, "He is not here; for he is risen, even as he said." The women were affrighted, as men of stouter nerves would have been, but the angel cried out, "Fear not." A little later Jesus himself greeted these women in the garden with the same assuring words.

Thus opened a day of the most sensational happenings and tremendous excitement. The women hastened to tell the disciples, but the startling news encountered persistent unbelief and even scoffs on the part of these men. "And these words appeared in their sight as idle talk; and they disbelieved them." Who were these first disbelievers in the resurrection? Jewish priests and Roman officers? No, but "the apostles." Peter and James and John and all of the eleven believed the story of these women was some hallucination of their excited minds, "idle talk," "the wild talk of the sick in delirium," as the Greek word means.

Peter was one of the first of the disciples to discover the truth. He at first disbelieved the report as idle talk and, likely enough, was one of the loudest scoffers. Yet he did not rest in his unbelief, but he "arose and ran unto the tomb." John went with him and these two disciples "saw and believed."

That afternoon two disciples were on their way to the village of Emmaus, and a Stranger fell in with them and stayed to take the evening meal with them and when "he took bread" he was revealed to them and then "he vanished out of their sight." That evening the eleven disciples were gathered in an upper room in Jerusalem, when "the doors were shut" and Jesus appeared in the midst of them and gave them visible proofs of his person and presence.

Already it was apparent that there was something mysterious in the resurrection body of Jesus by which he could appear through closed doors and vanish at will. A week later the disciples were again assembled in the upper room, Thomas, the persistent sceptic being present, and he was convinced and exclaimed, "My Lord and my God."

The scene now shifts to Galilee where two appearances

are recorded. The first was on the shore of the familiar lake of Galilee when the disciples were out fishing in their boat and Jesus greeted them as he stood on the shore. Impulsive Peter, true to himself, leaped into the sea and swam ashore, and when they all followed, Jesus held a touching and searching interview with Peter.

Later he appeared to "above five hundred brethren," whom Paul mentions (I Cor. 15:6), on a mountain. "And when they saw him, they worshiped him; but some doubted." Only an honest historian who was simply intent on telling the truth would have admitted this unfavorable fact that "some doubted." A partisan writer or pleader would have made it out that everybody worshiped and nobody doubted; the worship was absolutely unanimous! "But some doubted," calmly and boldly says Matthew. We can trust a writer and a book that is so impartial and fearless in telling the truth.

There are ten of these recorded appearances in which every opportunity and test of knowing Jesus as the risen Christ is used to validate this event. The witnesses are numerous, competent and trustworthy who could not have been deceived and who sealed their testimony with their blood.

A witness of special weight is Paul who after his conversion went to Jerusalem and spent fifteen days with Peter and James the Lord's brother investigating this event on the ground. He says he went to "visit" Peter (Gal. 1:18), a word which means "to know by inquiry and personal examination," or "it denotes visits paid to places of interest with a view to getting information about them on the spot" (*Expositor's Greek Testament*). Paul was a lawyer and he cross-examined these witnesses and he made sure of the certain reality of this fact.

These disciples that at first were bewildered and crushed by the death of Jesus were by his resurrection suddenly transformed into masterful men who arose in their might and planted Christianity on this rock where it stands to this day; and they went everywhere preaching this fact and with it turning the world upside down.

This thing was not done in a corner but in the open day and in the New Testament is pushed into the light of the fullest publicity as is no other event. There may be discrepancies in the narratives, but they are such as might be expected in fragmentary accounts in which the witnesses are giving impressionistic reports of what they experienced and no one of them is endeavoring to tell a complete story.

God left no uncertainties hanging around this event but placed it on a rock in the broad light of history. It is a vital fact in our Christian faith and we can join with the accent of conviction in reciting the most ancient creed of the church: "I believe in Jesus Christ our Lord, who suffered under Pontius Pilate, was crucified, dead, and buried; the third day he rose again from the dead."

We here give two brief quotations from recent works by weighty authorities, the one in the field of critical New Testament scholarship, and the other in the field of biological science. The first is from Dr. G. W. Wade's elaborate and learned *New Testament History*, who concludes his thorough examination of the narratives of the resurrection of Jesus with these words: "Thus the available evidence, in the case alike of the Eleven Apostles and of St. Paul, points to the conclusion that the accounts of their visions of the Risen Christ are not mere dramatic expressions of intellectual convictions attained solely by reasoning and reflection, but that certain visions were creative causes of those convictions" (page 483). The second quotation is from Professor James Y. Simpson's *Man and the Attainment of Immortality*: "The fact that we are just beginning to understand the effects of mind and particularly of emotion upon the metabolism and actual constitution of the body, that we are only on the threshold of our knowledge of what is involved in the far from static conception of personality, and that we have no ability whatever to estimate what would be the effect of a sinless spiritual life upon its physical concomitant, forbids us to relegate the story of the Empty Tomb to the realm of legend. However regarded, the Resurrection is the supreme proof of the triumph of spirit over matter" (page 300).

10. THE GREAT COMMISSION
Matthew 28: 16-20.

The time was growing short, and the hour was come when the risen Christ must announce his final program. A mountain in Galilee was the appointed place for the momentous utterance. It was fitting that this program should be proclaimed from a mountain overlooking that same sea around which he had labored and near which on another summit he had preached the Mountain Sermon and sent its great words rolling through the centuries. And this final message matched the mountain, massive and mighty in proportion and power, with its summit bathed in the blue of heaven and its base rooted deep in the earth.

On this mountain gathered the company of the believers to hear what the Master would say. When a man announces his program for the world we want to know what his credentials are, by what authority he speaks. Many men have drawn up plans for reorganizing society and reforming the world, but their little schemes have come to naught because they had no depth of wisdom in constructing them and no power to put them in operation. Many philosophers have had dreams of social reconstruction and a golden age, but seldom have their dreams in the slightest degree affected the course of the world.

"All power is given unto me in heaven and in earth," is the tremendous affirmation with which Jesus prefaces his program. He did not set out on the enterprise of world-redemption without counting the cost and seeing that he had the means, and nothing in it shall fail which all power can accomplish. Heaven is on the side of Jesus Christ and wheels all its battalions into line under his banner. The power that framed the universe and forged burning suns on the anvil of creation is at his disposal, the constellations are his silent and eternal allies.

This power flows down into and envelops the earth. The whole framework of nature is pliant and obedient to his touch. All the streams of human energy, population and commerce, wealth and war, enterprise and adventure, invention and discovery, science and literature and art, flow into channels that are guided and shaped and at least limited by his hand. The glorified Christ is not an indifferent or impotent spectator of the whirling panorama of this world, but he sets and moves its scenes, and with majestic dignity he declares, "All power is given unto me in heaven and in earth."

Since all power can do all things, we might think that Jesus would with his own hand bring immediate redemption to the world. But this is not his method. "All power is given unto me," "Go ye therefore," is the divine logic of the great commission. Divine power must have human means through which to work. The currents of celestial omnipotence must have earthly wires along which to flash.

What enormous power is stored up in a steam hammer? It can crush a steel bar or deliver the lightest tap that will not hurt a child's finger. What controls and guides it? The workman's hand on the lever. The all power of the steam and the puny power of the human hand work together in beautiful harmony. Either without the other could do nothing, but both together forge huge axles on which will roll the world's commerce, or mighty shafts and anchors that will drive ships through foaming seas and defy the fiercest storms.

So the power of omnipotence is lodged in the hands of the risen Christ, but it waits for our cooperation to shoot forth in the mightiest blows of power, or to slip down in the softest accents of love. He stands back of us with his power, but we must go at his bidding.

On what mission were these disciples sent? To overrun the world with armies and beat it into submission with the sword? To set up a world-empire of earthly power and splendor? No, but to "teach all nations, baptizing them in the name of the Father, and of the Son, and of the Holy Ghost, teaching them to observe whatsoever I have commanded you." Standing on that Galilean mountaintop, he was looking out over the world. Jesus was no provincial Jew or parochial philosopher, but he stood in universal relations and was shaping all coming centuries. "Make disciples of all nations," he calmly said, foreseeing that all the world would be attracted by his truth and love and by the power of his personality and kingdom.

Christianity is no national or racial religion, it refuses to stop at any mountain range or ocean shore or political boundary, but it is a universal faith that like the atmosphere must flow over all mountain ranges and peaks and envelop the whole earth. With this command committed to us we should not shut the gospel up in our own lives and land, but give it universal wings and send it over all lands and seas.

What is the connection between the divine power of Christ in heaven and the human disciples on earth? Is he so remote and separated from them that his power is unavailable and useless to them? He left no such missing link or break in the connection at this point. "And, lo, I am with you always, even unto the end of the world." Jesus in his human person in the world was limited to one place. On this account it was expedient that he should go away into the spiritual world whence through his Holy Spirit he can be with his disciples everywhere. Sustained by his presence apostles went forth preaching the gospel, martyrs stepped into the flames, and missionaries are yet declaring the gospel to all nations. We also are bound to him by the tie of loyalty, and he is ever with us to give us the victory that overcomes the world.

Such was the final program of Jesus Christ; and it corresponds with the course of history and fits this far-off century in a way that shows he was indulging in no empty dream, speaking no random guesses, but was legislating for the ages in these weighty words. This grand utterance bears the impress of his divinity and proclaims him to be the master of the world.

11. THE ASCENSION
Luke 24: 50-53

We have come to the closing scene; and it is worthy of its place as the conclusion and climax of this wonderful Life. Had the story of the resurrection of Jesus been an invention or a myth, it would have been a hard matter to know how to bring his life on earth to an end. Christ was risen and his work was finished: what shall be done with him? He must not be permitted to die again, and he cannot remain. The critical point in a story is its conclusion. It must keep up the interest to the end and close at the highest point, or it breaks down and fails.

How shall this life, that opened with angel minstrelsy in the skies and was attended with many wonderful works and has just emerged from the tomb and been crowned with the wonder and glory of the resurrection, he brought to an appropriate and worthy conclusion? What novelist or poet or painter would dare attempt such a task? But give the pen to one of these humble unliterary followers of Jesus and he will write a conclusion that is a fitting culmination and climax to the whole story, and that, viewed simply as a piece of literature and work of art, is one of the most perfect and beautiful things in all the books of the world.

How simple and natural it is, how free from all art and effort, affectation and self-consciousness, how true to reality! The man that wrote the story of the ascension of Jesus, we feel, did not invent it and never thought of inventing anything. Nobody imagined it, it was a fact, the disciples simply related what they saw, and here it is:

And he led them out as far as to Bethany, and he lifted up his hands, and blessed them. And it came to pass, while he blessed them, he was parted from them, and carried up into heaven. And they worshiped him, and returned to Jerusalem with great joy: and were continually in the temple, praising and blessing God. Amen.

Who can gild that gold, or paint that lily, or throw a perfume on that bit of literature? It is art surpassing art, simply because the writer had no other purpose than to tell what happened on that day at Bethany when the risen Lord made his farewell appearance to his disciples and was parted from them and carried up into heaven.

"He led them out as far as to Bethany." We can see the little company emerging from the eastern gate of Jerusalem, perhaps on a bright May morning when, instead of the darkness of the crucifixion, all nature was clad in fresh colors and seemed to sing in gladness. They descend into the valley of the Kedron, wend their way up over Mount Olivet and down its eastern slope as far as to Bethany, all the while talking earnestly concerning the kingdom and the disciples possibly all unconscious of what was impending.

Every step of the way was crowded with sacred associations. In ascending Olivet they passed by Gethsemane, where Jesus fought the real battle of the cross. At the summit they stood on the spot where he first saw Jerusalem in his triumphal entry and wept over the city. And Bethany was dear to him by many ties. There was the house of Martha and Mary, where he had so often dwelt and rested. Possibly more than any other spot it was home to him. No wonder his feet now found their way to this place when he was about to take his farewell look at earth. We all want to come home to die. Where we first saw the light, there let the final rush of darkness come. Jesus was human to the last.

Why did he lead them out only as far as to Bethany? Why did he not lead them all the way and remain with his disciples through all the generations and centuries, in every land working miracles and speaking as never man spake, until the kingdoms of this world were his? Ought not he above all others to stay until the end? Yet he was the first to go. He led them out as far as to Bethany and there he left them.

How can we explain this? Jesus himself explained it. "It is expedient for you," he said, "that I go away." Mark that it was not expedient for himself that he should go away. It was no cowardly desertion of his post of duty that took him out of the world. But it was expedient for the disciples that he should go: he could lead them from his throne in heaven better than he could on earth. The place for the captain of a steamship is up on the bridge, not down at the wheel or in the engine room. Lincoln could do more for his generals and soldiers in Washington than he could have done for them on the field. The ascension of Jesus was the crowning act of his work, for it put him in the right place and enthroned him over all the world.

"He led them out as far as to Bethany": he led them part way and then left them. This is the way God is always leading us. He leads us out as far as the Bible. The Bible throws light upon the path of life and yet it is never a complete guide book. It gives us general principles, but hardly ever tells us what to do next. Why did God not give us a book containing minute directions for every step in life? Because, to say nothing of the impossibility of such a book, he means to leave something for us to do. He leads us to Bethany and then we must find our own way. He assumes on our part common sense, a prayerful mind and an obedient will. If we go with

Jesus as far as to Bethany, we shall safely find the rest of the way.

"And he lifted up his hands, and blessed them." This is what he had been doing all his life long. He blessed the blind when he touched their eyes into sight, the hungry when he fed them, the penitent when he forgave them and the sorrowing when he comforted them. There are smitings and cursings enough in the world: let the holy hands of the Son of God be lifted upon it in blessing and in time its noisy strife and wickedness shall be stilled into peace.

"And it came to pass, while he blessed them, he was parted from them, and carried up into heaven." He came under the attraction of a higher gravitation, and instead of being bound to this little globule of earth he rose into the clouds and vanished into the unseen spiritual world. What possibilities this may involve or hint for our glorified bodies we do not know and need not speculate. But in being carried up into heaven he went to his own place. His whole life had been an ascent and another upward step naturally and necessarily carried him into heaven. He simply went to his own place, back to his native country.

"And they worshiped him." They had reason to worship him before, but now these humble disciples knew as they never knew before that their meek and lowly Friend was indeed the Son of God and they could only worship him. Worship is the greatest thing man can do. It is this that makes him more than a sheep. This is the highest exercise of his highest powers. This is the golden chain that binds him to a higher life and another world, by which he casts his anchor within the veil. What shall the world do in the presence of this Person? Only one word is great enough to express it: worship. Crown him Lord of all!

"And they returned to Jerusalem with great joy." They wanted to stay. There they stood gazing into the sky at the point where Jesus had disappeared as though they expected him presently to reappear. But while they looked, two white-appareled angels stood by them and said, "Ye men of Galilee, why stand ye gazing into heaven?

This same Jesus, which is taken up from you into heaven, shall so come in like manner as ye have seen him go into heaven'' (Acts 1:11).

So we are living between two visits of Jesus Christ to this world. He has come and gone, and he will come again. But in the meantime we are not to stand gazing into heaven. From our worship we must ever return to our work. This worship of the risen Christ has now widened down through the centuries and its works are blessing the world.

The Life of lives is now finished. It closed, as it began, with a note of joy so that all the way through it has kept its initial keynote. Of Jesus it is declared that ''God hath anointed thee with the oil of gladness above thy fellows'' (Heb. 1:9); he was the gladdest Man that ever lived, and his gospel is still good news, glad tidings of great joy to all the world. The world is still heavily burdened with sin and sorrow and deeply shadowed with gloom, but this Life has power to lift the burden and disperse the shadows and will at last cause all sorrow and sighing to flee away. This shall be finally accomplished when the ransomed of the Lord shall return to the new Jerusalem with songs and everlasting joy upon their heads.

Having followed this wonderful Life from its beginning through all its years to its glorious end, we shall now see how it fares when it steps upon the great stage of the world and starts down through the centuries.

PART IV

THE SPREAD OF CHRISTIANITY

CHAPTER I

INTRODUCTION

Christianity has now come to its critical hour. Its Christ has done his work on earth. He has been ushered upon its stage, wrought the signs of his divine Saviourhood, taught his disciples, proclaimed his mission and message, started his kingdom, crowned his cross with his resurrection, and ascended to the eternal world.

He has gone, and now the critical question is, How will his cause and kingdom get along without him? Will the hands of these human disciples be strong enough to hold the fabric of the new kingdom together and keep it on its foundation and build it so that it will stand through the ages? Will the story of the life of Jesus now prove to be only "a sweet Galilean vision" which will quickly fade and leave no trace that can be discovered under the dust of the centuries? Or will Christianity spread from Jerusalem and start out on a victorious march to the ends of the earth?

This question is answered in the Book of Acts and the remaining books of the New Testament. The Acts of the Apostles is the continuation of the Four Gospels and continues the mission of Jesus as carried on by his apostles. It is the fifth volume of the Life of Christ.

It is a stirring story. It starts out splendidly at Pentecost with marvelous success and promise, and then quickly encounters opposition and persecution. Dark and dangerous days follow. But the fires of persecution only scatter the sparks and flames and start new centers of Christian faith and fervor at widely separated and distant points. Christianity is a fire that cannot be confined and will burn its way to the great rim of the Roman Empire and to the utmost frontiers of the world.

External obstructions are bravely overcome, but more insidious and dangerous internal difficulties and threatened divisions arise. Two epochal questions soon confronted the new faith: Should the Gentiles be admitted to the Christian church? Had this question been answered in the negative it would have constricted Christianity to a Jewish sect and then it never would have become a world religion. This question was emphatically decided in the affirmative and a deadly danger was passed.

Practically the same issue arose in another form: Should the Gentile converts be required to submit to the Mosaic ordinances such as circumcision? Had this requirement been imposed on the Gentiles, again would Christianity have been strangled in its cradle and would never have gotten beyond its ancestral home. But again the right decision was reached, and the new faith was freed from the swaddling clothes and fetters of the old faith.

The new faith thus set free could not be confined within racial or national or continental limits, but went out from Jerusalem in all directions, overleaping all boundaries, and stepped from Asia into Europe and stopped not until it had reached Rome and swept a circle of Christian churches around the Mediterranean shore.

It is an inspiring spectacle to witness these conflicts and triumphs and this grand march. It is full of picturesque scenes, critical epochs, dramatic moments, masterful personalities, and splendid heroisms and martyrdoms, unsurpassed in any other period of human history.

What book can compare with the Acts in vital importance and thrilling interests? Properly seen and understood it is a grand unfolding panorama set on the mighty stage of the Roman Empire that kindles the imagination and enchains and fascinates the attention. It is one of the most stirring stories as it is one of the most important books in the Bible. In the following studies of the Spread of Christianity, as in the Life of Jesus, only selected points and scenes can be presented, and the endeavor will be made to paint the picture with some life and color so as to make it realistically vivid and practical.

CHAPTER II

THE CHURCH IN JERUSALEM

When the disciples returned from the ascension at Mount Olivet they assembled in an upper room in Jerusalem and proceeded to choose an apostle to take the place of the apostate Judas. Two disciples were selected who had companied with them "all the time that the Lord Jesus went in and out among" them and so were qualified by their personal experience of Jesus to serve in the apostleship. Lots were cast and the lot fell upon Matthias and "he was numbered with the eleven apostles." Nothing further is ever recorded of him, and this may leave in doubt whether the lot is the best way of choosing an apostle or a minister.

1. The Day of Pentecost. Acts 2

The time was propitious, for the harvest feast drew an immense multitude of people who thus furnished a compact mass and rich soil in which to sow the gospel and who, in turn, became winged seeds to waft it out over the world.

On this day the disciples were all in one place. There were not many of them, but they were all there. Not one member of the church was missing to leave a gap in the little audience, and the circuit was continuous and complete, ready for the flash of power from above. There is power in compactness, and every vacant seat in the church is a break and leakage in the current of spiritual energy. The disciples were not only in one place, but they were all together, or "with one accord," implying they were all blended into unity of mind and heart. There were no factions, strifes and strained relations among these church members to divide and scatter spiritual power. The Spirit cannot travel along a broken circuit, but must have continuous minds and hearts.

What was the secret of this mother church of all Christendom that stands to this day as the greatest church in spiritual power and fruitfulness? It was not numbers, for it had only a hundred and twenty members. It had no scarlet-cushioned pews and stained glass windows, in fact, it had no church building at all; it had no money in its treasury and did not even have a treasurer; it had no choir and pipe organ and no settled pastor or salaried preacher. It had no elders, deacons, trustees, no Sunday school or missionary societies, and no formal or informal organization whatever. There was almost nothing there that we would call a church, yet never has there been such a church since. What did it have?

It had unanimity; it had one hundred and twenty souls fused into one great thought and passion; it was simply an open channel free from human clogs through which the Spirit of God could flow in unobstructed fullness, and such a church was and ever will be drenched and flooded with Pentecostal power.

The human conditions were ready and now the divine manifestation came; the Spirit found the continuous circuit and flashed forth in power. This coming of the Spirit was meditated in and through physical signs, for God ever uses material crutches to support spiritual infirmities. The wind came as a fitting symbol of the Spirit's work.

Ordinarily the air lies around us invisible and impalpable, so soft and still it does not rustle a leaf or fret an infant's cheek. But let the sun play upon it and wake its slumbering power, and it begins to blow in breezes and to gather into a storm and at length it levels forests and lashes the sea. So may the Holy Spirit lie around us unfelt and we may think the great Spirit of the universe is dead, but when we are in the right condition he gathers his energies together and sweeps down upon us in a tide of power before which souls are tossed as leaves in a storm.

Tongues of flame also symbolized the Spirit. Fire as it sifts down so silently in the soft sunshine does not seem to have much energy, but it makes the whole earth bud and blossom, and as it is condensed into the lightning bolt or in the glowing furnace it has enormous explosive and motor power. The truths of Scripture are condensed spirit as coal and wood are condensed sunshine. When these are kindled by the fire of the Holy Spirit they develop their hidden energy. Our sins burn us. Spiritual things that seemed so shadowy and evanescent become intensely real and we see them solid. It is as though a new world were suddenly opened and we saw God!

On this occasion Peter, the fisherman-preacher, delivered a great sermon from an Old Testament prophecy that went as a burning arrow into the bosoms of his hearers so that "they were pricked in their heart" and began to cry out, "Men and breathren, what shall we do?" Peter, without the hesitation of a moment or the waste of a word, gave an answer that exactly and fully met the question of the hour. "Repent!"

This was the first recorded word in the public preaching of John the Baptist and also of Jesus himself, and it everywhere stands in the forefront of the gospel. "Change your mind," as the Greek word means, is the initial command of the gospel. This change is a voluntary act which we can effect by divine grace, and it rolls a tremendous weight of responsibility upon us, calling upon us to change our minds toward sin and Christ out of indifference into faith and action. So the gospel message has not changed in passing from Jesus to his apostles but is the same yesterday, today, and forever.

A wonderful scene now followed. Three thousand souls were converted and the little church became a multitude in a day. Then the ratio of increase was twenty-five converts to one church member, but now it is about twenty-five members to one convert. If the church today were only baptized and saturated with the Spirit as was the Pentecostal church, how swiftly would the kingdom march around the world and how quickly would Christ reign!

The scene closes with a picture that has given much perplexity to Christians. In the enthusiasm and joy of their new fellowship these converts practically abolished private property and lived together in a state of communism that some dreamers consider the ideal state of society.

But several considerations modify this view. Whatever the nature of this communism, it was their own voluntary action and was not enjoined upon them by any inspired authority and thus it has no authority over us. It may have served a good purpose for a time, but only for a time, for it soon came to an end and we hear of it no more. Presently we find these early Christians exercising the rights of private property, and we also find them in a state of poverty so that collections had to be taken up in other churches to help the Christians in Jerusalem. Their communism thus seems to have had the effect of reducing them to beggary, as it is doing today on a colossal scale in Russia. Private property has been and is a main root of human progress, the beginning, said John Fiske, of civilization.

Nevertheless, the spirit of these first Christians in this act was altogether admirable as an expression of their brotherhood and shines as a splendid star across all these countries.

2. The Martyrdom of Stephen. Acts 6-7

Pentecost was quickly followed by persecution. The high hopes of swift success were soon dashed to the ground. Peter, who preached so powerfully and eloquently on the day of Pentecost, in a few days landed in jail. The apostles began street healing and preaching with such success as to attract crowds and then to draw upon them the notice of the priests. They thought they had made an end of Jesus, and here he was back upon them with new terror, risen, it was said, from the dead!

They arrested and tried to stop the preachers, but they could not be stopped and sending them to jail had no effect upon them, for they declared, "We cannot but speak the things which we have seen and heard" (4:20) and "We ought to obey God rather than men" (5:29). Men of such motives and might were not to be intimidated or restrained by priestly threats or prison bars. And so the Gospel message that started off with such power and momentum on the day of Pentecost irresistibly pushed its way forward against bitter opposition, and the three thousand converts of the first day soon grew to five thousand.

Christ's promise to his disciples that he would be with them was being fulfilled.

No sooner had external trouble temporarily subsided than internal trouble arose in the church. Growth outran grace. The apostles and first Christians were still human with enough unsanctified depravity in them to breed dissension. Unworthy and false members appeared in the persons of Annanias and his wife Sapphira, who attempted to gain the popularity of being counted pious to the point of turning all their goods into the common fund without paying the price of such coveted reputation. They professed to have given all, but they were telling a lie; part they had secretly held back. Such a sin was so dangerous and deadly in the little company that it had to be cut up by the roots in an example of solemn warning, and sudden death removed them.

Another difficulty presently arose. The apostles were doing everything and so were overworked and saw that they must have help. Complaints were also being made that the charity funds were not being fairly distributed, a complaint with which the church is familiar to this day.

A congregational meeting was called and the apostles stated the situation. It was enough for them to preach, let others be appointed to manage the funds and take care of the poor. Thus a new office arose out of this first church dissension and seven deacons were appointed.

This gives us an interesting insight into the development of church government. No inspired system was enjoined, but organization grew and was adapted to the circumstances as it was needed, and this has been the history of the church to this day. Afterward bishops and elders grew up in the same way. They were chosen or appointed as they were needed to meet the growing demands of the expanding church.

Among these seven deacons Stephen stood first. Nothing more is known of him than appears in the narrative, but in this one event he leaped into a foremost place in the history of the church. We hear nothing more of his ministrations as a deacon, but he shot far beyond this office into power and fame as a preacher and inaugurated a momentous evolution in the history of Christianity. Pauline doctrine and Paul himself have their spiritual ancestry in Stephen.

In personal character he is described as being "full of faith and power." He was a sympathetic and winsome man whose piety was the beauty of holiness. Such men are sometimes weak, without offense but also without force. But Stephen was also a man of power. He combined amiability with strength, beneath his gracious nature lay stout bones, and iron burned in his blood.

Such a man needed looking after by the opponents of the new faith and they were not slow to rise against him. We are not told what doctrine Stephen preached, but we may gather it from the charges brought against him. Perjured witnesses were suborned against him, and while their accusations were false in spirit, yet they were true in substance, for Stephen did not deny them and his own defense bore them out.

It was false that he spoke blasphemy, but it was true that he did preach doctrines which seemed to these opponents destructive and sacrilegious. He did speak "against this holy place, and the law," though not in the sense and in the spirit which they imputed to him. It was doubtless true that the witnesses heard him say, in substance if not in words, "that Jesus of Nazareth shall destroy this place, and shall change the customs which Moses delivered us," for Jesus himself asserted this very thing. When he declared to the woman of Samaria, "Woman, believe me, the hour cometh, when ye shall neither in this mountain, nor yet in Jerusalem, worship the Father" (John 4:21), he boldly swept the temple and the customs of Moses off that mountaintop forever. To an orthodox Jew no more radically iconoclastic and terribly destructive blasphemy could have been uttered.

Stephen was thus the first Christian preacher to grasp and boldly proclaim the truth that the old dispensation must disappear before the new. He began to shake the Christian church loose from the narrowness and bondage of Moses (necessary and good in its day) and let it out into the glorious liberty of Christ. This process cost the church a long conflict in which Paul was the magnificent champion of liberty, but it was Stephen's inspired genius that first saw this epochal truth and his bravery began the battle.

We see, then, why the Jews were so furiously incensed against Stephen's doctrine; they believed their religious life was at stake; Moses, who has been the innocent cause of so many ecclesiastical controversies, was being attacked. Yet the customs of Moses were not being destroyed in the sense the Jews supposed and feared, but were being fulfilled; they were simply blossoming out and ripening into their own proper fruitage and glory.

Christianity was not a revolution but an evolution. It did not destroy Judaism any more than the flower destroys the root when it blooms; it superseded it only as noonday splendor displaces morning twilight. The same process has been going on through all the Christian centuries and is still in operation as new truth enlarges and illuminates the old. We may be needlessly alarmed as we see changes going on in the church and the world of religious truth as though the new were destroying the old, when in fact it may be that Christ is only revealing the many things he has yet to say unto us and is thus guiding us into larger truth and fuller meaning and wider application (John 16:12-15).

As the charges were being made against Stephen, the members of the council fastened their eyes on him and saw an unexpected and wonderful sight. His face grew transfigured before them and became as it had been the face of an angel. Stephen seems to have discerned that his hour had come and that his blood would be the first to baptize the church. Some great thought or passion kindled his soul into flames that shone through his flesh and lit it up with heavenly radiance. The man was so nearly pure spirit that his body was the thinnest possible veil that could scarcely contain and conceal the burning inner glory.

With his soul thus aflame, Stephen began his defence. His long address is one of the most notable speeches in the Bible and repays careful study and analysis. The drift of his argument is proof from Scripture that God did not always confine himself to the holy land and sacred places but went outside of these in revealing himself. The address was broken off before the argument was completed, but its logic and conclusion are clear. His whole handling of the history makes it plain that Stephen is not hostile to Moses and is a loyal Jew. But he shows that God had not restricted his grace to any one "place" and "custom," but had revealed himself in many places and through many prophets.

This rapturous speech of Stephen was too much for his judges, and, stopping their ears that they might not hear the hateful words, with shouts of rage they rushed upon him and, in violation of Roman law, hurried him through the gate of the city to the place of stoning, where murderous missiles flew hurtling through the air and Stephen was quickly struck down.

At this point in the dreadful business first appears on the pages of Scripture a new name which, though it rises red as blood in the gloom, yet presently shines out as one of the most splendid stars in all the firmament of human history. "The witnesses laid down their garments at a young man's feet, whose name was Saul." In this incriminating attitude is first seen him who afterward so powerfully preached the faith he here attempted to destroy.

With the wonderful prayer upon his lips, "Lord, lay not this sin to their charge," altogether in the spirit of the Master's prayer on the cross, "Father, forgive them, for they know not what they do," Stephen "fell asleep." What a triumph of the grace and power of Christ that could draw from the bleeding lips and choking voice of the mangled and expiring martyr such a self-forgetful, forgiving, noble prayer as this! Verily his blood shall be the seed of the church.

CHAPTER III

THE GOSPEL SETS OUT ON ITS WORLD MARCH

Jerusalem was the cradle of the Christian church, but it contained a vigorous nursling that could not long be confined within infantile limits, and we shall now witness it unloosing its swaddling clothes and learning to walk and overleaping its bounds and setting out on its world march. It had been born in Judaism and nursed at its breast only that it might go forth as a world religion to proclaim universal salvation and build the kingdom of God around the globe. This world adventure of Christianity is the most inspiring spectacle in the New Testament and in the whole Bible.

1. THE GOSPEL IN SAMARIA. Acts 8:1-25

Persecution is a powerful propagandist. Following the death of Stephen it broke out violently in Jerusalem and that holy mountain flamed with fire against the new faith. The city that had crucified the Lord now began to slaughter the Lord's disciples.

But persecution only scattered the believers in the gospel, and presently other cities near and far were infected with the new faith and the holy contagion began to spread through the world. Fire scatters sparks and flames and rapidly extends into a wide conflagration.

Philip, the evangelist, went down to the city of Samaria and there started an evangelistic campaign that stirred the whole city and resulted in a multitude of conversions. Samaria was a hard place in which to begin. The Jews had no dealings with the Samaritans, for there was deep racial and religious enmity between them. The simple fact that Philip was a Jew was an almost fatal fact against him. And his message was also an unpopular one in Samaria, for Philip now asked these enemies to give up their ancestral faith and accept Jesus, a crucified Jew, as their Messiah. The situation was further complicated by the presence in the city of one Simon, a sorcerer, who had given out that he was some great one, admitting the fact himself, and he had so hypnotized the people that he had them under his thumb. He stood in the way of the gospel.

Yet nothing daunted or discouraged, Philip went to work, and soon the gospel proved itself the power of God. "The people with one accord gave heed," and results followed. Unclean spirits were cast out and palsied people were healed, and "there was great joy in that city." How could there help but be joy with such work going on in the town? There was the joy of purity and liberty and health, release from superstition and fear, for they were liberated from the black art and evil influence of the sorcerer Simon. The gospel thus brought forth its proper fruits in this first town outside of Jerusalem in which it was preached. The town was cleaned up and righteousness blossomed into joy.

Word came up to Jerusalem of the great meetings down in Samaria, and the apostles sent Peter and John to help in the work. Time was when John wanted to burn a Samaritan town for an incivility (Luke 9: 54), but now he went to the capital of Samaria to help in a great revival in that city; it was not the destructive fire of a conflagration that he wanted to see sweeping through its streets, but the beneficent warmth of the Holy Spirit.

It is deeply significant that the first Christian mission was sent out from Jerusalem to Samaria. These two mountaintops crowned with rival temples had flamed excommunication and defiance at each other, but now they were being fused into unity and brotherhood in their common Christian faith and spirit. Two of the deepest and bitterest differences among men, race and religion, were now closed up by this gracious work of the gospel.

The same gospel has come down through the centuries and spread over the world, dissolving the same barriers and melting men of all races into one mind and heart. It is true that it has met with much refractory material in its march of brotherhood and its own disciples have not always manifested this spirit, but this is its true nature, and we should be filled with the missionary spirit that will move us to love all men and send them the gospel.

What did Peter and John do when they arrived in Samaria? They did not assume an attitude and air of ecclesiastical authority over the converts and take charge of the meetings, but they prayed for them that they might receive the Holy Spirit. It appears that there was something defective in the baptism of Philip in that he had baptized his converts into the name of the Lord Jesus only and not also of the Holy Spirit. This defect was corrected by Peter and John by administering the full rite, and then the Holy Spirit was received.

Peter and John did not pray that the church in Samaria might have an imposing building and an impressive ritual and a learned and eloquent pastor, but that it might have the Holy Spirit: they were keeping this first missionary church close and true to the Pentecostal church. If any church have not the spirit of Christ, it is none of his, whatever else it may have or whatever historic name it may bear; but, having this gift and spirit, all things else will be added unto it in their due time and proportion.

Having completed their mission in Samaria, Peter and John "returned to Jerusalem, and preached the gospel in many villages of the Samaritans." Having done their work in the capital city, they did not disdain to work as they passed along in the smaller towns and villages; they were not looking out for large fields and conspicuous places in cities and did not despise the day of small things; but they gleaned sheaves along the roadside and improved every opportunity in wayside ministries.

Philip, also, having completed his work in Samaria, passed on to other points and went toward the south "unto Gaza, which is desert." He may have thought that he had been sent from a fruitful work in Samaria down into a desert where there was no prospect of converts, but here he fell in with an important officer of the queen of the Ethiopians, who under his ministry was converted and baptized. Though he found him by the roadside in a desert, yet he was doubtless the most important convert Philip ever won to Christ, and so Providence made no mistake in

sending him from Samaria to Gaza. God never makes
any mistakes with reference to us, and our best guidance
is his providence.

2. THE CONVERSION OF PAUL

Acts 9:1-31; 22:1-21; 26:1-23

Paul was a Hebrew university graduate and a lawyer
and influential rabbi in Jerusalem, and also a Roman citizen. Born in Tarsus in Asia Minor, he was bred in Greek
culture and could quote from Greek literature. Three civilizations, Hebrew, Greek and Roman, thus met and mingled in his blood. He was a man of acute and powerful
intellect, of logic all compact, yet of poetic and fiery temperament, a keen thinker and forceful writer who could
sound the depths of philosophy, or let loose his thoughts
on the wings of imagination, and an impassioned orator
who could put the spell of his eloquent speech on vast
audiences.

Paul is probably the most strongly marked character in
the Bible. He was unique in his angular individuality and
in the mixture in his nature of incongruous elements and
discordant moods, and was intense and uncompromising
in his principles and convictions.

Especially did he stand in sharp contrast with his Master and Lord. Jesus was country-bred and was rural in
spirit and speech and manner. He lived mainly a quiet
life, avoiding cities and crowds and carrying on his work
in the by-ways of Galilee, and he was supremely serene
in heart and temper, yet aggressive and bold enough on
the proper occasion, frequently retiring for rest and meditation, bathing his soul in the beauty and mystic influence
of mountain and sea and dwelling on the heights in communion with God.

Paul was city-bred and his ears were full of the tumult
of the market and the uproar of crowds and mobs. He
was intensely active and ardent, militant in spirit, always
ready for a fight and scenting the battle from afar. With
almost the last scratch of his pen he exhibited his characteristic spirit and summed up his career in the triumphant
declaration, ''I have fought a good fight.'' Although he

often traveled through grand scenery and frequently sailed the Mediterranean, yet there is not in all his letters a single allusion to the beauty of nature or any indication that he ever heard a bird sing or observed so much as a blade of green grass. The glorious architecture and art of Athens had no interest for him except as furnishing an apt text for a sermon, and versed as he must have been in Greek literature he never quoted it but once and again for a sermonic purpose. He was so absorbed in his one idea and objective that he had no time or thought for anything else. "This one thing I do," was his principle and rule, and never did a great man more imperiously concentrate and compress his powers into one narrow channel and swift impetuous torrent of energy and life.

Many-sided, variously-gifted, unspotted in character, deeply religious, terribly conscientious, tremendously in earnest in his convictions and volcanic in his emotions, by turns cool and calm or hot and passionate, at one time proudly boastful and at another in the depths of self-humiliation, adventurous and masterful as a pioneer preacher and missionary, absolutely devoted to his Lord, and brave unto death, he was one of the great men of his age and of all ages and has helped to shape all the Christian centuries.

Such was the man who is the weightiest single witness to the resurrection of Christ and the greatest preacher and missionary and practical organizer and profoundest theologian in the history of Christianity. We have already considered him as a letter writer, and we now take up his life as he steps into our narrative on the stage of his dramatic conversion.

This epochal event in his life burnt itself deep into his brain and left a vivid impression which he never could forget or misunderstand or confuse in its objective reality with any subjective illusion or delusion. The story is told three times in the Acts in chapters 9, 22 and 26, in the last two instances by himself, and he never tires of it. It is one of the most dramatic and interesting pages in the history of Christianity and remains to this day as one of its epochal events.

At first Paul was a bitter enemy of Christ and his gospel. An intensely orthodox Jew in birth and blood and training and zeal, he regarded Christ as the greatest heretic and most dangerous man in the world, and his soul blazed with hatred toward his disciples and he breathed out fire and slaughter against them. He stood holding the clothes of those who stoned Stephen the martyr, as we have seen, and next we find him out on the way to Damascus to carry the work of death far beyond Jerusalem. It took him several days to journey on horse from Jerusalem 140 miles northward to Damascus.

This must have been a time of cooling down and quiet meditation in his fiery soul. The excitement and passion of his work in Jerusalem had subsided and he found himself out in the solitude and silence of the desert under the solemn Syrian stars. If there was any still small voice in him, it now had a chance to be heard. Possibly the expiring prayer of Stephen strangely awoke and rang through his soul. He unexpectedly found himself troubled over his work. He was surprised to find his convictions were not so unanimous and solid as he had supposed. Cracks and fractures began to cleave his conscience into doubts. He felt himself on the eve of an impending crisis; already conscience was ripe for revolt.

This view of his psychological condition is not explicitly disclosed in the record, but it is in accordance with human experience and it is suggested by the statement in his narrative that "as I made my journey" the crisis came.

Upon this thoughtful and troubled man conversion fell. Damascus was near and decision could not be delayed. The Holy Spirit found him trembling upon the point of doubt and bore down upon him at this critical moment.

As in all conversions, human and divine elements were interblended and worked together. There were spectacular features in his case that were supernatural and unique, but the same essential principles operate in every converted soul. A blinding blaze of light burnt through the sky above him and the proud persecutor was unhorsed. A voice was then heard saying, "Saul, Saul, why persecutest thou me?" This was probably the very question that was troubling Saul himself. The Spirit touched the sorest point in his conscience, piercing his sin.

Saul answered, "Who art thou, Lord?" Already he

seems to know the person addressing him as the Lord. A wonderful answer was given to this inquiry: "I am Jesus of Nazareth, whom thou persecutest." This was a startling revelation and might well have struck terror into Saul's soul. But he was now fast falling into an attitude of faith and obedience. "What shall I do, Lord?" was now his inquiry. Already his restless energies are being reversed and were eager to flow in the channel of service for Jesus. And the answer came, "Arise, and go into Damascus." Not another word about persecution, but only words of kindness and guidance were spoken to the prostrate humbled man. Saul's sin was overwhelmed with God's mercy and washed away in a flood of grace.

Saul was now given further directions as to where he was to go and what he was to do, for conversion does not answer all questions and clear up all difficulties. It usually makes plain only a few steps which on being taken will lead us to more light. Saul took these few steps; he rose from the ground and went into the city. He immediately obeyed his newly found Lord, threw his will into the current of his Master's will and turned his faith into faithfulness.

There were doubtless days of profound meditation and self-examination in which Paul sat alone with himself and thought upon his ways. The past was full of pain and the future of problems. He wanted to be sure of himself and of his Lord, and he fought every doubt through to victory. In Damascus he was baptized and "straightway he preached Christ in the synagogues, that he is the Son of God." Thus he turned around and began to preach the very faith he had sought to destroy and received his great commission that he was to bear the name of Christ to the Gentiles. Christianity won its most powerful preacher and apostle that day.

At this point the Epistles of Paul begin to throw light upon his life, and he tells us in his letter to the Galatians that immediately after his conversion he "went into Arabia" (1:17) and then returned to Damascus and that it was three years after this that he went up to Jerusalem. How long he remained in Arabia and why he went there are not disclosed, but it seems evident that he retired into that desert region for a season of further meditation and preparation for his public ministry. This period corresponds with the "silent years of Jesus" in which he was getting ready for his work. Paul also felt the need of striking his roots deep into the soil of conviction and gathering strength and ripened wisdom and unconquerable resolution for the work to which he had been called and that he might pay the last full measure of devotion to his Lord and be faithful even unto death.

3. PETER AND CORNELIUS. Acts 10

The apostles were now carrying the gospel out from Jerusalem in every direction and Peter went down to Lydda and on to Joppa on the Mediterranean where he went into the house of Simon, a tanner, and lodged there. Little did he know or dream what epochal event would happen to him when he went into that house "by the sea."

About forty miles to the north was Cæsarea and the scene suddenly changes to that city. Cornelius was a Roman soldier, captain of the Italian cohort stationed at Cæsarea. He is described as "a devout man, and one that feared God, who gave much alms to the people, and prayed to God alway." His relation to Judaism is not clear, but he was a Gentile that had derived some light from Jewish revelation and had become a worshiper of Jehovah. He was one of the pious people we find in unexpected places, even out in the heathen world where to this day we discover wild-growing saints who compare with Christian worshipers in piety as we find wild flowers in the forest that rival cultivated blossoms in beauty. God has not left himself without a witness in any part of the world, and his Spirit works unseen and unknown in many hearts.

While engaged in fasting and prayer at three o'clock in the afternoon Cornelius had a vision. A bright-appareled figure stood before him and said, "Cornelius, thy prayer is heard, and thine alms are had in remembrance in the sight of God." The angel now told Cornelius to send to Joppa for Peter and gave particular directions how to find him and promised that he would speak further.

Messengers were dispatched to Joppa, and at noon the next day as they were drawing near that town, Peter was having a vision in which he was being prepared to play his part in this complex plot of providence. Vision matched vision, and both led on to a great victory.

At this hour Peter went up on the flat housetop to pray and fell into a trance or exalted state of soul in which he saw his vision. A great sheet held at the four corners and swollen like a sail in the wind was let down upon the earth, and its contents were all manner of beasts and creeping things that were abhorrent to Jews as unclean. A voice commanded Peter to rise, kill and eat. But his shocked sensibilities refused to respond to such a command and he objected that he had never eaten anything unclean. Peter was still a Jew in this point.

Then came the voice, ''What God hath cleansed, make not thou common.'' Three times this scene was repeated, and then the swollen sheet disappeared up into heaven.

While he was wondering what the vision meant the three messengers from Cornelius knocked on the door and inquired for Peter. He went down to them and heard their story and the next day he went with them to Cæsarea, where he met Cornelius, who recited to him the story of his vision and how he had been instructed to send for him.

This incident gives us a glimpse behind the scenes and lets us see how Providence works. These two men, apart from and unknown to each other, were prepared for each other so that when they met their experiences matched and the two played into each other's hands and worked together. God is always preparing us for our work and preparing our work for us so that when we reach it along the path of obedience we shall find it ready for us.

The story told by Cornelius was heard by Peter with astonishment and wrought in him a profound revolution. Peter's creed and habits of thought and heredity distilled into him out of more than a thousand years of racial history experienced a sudden jar at the discovery. His most deeply inbred thought was that God was a respecter of persons; that he had put a wide difference between the Jew and the Gentile with all the favor on the side of the Jew. But this distinction that had been so wide and deep in his mind was here suddenly blotted out; in a moment it melted away and he saw with amazement that there is no such distinction, that "God is no respecter of persons, but in every nation he that feareth him, and worketh righteousness, is accepted of him."

There is, of course, a sense in which God does respect persons: he respects their inner moral character. But he does not respect their outer conditions, as the Jews thought. Birth and blood, ancestry and heredity, race and rank, wealth and social standing, are not matters that determine or influence his relation to and dealing with people; his classification runs along no such superficial lines as these, but strikes deep into the heart.

God has no favorites in the sense some people think. Sectarianism is apt to breed in us the old Jewish feeling of exclusiveness, but the Bible is a broad book, the world is wide and the Father has many children, and divine grace flows over all human inequalities as the atmosphere flows over all valleys and mountaintops. "What God hath cleansed, that call not thou common." We have not yet learned this lesson in all its breadth and fulness.

Peter now delivered his message. He first gave an outline of the grace of God in the gospel. God sent the word to the children of Israel through Jesus Christ who was anointed with the Holy Ghost and whose life was compressed into one marvelous shining line, "who went about doing good." Yet the Jews hanged him on the cross, but God raised him up and showed him openly. To these facts Peter gives his personal testimony as an eyewitness.

Then Peter declared that he was charged to preach Christ unto the people as the Judge of the living and the dead, and broadened out his message into the universal promise that "through his name whosoever believeth in him shall receive remission of sins."

This breadth and universality of the divine grace had lain latent in the Jewish Scriptures, but now it shone out in splendor, and Peter realized it for the first time and it came to him as a wonderful revelation and revolution. While he yet spake the Holy Spirit fell on all who heard the Word, and the kingdom of God there and then began to push out across the boundaries of Judaism into the Gentile world. Peter has now found the same road that Stephen and Philip traveled, and a great day is dawning.

4. FIRST COUNCIL AT JERUSALEM: SHALL GENTILES BE
RECEIVED INTO THE CHURCH? Acts 11:1-18

The news of what Peter had done down at Cæsarea rapidly spread through Judea and was soon matter of talk up
at Jerusalem. The report was abroad that "the Gentiles
had received the word of God." This raised the great issue
that could now no longer be evaded, What was to be the
relation of the Christian church to Gentiles? Were they
to be admitted on equal terms with Jews, or were they to
be excluded and the Christian church confined to a Jewish
sect? This was the greatest issue and epochal decision
that could confront the church, and history trembled in
the balance the day the apostles and brethren met to decide
it.

The decision was made at a council held in Jerusalem.
Peter, learning of the dissatisfaction, took with him six
brethren who had been with him at Cæsarea and went up
to Jerusalem to give account of himself. There "they that
were of the circumcision contended with him, saying, Thou
wentest in to men uncircumcised and didst eat with them."

Who were these "of the circumcision"? They were
Christian Jews that still held to the law of Moses and believed that Christian converts should be circumcised. They
therefore retained all the Jewish prejudices against the uncircumcised Gentiles. Peter by eating with Cornelius had
thus violated their religious creed in one of its most vital
points and had shocked them beyond measure. A breach
of the Ten Commandments would not have been such a
dreadful scandal in their view.

So these Jewish converts had not yet gotten a glimpse
of the splendid breadth and universality of Christianity
and were still hemmed in and blinded by their own narrow bigotry. They still drew the boundary of God's grace
around their own Jewish race, and left the Gentiles out in
the darkness. They still thought they were the favorites
of heaven and had a monopoly of its grace, and that all
who were outside of this pale were left to perish. Let us
not think that this spirit expired when the last Pharisee
passed out of the world and it is still lurking in some
quarters of the church.

Peter himself had at first been of this way of thinking,

not only when he was a Jew, but even after he had become a Christian. He now told the story of his conversion to these offended Jews. The vision on the flatroofed house of Simon the tanner at Joppa, the great sheet with its beasts, the command to eat which had so shocked him, the arrival at the same hour of the messengers from Cornelius, his visit to the Roman officer at Cæsarea and the descent of the Holy Spirit upon the Gentiles "as on us at the beginning" were graphically described.

"Then remembered I," proceeded Peter, "the word of the Lord, how that he said, John indeed baptized you with water; but ye shall be baptized with the Holy Ghost." Peter had heard Jesus say these words, but he did not fully understand the promise at the time and now it began to blaze out in its breadth and brightness. All these rays of truth and lines of evidence converged into such a flood of light and overwhelming proof that Peter could no longer stand by his old convictions, but his whole mind and heart gave way to the manifest universality of the grace of God in Christ.

The effect of the narrative was decisive upon his prejudiced hearers. If Peter had entered upon a theological argument with them to try to convert them to his view, he probably would only have confirmed them in their opinions and exasperated them. But this plain recital of facts silently undermined their prejudice and the whole structure of their hereditary exclusiveness crumbled down.

"And when they heard these things, they held their peace, and glorified God, saying, Then to the Gentiles also hath God granted repentance unto life." They also could not resist the logic of events and withstand the manifest grace of God. Their noisy clamor against Peter's irregularity and scandal in associating with the uncircumcised quieted down, they held their peace, often a very hard thing to do, they grew attentive and receptive, and they ended with glorifying God for his universal grace.

It was a great day in the Christian church when this victory was won. Had these Jewish Christians been able to fasten their view upon Christianity and bind it with their racial constriction, they would have doomed it to remain a Jewish sect and it never would have reached us. This vic-

tory released it from its Jewish shell in which it had been
hatched and let it spread its wings for its flight out over
the world. We need to appreciate and glory in this universal breadth of the gospel and proclaim it far and wide
that unto all men of every race and nation and class and
condition God hath granted repentance unto life.

We see how the truth and the church grew through the
discipline of controversy. The early church was disturbed
and torn with these discussions and dissensions as to doctrine and polity so that the first Christian centuries seem
a sea of strife. And yet it was through these controversies that great doctrines were wrought out and established, and never did Christianity have a more rapid and
vigorous growth and win mightier victories than during
these times.

Controversy is never to be sought for its own sake, and
it should be avoided when this can be righteously done;
but there are worse things than controversy. Dullness and
deafness to spiritual things are more fatal to life. The
spirit of investigation and criticism, of revision and reconstruction, of unrest and change, of the progressive discovery of new truth, is the spirit and life of the church. These
things show that the Spirit of God is working in the church
and fulfilling the promise of Christ that he would yet reveal many things, and that Christian men are still religiously alive and thinking. And when discussion and even
controversy are carried on in a Christian spirit of mutual
toleration and love, they are sure to issue in some broader
view of truth and wider and deeper experience of God's
grace.

5. The Gospel in Antioch.   Acts 11 : 19-30

The echoes of the great persecution in the days of Stephen long reverberated through the world. That violent
explosion shot flying embers of the church far from Jerusalem and we find them at many points around the Mediterranean shore. One of these points stands out conspicuous as one of the most important centers in the spread of
Christianity.

Antioch at this time was a city of half a million people
and was the third city in the world, Rome being first and

Alexandria second. It was situated three hundred miles north of Jerusalem on the river Orontes, twenty miles from the sea. As it was the political capital of Syria and a center of commerce and art, it was a city of great wealth and architectural magnificence. It had many fine temples and theaters, a main avenue running through its heart four miles from east to west, paved and lined on each side with two rows of columns, and walls, aqueducts and bridges, of which the massive but mournful ruins remain to this day.

While it was the third city in rank it was the first in corruption and vice. Near it was the famous grove of Daphne, ten miles in circumference, an immense pleasure establishment that was a plague spot to all the world. Here vice was cultivated as a fine art and sensuality as a rite of religion. So infamous and infectious was its evil influence that even Rome complained that the Syrian Orontes befouled the Roman Tiber. Yet in this hotbed of vice grew the white flower of Gentile Christianity and the name Christian was born.

To this city of Antioch came certain of the scattered disciples and began to preach the Lord Jesus to ''the Greeks.'' This announcement marks a radical and revolutionary departure in preaching the gospel. There had been, as we have seen, the sporadic instances of Philip at Gaza and Peter at Cæsarea, but these disciples deliberately and openly preached the Lord Jesus to the Greeks, the heathen residents of Antioch. All distinctions between Jew and Gentile had been blotted from their minds and they saw and seized the great truth that Jesus Christ is the Saviour of all men without regard to their race or rank or religion. Uncircumcision was no longer a bar to conversion. The ceremonial law was gone and grace had come. Moses was no longer master, and Jesus was Lord of all.

It was remarkable that this revolutionary policy was not inaugurated by the church authorities up at Jerusalem or by ordained apostles or deacons, but by unordained and unauthorized laymen. Certain men from Cyprus and Cyrene, points far from the seat and sources of Christianity, began this business, apparently of their own accord, moved by the wider and freer spirit that was bred in the hearts of those out in the field of heathenism in close contact with its needs.

This principle has been frequently exemplified in the history of the church. Great movements, such as the Reformation in Germany, the Wesleyan revival in England, the Sunday school and the Salvation Army, did not originate with ecclesiastical authorities, but with unofficial ministers and laymen among the common people. The human heads of the church, as represented by popes and bishops, conferences and assemblies, are generally conservative and often obstructive, and the Holy Spirit usually pours in new life and grows new organs of operation down among the people.

Often new movements start far from the original centers of faith. It is the spirit of Christian unity that develops among our foreign missionaries and native Christians abroad that widens our vision and brings our churches closer together at home.

The news of what was going on down in Antioch soon came up to the church in Jerusalem and it was determined to send a committee to Antioch to look into the situation. Church authorities do not ordinarily start new movements but they usually want to manage them after they are started; and this is right, provided they sympathetically guide them and do not try to obstruct and strangle them.

The Jerusalem church was fortunate in the choice of its commissioner to Antioch. Barnabas was chosen. He was himself from Cyprus, not far from Antioch, and was thus qualified to understand the people and the conditions in that city. Better still, ''he was a good man and full of the Holy Ghost and faith,'' and was therefore a man of broad sympathies whose goodness of heart enabled him to appreciate men and movements that a narrow ecclesiastic would have quickly run foul of and condemned.

When he came to Antioch he saw the grace of God. A differently constituted and tempered man might have seen something to suspect and brand with the name of heresy, but Barnabas saw grace. And he was glad and exhorted them all with purpose of heart that they would cleave unto the Lord. He saw the new policy was inspired of God and he urged it forward; and yet he endeavored to guard it from ephemeral enthusiasm and to guide it along solid and permanent lines.

The work grew and Barnabas needed help. Not far around the Mediterranean shore was Tarsus, Paul's home, whither he had gone after his conversion and had been in quiet retirement for about ten years, which may be included in the "silent years" of Paul. Barnabas went after him. They had been together before. When Paul went up to Jerusalem after his conversion and tried to join the disciples, they were afraid of him, but Barnabas took him up and stood by him (Acts 9: 26-27). Barnabas brought Paul to Antioch and for a year these two men, so different in type and temperament, worked together in preaching the gospel in that city.

At this point a new name appears in the record that shines as a star whose lustre has brightened with increasing ages and shall never be dimmed. "The disciples were called Christians first in Antioch." This name was not assumed by the disciples themselves and, it has been thought, was first applied to them in ridicule. Not in Jerusalem, but down in the Greek city of Antioch, famous for its witty nicknames, was the new name invented. The Greek idlers, seeing that the new religionists were followers of a certain Jew named Christ, called them Christians in derision and contempt. Possibly the designation was considered a happy hit and was greeted with bursts of laughter.

But a new word was born that day into the vocabulary of the human tongue that was destined to live for all time. Like many another word spoken in ridicule, it has become a badge of honor and shines above every other name given among men. It may have been a derisive contemptuous jest, but it now sparkles as one of the most precious jewels in the vast heap of words that men have piled up; it runs as a glittering thread of gold through all the web of human speech.

Those Greek jesters spoke better than they knew and we thank them for their word. But now that we have the name, we should not dishonor it but strive to live up toward it.

CHAPTER IV.

PAUL'S MISSIONARY JOURNEYS

At this point Paul, called from his retirement at Tarsus, looms up in the narrative as the central figure and foremost leader in the story of the spread of Christianity, and beginning with his first missionary journey the Book of Acts is practically his biography; and next to the life of Jesus it is the most important and thrilling biography in the Bible.

1. PAUL'S FIRST MISSIONARY JOURNEY

Acts 13-14. Galatians

The church in Antioch grew in members and strength, and then a call came to it for larger service. "Separate me Barnabas and Saul," was the call of the Spirit, "for the work whereunto I have called them." A new line of work was to be opened and the foremost leaders and strongest men in the church were chosen to go out into the foreign field. We might have expected some doubt and opposition to this choice. How plausible and strong would have been the plea that these two ablest men in the church were needed at home. Was not Antioch a great city and center that ought to be seized and conquered for Christ before any further work should be undertaken? If this policy were suggested it did not prevail, but the divine call was trusted and followed.

The foreign field is no place for weak men: let the church send there her strongest and most gifted sons and daughters, and this it has ever done as the long roll call of famous missionaries, such as David Livingstone, eloquently attests. It may have seemed to some a poor use and needless sacrifice of Paul to bury him in the obscurity and darkness of superstitious heathenism, but it was the same kind of sacrifice as that by which a grain of wheat falls into the ground to spring up a hundred fold, and Christian Europe is its splendid fruit and justification today.

"So they, being sent forth by the Holy Spirit, departed unto Seleucia; and from thence they sailed unto Cyprus." The narrative interblends human and divine action in one statement, in one verse attributing their departure to the church and in the next verse to the Holy Ghost. Seleucia was the seaport of Antioch, twenty miles down the Orontes at its mouth. Possibly members of the church went with the departing missionaries as far as this port, where they bade them farewell and saw them disappear on board a corn ship on the blue Mediterranean.

They sailed westward, for this has been the course of empire in the spiritual, as in the political, kingdom until it has encircled the globe. Never did a ship set sail with a more important and precious cargo. It had aboard the gospel of Christ and kingdom of God compared with which all other freight was as dust and chaff; it had seeds of truth and grace that were soon to be sown in Europe and in time around the world to bloom on every shore.

A sail of eighty miles brought Barnabas and Paul with John Mark as their attendant to Cyprus, the native island of Barnabas, where they began preaching. They worked their way westward through the island without anything of note happening until they came to Paphos, at its western extremity. Here lived the Roman proconsul Sergius Paulus. He was a man of serious thought and spiritual aspiration who hungered for something better than was offered by the effete Roman religion. He was some such man as Cornelius, possibly another wild-growing saint, and there appear to have been many such in the Roman empire, and foreign missionaries find them today out in the heathen world.

When Sergius heard of the missionaries preaching a new message of salvation he sent for them to come up to his palace and desired to hear the word of God. Here was a most unexpected and promising opening, and it must have been with great hope and gladness that Barnabas and

Paul declared to him the way of life. But an unexpected obstacle was also encountered. Lurking in the shadow of Sergius they found his evil spirit and tempter, one Barjesus, a sorcerer. He was an apostate Jew who had gone into the business of fortune telling and magic, a kind of religious impostors and quacks that swarmed in the Roman world.

Paul, who at this point forges ahead and takes precedence of Barnabas in the narrative, unmasked the smooth villainies of the tempter, branded him whose name was Son of Saviour as a son of Satan, and he was stricken with blindness. Trying to blind others, he was blinded himself. But Sergius himself believed and was the first convert of the expedition.

When the missionaries "loosed from Paphos, they came to Perga in Pamphylia: and John Mark departing from them, returned to Jerusalem." Various conjectures have been advanced to explain why Mark left Paul and Barnabas at this point and went back home, such as that he may have thought that Paul was crowding Barnabas, who was his uncle (Col. 4:10), out of the leadership of the party, or that he thought the preaching of the gospel to the Gentiles was being carried too far, or that he lost courage and could not endure the hardship of the tour. Evidently Paul at this time thought Mark did not have in him the stern stuff of a missionary.

Whatever was Mark's reason, Paul did not forget this act when they had returned to Antioch and were preparing for a second missionary journey over the same ground. Barnabas wanted to take Mark along, but Paul opposed this, and these two leaders parted company. Paul believed that Mark had been unfaithful once and should not be tried again; Barnabas, true to his good heart, believed that the young man should have a second chance.

So these apostles were quite human and had their quarrels; but their dissension fell out to the furthering of the gospel, for, as we shall see, on the next journey Barnabas took Mark and sailed for Cyprus, and Paul took Silas and struck up through Asia Minor, and so two missionary expeditions instead of one set out from Antioch on account of this quarrel. It is pleasant to know, however, that in time Paul and Mark became reconciled and close friends, for in his second letter to Timothy Paul bids him to "pick up" Mark somewhere between Ephesus and Rome and bring him along (II Tim. 4:11).

Thus this first missionary expedition soon struck rocks, both external in the case of Bar-jesus the sorcerer and internal in the matter of Mark. Foreign missions are still attended with these troubles, and we must not expect smooth sailing and easy marching in our Christian work, either at home or abroad.

Paul and Barnabas now passed into Asia Minor and stopped first at Antioch in Pisidia, where Paul delivered a long sermon in the synagogue (13:15-41), and when the message was rejected by the Jews the missionaries turned to the Gentiles with many converts; but when the Jews stirred up opposition the missionaries moved on to Iconium. Similar results followed at this town and then in Lystra and Derbe, the farthest point reached. At Lystra Paul and Barnabas had a specially exciting experience, the people at first worshiping them as gods and then stoning Paul and leaving him as dead.[1]

These four towns were all in the Roman province of Galatia, and the churches founded in them on this journey were the Galatians to whom Paul wrote his Epistle of this name. From Derbe the missionaries retraced their steps back through Lystra and Iconium to Antioch in Pisidia, "confirming the souls of the disciples, and exhorting them to continue in the faith." They then proceeded to Perga and "thence sailed to Antioch," their starting-point, where "they rehearsed all that God had done with them, and how he had opened the door of faith unto the Gentiles."

The first missionary journey, attended as it was with both external and internal troubles, was successful, proving that the gospel was the power of God to the Gentiles, and leaving behind a group of churches that played an important part in the early history of Christianity.

---

[1] It is a striking confirmation of the accuracy of Acts that the worship of Mercury and Jupiter as associated gods was a local cult in and around Lystra. See Ramsay's *The Bearing of Recent Discovery on the Trustworthiness of the New Testament*, pp. 48-49, a book abounding in such confirmations.

2. Second Council at Jerusalem; Must Gentile Converts Submit to the Mosaic Ceremonies?

Acts 15:1-29

No sooner had Paul and Barnabas arrived at Antioch from their first missionary journey than they were confronted with a great crisis. "And certain men which came down from Judea taught the brethren, and said, Except ye be circumcised after the manner of Moses, ye cannot be saved." This is akin to but not just the same question that had been settled at the first council at Jerusalem: There the question was, Shall Gentile converts be admitted to the Christian church? Here the question is: Shall they be admitted without being circumcised? Defeated on the first point, these Judaizers are bringing up practically the same issue in another form.

We must try to put ourselves in the place of these Judaizers and see the situation from their point of view. It seemed to them that the admission of Gentiles into the church without circumcision was destructive of the whole system of Moses that had been consecrated by more than a thousand years of glorious history. This was a terrible wrench and shock to their orthodox consciences, and we may well appreciate if not sympathize with their sore experience. Yet however conscientious they were, they were not blameless in their blindness to the breadth and liberty of the gospel. Paul calls them "false brethren unawares brought in, who came in privily to spy out our liberty, that they might bring us into bondage" (Gal. 2:4).

Pharisees before conversion, the Pharisaic spirit clung to them after conversion. Conservatism in them was crystallized into fixity and finality. They were narrow rigid literalists who could see no room in religion for any difference of opinion. And so they went about among the brethren as spies and heresy hunters, stirring up dissension and subverting souls. We have not yet seen the passing of all the people that say that others must believe after their manner, or "ye cannot be saved."

Paul also at this time and place encountered this Judaistic propaganda in another quarter. According to the order of events in the life of Paul that we have adopted,

Judaizers had already got in among his Galatian converts, following close on his heels through the towns in Galatia where he had only recently founded churches, and it was at this time in Antioch that he wrote his Epistle to the Galatians. "I marvel," he begins, "that ye are so soon removed from him that called you into the grace of Christ unto another gospel: which is not another; but there be some that trouble you, and would pervert the gospel of Christ" (1: 6-7).

Paul proceeds to give a brief sketch of his life and in chapter 2 tells of a visit he made to Jerusalem fourteen years after his conversion to consult with Peter and other "pillars" of the church on "the gospel of the uncircumcision." We take it that this visit does not refer to the council we are about to study, of which the account is given in Acts 15, but to a previous one, possibly the famine relief visit mentioned in Acts 11:27-30, or some other unmentioned visit. It would appear that this may have been a preliminary private conference in which the question of uncircumcision was practically settled before the public council was called.

The Epistle itself from start to finish is a trumpet blast against fastening the Mosiac ceremonies on the Gentile converts, and into this liberty Paul pours all the invincible logic of his mind and passionate heat and vehemence of his heart. "The business of the Letter," as John Locke long ago saw and said, "is to dehort and hinder the Galatians from bringing themselves under the bondage of the Mosaical law," and it does this with a vengeance.

The delegates appointed to attend this second council, consisting of Paul and Barnabas and "certain other of them," set off from Antioch and traveled by land three hundred miles southward, strengthening and heartening the brethren by the way. Arrived at Jerusalem, they were received by the church and told their story of God's doings among the Gentiles. They were again confronted with the demand of the Pharisiac Christians that the Gentiles be circumcised and the law of Moses be imposed upon them.

The conference then met and the different views were considered. Peter was the first speaker. He reviewed the circumstances of his own conversion to the principle of liberty and protested against putting a yoke on the Gentiles that the Jews themselves were unwilling to bear. Peter had wavered on this matter at an earlier day (Gal. 2:11-12), but he stood true in this decisive hour.

A great silence fell on the conference as Paul and Barnabas rose to speak. The exploits of these missionaries had made them illustrious and they had come back as generals from a great victory. They recited the story of their famous campaign and rehearsed the wonders that God had wrought among the Gentiles.

Then James, the brother of Jesus and head of the church in Jerusalem, spoke. He was a sympathizer with, if not a supporter of, the Judaistic party (Gal. 2:12), and might have been expected to oppose Peter and Paul. But he took strong ground in favor of Gentile liberty and quoted from the prophets to prove his position. The principle of universal salvation was in the Old Testament all the while, but the Jews did not see it until the light of the gospel fell on its pages and brought it out in luminous lines.

Thus the conference brought these brethren into unexpected agreement and consolidated the church in the principle and the policy of universal salvation with freedom from the ceremonial law of Moses. Christianity was again saved from Jewish sectarianism and provincialism and from schism and was finally loosed from its Judaistic swaddling clothes and set free to start out unimpeded on its worldwide march and conquest. It is because of the epochal decision made at this council that we are Christians today.

This council illustrates the true method and spirit of handling religious differences. "And the apostles and elders came together for to consider of this matter." They did not fight it out to the bitter end, but they came together for a friendly discussion. They sat down and talked it over and reached a decision with unexpected unanimity. Conference is far more effective in settling differences and disputes than controversy. Controversy heats the blood and intensifies differences, but conference cools passion and emphasizes points of agreement. In all our disputes, especially in religion, we should strive to come together to consider the matter in an amicable spirit.

The decision of the conference was embodied in a letter that has been preserved for us and is one of the most important documents in the history of Christianity. It is the Magna Charta of our right as Gentiles to share in the salvation of Christ without coming under the bondage of the Mosaic law.

The letter consists of an introduction giving the history of the matter and a resolution or exhortation stating the decision. It first addresses the Gentiles as brethren and next repudiates the troublers of the church. Paul and Barnabas are strongly commended, thus receiving complete vindication. Finally, in the name of the Holy Ghost it lays upon the Gentiles no unnecessary burden but bids them abstain from things sacrificed to idols, from things strangled, and from adultery.

There are thus in the letter some elements of compromise. While the Gentiles were released from the ceremonial law of Moses, they were yet to have regard for the prejudices and feelings of the Jews and not wantonly offend them in their social practices. But there was no division of the church, neither party sought to exclude the other, but room was found for both, and the unity of the church was maintained. The moral law of Moses, however, remained as one of the things that cannot be shaken.

3. PAUL'S SECOND MISSIONARY JOURNEY: FROM ANTIOCH TO BEREA. Acts 15:30—17:13

The brethren returned from Jerusalem to Antioch with the decree of the council, "which when they had read, they rejoiced for the consolation."

Paul and Barnabas now proposed to start out on a second missionary tour, but they disagreed over taking Mark along, as we have already seen, and so they parted company, striking out along different routes, Barnabas taking Mark and proceeding over the route of the first journey, and Paul taking Silas and traveling by land up through Asia Minor.

Paul revisited the churches at Derbe, Lystra and Iconium. At Derbe he did a surprising thing in circumcising Timothy, a young convert whose mother was a Jewess and his father a Greek: it is surprising because the act seems

in contradiction to Paul's whole position on the subject
of circumcision, against the decrees of the council which
he was at this very time delivering to these churches and
especially against the whole teaching of his Epistle to this
very church at Derbe.   Yet Paul gives his reason, which
was that he wished to avoid giving needless offence to the
Jews "in those quarters, for they knew all that his father
was a Greek."

Paul was willing to circumcise Timothy who accepted
the rite voluntarily as an act of expediency, but he was
unwilling to subject any Gentile to the rite against his
will, and for this liberty he stoutly stood to the end.   Paul
was ready for compromise when such a policy involved no
principle, but for the principle itself, he was unyielding.
This is simply saying that he was a man of good sense and
knew how to be all things to all men on points of expediency.   Practical life is full of such compromise in which
principles, without yielding their essential nature and demands, adapt themselves to wise policies.

Paul now passed on until he came to Troas, a seaport
on the Agæan sea separating Asia from Europe, where
Luke, the author of the Acts, joined the party and steps
into the narrative (16:10).   Here a vision swept down
upon Paul in the night, in which he heard a man of Macedonia calling, "Come over into Macedonia, and help us."
Instantly obeying the heavenly vision as his habit was,
Paul with his three companions, Silas, Timothy and Luke,
sailed from Troas across the Agæan sea to Neapolis on the
European shore.

In going over this narrow arm of the sea these travelers
crossed a more momentous Rubicon than Cæsar ever saw;
this voyage of a few hours marks one of the greatest cross-
ings and epochs of history.   In passing from Troas to
Neapolis the gospel leaped from Asia to Europe and added
a new continent to the kingdom of Christ.   The star of
spiritual empire here started westward and then kept moving onward until it has now encircled the globe.   This is
why we are Christians today.

The apostle and his companions went on to Philippi
where the gospel immediately took root and began to grow,
for it is adapted to every climate and soil.   The narrative

speaks of the missionaries here tarrying certain days—unimportant days that are simply huddled together under a general designation—and hurries on to a special day that shines out upon the page like a star, that never-to-be-forgotten "Sabbath day" when, Luke writes, "we went forth without the gate by a river side, where prayer was wont to be made; and we sat down, and spake unto the women which resorted thither." This seems like a rather unpromising beginning for the gospel in Europe, but no movement that begins with women can be counted unpromising.

The narrative now singles out "a certain woman" whose interesting story is told. Lydia has the conspicuous honor of being the first Christian convert in Europe. She was "a seller of purple," a business woman and shopkeeper who was earning her own living. She was a useful worker, and this fact shines as a crown on her brow.

The beautiful steps of her conversion are linked together like loops of gold. She went to the place of prayer, she heard the gospel, the Lord then inserted a divine link in the process and opened her heart, she attended to the things that were spoken, she was baptized together with her household, and then began to exercise the grace of Christian hospitality, and her conversion was complete. It is a quiet orderly conversion, perfect and beautiful at every point. And so "the man of Macedonia" that Paul heard turned out to be a woman, and this was a most significant start, for foreign missions to this day usually wins its way first among women. "The Lord giveth the word: the women that publish the tidings are a great host" (Ps. 68:11).

The first European convert was a woman and the second was a man; the first was a shopkeeper, and the second was a jailer: the gospel reaches up and down and through society in every direction and is no respecter of persons. The first conversion occurred in a quiet prayer meeting on a river bank, and the second grew out of a mob and took place in a jail amidst the cracking walls and shocks and shouts of an earthquake. The gospel works under all conditions and tells its story in sanctuary or street and knows no difference between the iron-barred windows and stone floors of a prison and the richly-stained glass and softly carpeted aisles and cushioned seats of a church.

As Paul and his companions passed to and fro between their lodgings and the place of prayer, they were followed by a fortune-telling slave girl who kept crying out that "these men are the servants of the Most High God." Paul took pity on her and released her from demon possession. But the slave girl belonged to a company of owners, who, seeing that they were losing the value of their property, had Paul and Silas arrested and dragged before magistrates, charging that they were "Jews," which was almost a crime in itself, and that they "do exceedingly trouble our city," which was bad for business.

Paul and Barnabas were soon in jail and at midnight held a prayer meeting when strange music floated through the dark damp corridors "and the prisoners heard them." An earthquake at this point suddenly rocked the prison, and the Roman jailer, fearing that he would answer with his life for escaped prisoners, drew his sword to slay himself, when Paul called out in the nick of time, "Do thyself no harm: for we are all here."

The jailer cried out, "What must I do to be saved?" and Paul gave the compact and thrilling answer, "Believe on the Lord Jesus Christ, and thou shalt be saved, and thy house." The jailer believed, faith rushed into fact, and he and all his were baptized "straightway."

Lydia and the Roman jailer illustrate widely different types of conversion, and there are many such types, for the wind of the Spirit bloweth as it listeth.

The Roman magistrates wanted Paul and Silas to leave the jail without investigation of the charge, but Paul stood on his rights as a Roman citizen, which greatly alarmed the magistrates and then they came and besought the prisoners to leave the city. Roman citizenship was a powerful protection throughout the empire, and more than once Paul used it to secure his rights.

Paul and his company now passed on to Thessalonica, where persecution followed them and drove them on to Berea, where again they had to be sent away by the brethren. Persecution was still the great propagandist of the gospel, and Paul was not carried through Europe on a flowery bed of ease but traveled a rough and thorny road to its fatal end.

4. PAUL AT ATHENS AND CORINTH
Acts 17:15—18:18. I and II Thessalonians

Driven out of Berea, Paul, leaving Silas and Timothy behind, was conducted by friends down to the sea where he set sail for Athens. This city was "the eye of Greece" and the university city and intellectual center of the world, glorious in its history and its achievements in literature and art, but none of these things interested Paul. The city was so full of idols that it was said to be easier to find gods than men and this gross idolatry shocked Paul's Hebrew soul.

He at once began preaching in the synagogue to the Jews and then in the market-place to the Greeks. These keen-witted people, whose main business was to scent the latest news, were quick to discover in Paul a philosopher who had something to say. A charge of heresy, " a setter forth of strange gods," began to be whispered around, and he was invited up to the Areopagus where he delivered the speech that is recorded in outline in our narrative.

The introduction, a critical part of every speech, is a striking exhibition of oratorical genius. "Ye men of Athens, in all things I perceive that ye are very religious." The translation of the Authorized Version is wrong and turns Paul's winning compliment into a repellent charge. He appealed to the religious nature which is so universal and profound, he took his stand upon common ground with his hearers that he might lead them up to higher truth.

He then took as a text an inscription he had noted on one of their altars, TO AN UNKNOWN GOD, Paul quoted this and thus further won the confidence of his hearers, and announced the subject of his sermon, "Whom therefore ye ignorantly worship, him declare I unto you." By this masterly stroke Paul put himself in touch and sympathy with his audience and then led them on through his discourse in which he unfolded the revelation of God in nature and in the human heart. At length he reached the revelation of God in Christ culminating in his resurrection.

Paul's discourse appears incomplete and was probably

interrupted at this point. The mention of the resurrection of the dead was too much for these volatile Greeks and was greeted with a burst of laughter and jeers. Some answered the missionary with mockery, and others put the preacher off with the easy excuse that they would hear him again concerning the matter; but they never did.

Yet Paul's sermon was not without results. There were some converts, including one man of note, Dionysius the Areopagite or member of the chief court of the Greeks, and a woman, evidently also of some note, Damaris. There is no evidence that Paul left Athens discouraged, as some have thought, yet he may have felt that the university city was not then the best soil in which to sow the gospel. But his sermon on Mar's Hill was not a failure and stands out as one of his most conspicuous achievements. After all, the gospel Paul preached there that day did in time sweep away all those idols, and the pagan Parthenon became a Christian church.

Fifty miles westward from Athens on a narrow isthmus stood Corinth, the second famous city of Greece. Though it never rivaled Athens in intellectual development, it almost equalled it in art and surpassed it in commerce and wealth. It was a city of magnificent architecture, and its Acrocorinthus was crowned with a splendid temple of Venus that matched the Parthenon, which was visible fifty miles away.

The city had a bad eminence in vice. Its heterogeneous population, containing adventurers from every country, and its wealth and luxury made it a hotbed of corruption in which every kind of profligacy grew riotously and shameless orgies attended its pagan worship.

Into this pleasure-seeking, sin-saturated city came Paul the missionary bringing the gospel of purity and peace, and here he abode and labored for a year and a half. Being an utter stranger in the city, Paul sought and found lodging with a family consisting of Aquila and Priscilla, husband and wife, who had been lately expelled from Rome by the edict of the Emperor Claudius. As this edict was issued early in 52 A. D., we have in this an event that gives us a definite date.

Here Paul labored at his trade of tentmaking to support

himself as his avocation and began preaching the gospel as his vocation. "He reasoned in the synagogue every Sabbath and persuaded Jews and Greeks." The usual opposition soon developed in the synagogue, and from the Jews Paul turned into the adjoining house of Justus where he continued to preach. Presently he began to gather converts, and one was Crispus, the ruler of the synagogue who believed with all his house. A church was thus founded which became important and figures largely in early church history.

Who were these people that formed this church? Not the wealthy merchants and artists and aristocrats of the city, but mostly they were its scum and dregs. In a letter written to them afterward (I Cor. 6:9-11) Paul gives a slimy catalogue of the classes these members had come out of and says, "Such were some of you, but ye are sanctified." This was the kind of work the gospel did in these heathen hotbeds of vice, and it is still doing the same work in great heathen and Christian cities.

In Corinth Paul seems to have fallen into some great fear and despondency, but a cheering promise was vouchsafed to him of the Lord: "Be not afraid, but speak and hold not thy peace: for I am with thee, and no man shall set on thee to hurt thee: for I have much people in this city."

While in Corinth Paul received word from his friends at Thessalonica through the arrival of Silas and Timothy (Acts 18:5) and heard of their steadfastness, and this good news moved him, as we have seen, to write to them his First Epistle to the Thessalonians. It contained, however, a passage on the coming of the Lord (4:13-18) which created some misunderstanding and alarm among them, to correct which Paul hastened to write his Second Epistle to assure them that other events would intervene before the Lord would appear. From this point on Paul was a frequent letter writer and thus kept in touch with his churches and friends and greatly widened his field of labor and sphere of influence.

Paul at length left Corinth and, stopping for a brief time at Ephesus, he traveled by way of Cæsarea up to Jerusalem where he went to attend a feast, probably a passover, and having "saluted the church, he went down to Antioch," his home base, having been absent on this second missionary journey upwards of three years.

5. PAUL'S THIRD MISSIONARY JOURNEY
Acts 18:23—20:3. I and II Corinthians. Romans.

From Antioch Paul started out on his third missionary journey and passing through Galatia and strengthening the churches there he came to Ephesus.

Ephesus was the principal city of Asia Minor and was the center of commerce, wealth and art. Its crowning glory was the famous temple of Diana that was counted one of the seven wonders of the world. It rose a mass of pure white marble, magnificently columned and carved, and its brilliant beauty glittered far out at sea. Hewn out of the side of the overhanging mountain was the great theater, capable of seating fifty thousand persons, the stone seats of which yet remain.

Under the shadow of this magnificent temple of pagan worship Paul began his preaching, first in the synagogue and then in the lecture room of Tyrannus, where he taught two out of the three years he labored in Ephesus. The presence of the Jew missionary was at first unknown to the Greek priests and they would have scorned him, but his preaching soon began to diminish the throng of worshipers in the temple, and in time the gospel of the Nazarene did sweep the worship of Diana off the earth.

Some strolling Jewish exorcists tried their hand at imitating Paul, who had wrought special miracles of healing in the city. Two of them tried their art on a man with an evil spirit, but the man, frenzied with his evil possession, leaped upon the impostors and beat them so that they fled from the house with torn clothing and bloody wounds.

The result of this disastrous failure was that fear fell on many and the name of the Lord Jesus was magnified. These penitent believers did not stop with confession but brought their curious arts and magical books and piled them up in a heap and burnt them in the sight of all. Magical books have a great fascination for Jews, and Ephesus was noted for its trade in such writings, often mere strips of parchment inscribed with mysterious words or sentences which were supposed to have miraculous power. The value of the books burnt on this occasion amounted to fifty thousand pieces of silver or about as many dollars today. If all the impure books and gambling tools and evil implements in the world were burned up in one great heap it would make a tremendous conflagration, but it would cleanse the world of much unrighteousness. With converts bringing forth such fruits of repentance we are not surprised that in Ephesus the word of the Lord grew mightily and prevailed.

The gospel was now making such inroads upon idolatry in and around Ephesus that the profitable trade in images of the goddess Diana was falling off. The manufacturers felt the loss and cast about for the cause. Demetrius was the man that hit upon the trouble. He called together the workmen and delivered to them an artful speech in which he played upon their fears and their self-interest with a masterful hand. He reminded them ''that by this craft we have our wealth.'' Right well did they know this, and the man that starts off with this proposition is bound to have a hearing and carry his point. Whoever touches our business and bread touches our bones and blood.

The financial argument of Demetrius, appealing to their self-interest, would be effectual with the workmen, but would it appeal to the public? The wily shrine manufacturer was equal to this side of the case and produced an argument that took the whole city by the ears. Not only was their craft in danger, but it would also follow ''that the temple of the great goddess Diana should be despised, and her magnificence should be destroyed, whom all Asia and the world worshipeth.'' Piety and patriotism were here both aroused and enlisted in defence of the shrine business. Orthodoxy was being undermined and destroyed by heresy and a reign of irreligion and atheism was imminent. The fall of the temple would also mark the fall of the city and its glory would perish from the earth.

The Ephesian silversmith artfully linked profits, piety and patriotism together in defence of his trade, and from such a speech we may expect great results. Demetrius is a plausible fellow, and his voice is still heard in many a modern meeting, whether it be a manufacturers' trust, a labor union, a political convention, or an ecclesiastical assembly.

The effect of the speech was tremendous and must have exceeded the expectations even of Demetrius. There was an instant outburst of wrath from the silversmiths. Profits, piety and patriotism shouted with one voice, "Great is Diana of the Ephesians!" The excitement grew and spread and soon the whole city was in an uproar. There seems to have been a search made for Paul, but he was not to be found. Two of his known companions, however, were caught up by the swelling tide of madness and swept on its foaming crest into the theater. Higher and higher rose the waves of wrathful humanity until the vast theater was a surging sea of furious faces.

When Paul heard of it he was for going at once to the help of his friends. His brave spirit could not brook the thought of personal safety at the expense of unfaithfulness to others. His disciples and powerful friends, however, intervened to save him from a useless sacrifice. The Jew might soon have been torn to pieces in that storm.

For two hours an incessant cry was kept up. At length the city clerk got the attention of the senseless wearied crowd and made a speech marked by singular wisdom and justice. He reproved the Ephesians for their small faith in their religion, pointed out the legal way of proceeding against any wrong doer, and closed by threatening them with being called to account for the Romans for their disorder.

This speech brought the Ephesians to their senses and the human sea flowed out of the theater and left the stone seats empty. Paul hastily left the city. Demetrius seemed to have triumphed, and yet he was really conquered. For Paul had inserted a wedge in that temple of Diana that in time split it down to its deepest foundation stone, and in its place rose a powerful Christian church.

While in Ephesus Paul wrote his First Epistle to the Corinthians, in which he endeavored to correct certain evils that had arisen in that church, especially a factional spirit and moral laxness; and a little later he followed it, after he had gone to Macedonia on his way to Corinth, with the Second Epistle in which he expresses his joy at the happy turn of affairs of which he had been apprised.

From Ephesus Paul passed through Macedonia to Corinth, where he remained three months, and at this point he wrote the Epistle to the Romans in anticipation of his contemplated visit to that city. Leaving Corinth he passed back through Macedonia, stopped at Miletus, the seaport of Ephesus, where he bade an affecting farewell to the Ephesian elders, and sailed on down the Mediterranean coast, touching at various points with interesting incidents, and landed at Cæsarea, where the company "took up" their "baggage and went up to Jerusalem."

6. PAUL AT JERUSALEM AND CÆSAREA
Acts 21: 16—26: 32

When Paul arrived in Jerusalem he was kindly received of the brethren and he hastened to pay his respects to James and the elders of the church. A narrative of his labors among the Gentiles again drew from the church thanksgiving and praise to God. The church seemed to be united and harmonious, and yet the old antagonism between conservatives and liberals was working beneath the surface.

Some of the elders explained to Paul that many of the Jewish Christians were zealous for the Mosaic law and were suspicious of his orthodoxy, having heard that he rejected Moses altogether; and they proposed that he go to the temple with four brethren that had taken a vow, and, by thus appearing with them and bearing their expenses, disarm these criticisms. Paul, in accordance with his practice of being all things to all men in points of expediency when no principle was involved, complied with this request.

The next day, while in the temple with these Nazarites, he was observed by some Asiatic Jews, probably some of those who had opposed him in Ephesus, who immediately seized him and began to shout, "Men of Israel, help!" declaring he was the man that everywhere rejected Moses and had defiled the temple by bringing Greeks into its sacred precincts.

Instantly there was a tremendous Oriental uproar. A mob seized Paul and were bent on killing him, when Roman soldiers intervened and saved him from the popular fury. The Roman captain permitted Paul to address the crowd from a stairway, when he gave an account of his life. The next day the captain took Paul before the Jewish council, where Pharisaic fanaticism again broke out against the prisoner, and he was taken back by the soldiers into the tower of Antonia where the Roman garrison had its headquarters.

The plot of conspiracy grew thick, forty Jews bound themselves with an oath that they would not taste food until they had killed the hated apostate, but Paul's nephew hearing of the plot warned the captain of the garrison, who hurried his prisoner off under heavy guard down to Cæsarea to the governor. Thus from the historic city where he had been educated as a university student and had entered upon life as a rising lawyer and had taken such a prominent part in persecuting Christians and then had returned to it as a foremost Christian apostle, Paul departed as a prisoner never to return. Strange must have been his memories and reflections on that memorable day.

Lawyers came down from Jerusalem to conduct the prosecution of the case against Paul, but Felix the governor, after a preliminary hearing of the matter, postponed the case on the ground that he would wait until Lysias the chief captain would come down, committing the prisoner to a centurion.

One day this wearied, satiated Roman governor bethought himself of the prisoner that had some new notion on the subject of religion and it occurred to him that he might while away an idle hour, and besides get some money out of the Jew as a bribe, by hearing him speak. In a luxurious room in the palace Paul was ushered in before Felix and Drusilla his wife.

It was a curious situation. Felix was judge and master of Paul's life and with a nod of his head he could have sent him to his doom. Yet the prisoner was to preach to the judge. How strong was the temptation to curry favor with the governor and slip in a word for himself. How many a man would have cringed and fallen? But never

was Paul more fearless, brave and calm and truer to his
real Master, Jesus Christ.

The sermon Paul preached is not recorded, but its three
divisions or points are given: righteousness, temperance
and judgment. He uttered not a word concerning himself,
he wasted no time in a long introduction, but he came right
to the point and preached straight to the conscience of the
man before him. He spoke of righteousness to this wicked
man; of temperance to this sensual man; and of judgment
to come to this godless man. It was a pointed and searching sermon, and such preaching will be heard from.

Felix trembled under the tremendous indictment, and
then dismissed the preacher with the excuse that when he
had a convenient season he would call him again; but he
never did. Two years rolled by with Paul still in prison
when Felix passed out of office and Festus came into his
place. At this point the Jews tried to have Paul returned
to Jerusalem, where they had a better chance to convict
him and Festus asked him if he was willing to go, but Paul
prevented this procedure by exercising his right as a Roman citizen of appealing unto Cæsar. "Hast thou appealed unto Cæsar?" said Festus; "unto Cæsar shalt
thou go."

The new governor, having Herod Agrippa, king of a
petty kingdom lying northeast of Galilee, and his wife
Bernice (who was also his sister), with him as his guests,
mentioned to his visitors the case of the Jewish prisoner
left on his hands, and Agrippa expressed a desire to hear
the man himself. The next day the hearing took place before the governor, the royal visitors and other men of note,
attended with great pomp.

Festus introduced Paul with a brief statement of the
case and Agrippa called upon Paul to speak. Paul rose
and, assuming his characteristic attitude with uplifted
hand, delivered his defence in which he went over again
the chief points of his life. At one point in his impassioned speech Festus interrupted him with the exclamation,
"Paul, thou art beside thyself; much learning doth make
thee mad."

But Paul was more concerned with the king than with
the governor and directed his remarks to Agrippa. He

appealed to him as a Jew: "King Agrippa, believest thou the prophets? I know that thou believest." The king answered him to the effect that he evidently thought he was about to convert the king "to be a Christian." Paul, however, expressed the passionate wish that the king might become altogether such as he himself was, with one noble and thrilling exception. As he uttered his prayer he lifted his hand and, as the chains with which he was fettered clanked, added the significant words, "except these bonds." The scene was intensely dramatic and pathetic and was enough to move even Romans to tears. The king, who had been in a jesting mood, did not care to pursue the subject further and rose to retire, followed by the rest of the company.

Paul, however, had made a deep impression, for in discussing the case after their retirement Agrippa said unto Festus, "This man might have been set at liberty, if he had not appealed unto Cæsar." Paul was now on his way to Rome, that great world magnet that had long been drawing him, though he was going in a way of which he had never dreamed.

7. STORMY VOYAGE AND SHIPWRECK
Acts 27-28: 16

We here see Paul in a new situation in which he discloses unsuspected capacities. The eloquent preacher and profound philosopher becomes a successful weather prophet and able shipmaster. Put him in any situation and he will grasp it with a firm and deft hand. He had a rare combination of genius and common sense. The man that could deliver a masterly address to Athenian philosophers and write an immortal prose-poem on love had the shrewd judgment and force of will that made him the real captain of an Alexandrian corn ship and pushed him into leadership everywhere. Religion does not unfit a man for business, but knits up all his powers into unity and strength and makes him a man among men.

The appeal to Cæsar, which could not be reversed, carried Paul to Rome, whither he had long been planning to go. The voyage is described with such realistic minuteness and vividness as could not have been invented, but must be the pen-photograph of an eyewitness. Luke's history attests its trustworthiness all the way through and he was aboard this ship and kept something like a diary of what happened. We have a narrative of wind and wave, ship and storm, freight and sail and rope, that in every word is redolent of the sea's salty breath, yet it is saturated with religion and all its events reflect spiritual lessons. The sea has ever been a favorite symbol of life, and its surface and deeps, placid and smiling or storm-swept and foam-flecked, mirror the varied aspects of life's voyage.

Paul with other prisoners in charge of a centurion together with Luke took passage on a coastal vessel at Cæsarea and at Myra took an Alexandrine wheat ship bound for Rome. The dangerous season of navigation was near and at Fairhavens on the southern coast of Crete Paul advised the centurion to lay up in that harbor, but the captain and the owner of the ship decided to make for the next port where they would have more roomy quarters.

Presently what Paul had expected happened. The terrible Euroclydon, a sudden violent wind in that region, swept down off the steep Cretan mountains, seven thousand feet high, and, as it tore across the sea, lashing it into fury, it seized the boat in its giant fist and threatened instantly to crush and sink it. For a fearful run of twenty miles the ship drove helplessly before the gale. The storm continuing unabated and danger of foundering still threatening, the crew began to lighten the ship by throwing overboard freight and tackling, though saving the precious wheat until the last extremity, when it also had to go.

Thus amidst intense excitement and activity on board of that storm-struck foundering vessel, everything was done that could be done. Modern seamanship approves of every measure that was taken. The captain of the Alexandrine wheat ship made a mistake in venturing out upon that treacherous sea at that season, but he handled his vessel with masterly ability after he was caught in the gale.

There was one man at least on that ill-fated ship who stood tall and strong on its rolling, wave-swept deck. "Paul stood forth in the midst of them." What strength of character and purpose is indicated in these words! It was the prisoner that thus stood forth in the midst of them and they all gathered around him to receive his message; the prisoner was now the central figure on that deck; the captive was now captain. The strong man will always come to his hour and rise to leadership.

Paul now announced to the panic-stricken crew and passengers that he had good news for them. He had received a message from God in a vision in which he was assured that all on board the ship would be saved, only they must first be cast upon an island. This message was a striking revelation of divine sovereignty and foreordination. God is not going forward blindly and working at haphazard, but he has all things laid out and put together in his eternal plan. This news, instead of releasing them from their utmost activity in managing the ship, only encouraged and inspired them to do their part all the more urgently.

With the dawn of the next day they were in sight of land, but could not tell where they were. The imperfect instruments and maps and seamanship of that day did not enable them to do what would be easy in our day. They saw a bay with a shelving shore, and their plan was to beach the ship. The anchor ropes were cut and the foresail hoisted and the ship made for the shore, only to be caught in a swirl of the sea and run aground. Though Paul had announced that all would be saved, yet they used and had to use every device and effort of seamanship to bring the ship ashore.

The soldiers, answerable with their own lives for the safety of the prisoners, now proposed to kill Paul and his companions, lest they would swim ashore and escape, but the centurion interposed on Paul's account, and his presence saved Paul's life. Orders were now given for every one to make land for himself, and some swam and others floated ashore on planks and other things from the ship, "and so it came to pass, that they escaped all safe to land."

This is the most notable shipwreck of history. Greater disasters have happened, but no other tale of the sea has been studied so minutely and recounted so many thousands of times and has entered so vitally into the life of the world: and it draws its fame and significance from the single fact

that one of the prisoners on board this wrecked ship was a
missionary of Jesus Christ. Infinitely the most important
and precious freight in its cargo was the gospel which is
the power of God unto salvation, and ships still carry this
gospel over every sea unto the ends of the earth.

Paul spent the winter in Malta, where he healed Publius,
the Roman governor of the island, and wrought other
miracles, and in the spring resumed the journey and
finally arrived in Rome.

8. PAUL IN ROME

Acts 28 : 16-31; Philippians; Ephesians; Colossians; Philemon; I Timothy; Titus; II Timothy

In Rome at last! The metropolis of the world with its
two million inhabitants sat on its seven hills and bore the
proud name of the Eternal City. All roads ran to this
center, all power radiated from this throne, around this
hub revolved the mighty rim of the world. From its marble Forum, the very ruins of which are still an attraction
to all the world, stretched in every direction miles of public buildings, fashionable residences, splendid avenues, triumphal arches, magnificent aqueducts, intermingled with
slums of poverty and vice.

All the world had been taxed and robbed to enrich this
city. Conquering Cæsars came back from every land
loaded with the loot of cities they had captured. Marble
Forum and Nero's Golden House, columned temples and
vast bathing establishments and (later) majestic Colosseum, the world had been rifled of its wealth and treasure
that this immense blossom of architecture and art might
bloom out upon its seven hills. Art and learning were already stealing away from Athens and making this the
university city of the world. Every ambitious face was
set towards Rome. This powerful magnet drew the world;
the Golden Milestone in the center of the Forum was the
axis of the Roman earth; here all things came to their
culmination and grand climax.

Paul had long felt this imperial attraction. Great men
inevitably gravitate to great cities as affording the proper
field for their faculties, and the great apostle felt and

declared, "I also must see Rome." At last he had arrived, not in his own way, but in God's way; not as a free traveler, but as a chained prisoner.

Paul was in Rome, living in his own hired house, but a soldier was always at his side and with every movement of his hand his chain clanked. Yet he was incomparably the greatest and most important man in that city beside whom Nero in his Golden House shrinks into insignificant worthlessness.

His bonds could not bind the truth he preached, but fell "out rather unto the furtherance of the gospel." This man had some subtle and potent chemistry by which he could transmute the crudest ore and coarsest slag into fine gold. In his prison-house he preached to soldiers and thus sent the gospel up into the very palace of Cæsar; and he wrote letters that went out bearing instruction and inspiration and comfort to distant points and passed into the Scriptures and are today circulating in the spiritual life-blood of the world.

After three days in which we may suppose he was resting and arranging his temporal affairs Paul was ready for work. The prisoner was bound, but the preacher was free. The apostle began as usual with the Jews. When they were assembled Paul made a brief statement of his case. In every such statement he always stood on and started from conservative ground and so he put in the forefront of his case the fact that he had "committed nothing against the people, or customs of our fathers." He addressed them as brethren and spoke to them as a loyal Jew and thus set himself before them in a favorable light. Yet, notwithstanding this fact, he had been delivered a prisoner to the Romans, who, when they had examined him, found no cause of death in him and would have released him, had not the Jews objected and thus forced him to appeal to Cæsar.

The appeal to Cæsar, however, bore a suspicious look to Jews, implying treachery to his own country, and Paul was careful to explain that he had no charge against his nation. For this reason he had entreated them to see and hear him; and he concluded with the declaration that "for the hope of Israel I am bound with this chain."

The Jews answered that they had received no letters or reports against him, but that they desired to hear him: "for as concerning this sect, we know that everywhere it is spoken against." This shows that already Christianity had got into the general news of the world and report represented it as something scandalous. It was a "sect" of the Jews, which was bad enough, and Christians were declared to be "the enemies of mankind," and were charged with worshiping a crucified ass, and drinking the blood of slain infants at their religious feast. Rome rang with these reports, and several years later when Nero, to shield himself, charged them with having set fire to the city, the infuriated populace saw Christians thrown to wild beasts in the arena and burned as torches in Nero's gardens with shouts of frenzied delight. It cost a great price to be a Christian in that day.

A day was now set for a more extended hearing, and at the appointed time the Jews were present in Paul's house in large numbers. The apostle preached an all-day sermon in which he expounded the kingdom of God, quoting Moses, with the result that "some believed the things that were spoken, and some believed not." It is an honest record and an honest book that writes this result down. When these Jews had finally rejected the gospel Paul pronounced judgment upon them and turned to the Gentiles, "preaching the kingdom of God, and teaching those things which concern the Lord Jesus Christ, with all confidence, no man forbidding him."

These closing words in Luke's biography of Paul are true to the great apostle in every syllable and accent, and sum up his life from the hour when he fell under the spell of Christ's presence and power near Damascus to the hour when he fell under the executioner's sword at Rome.

Two years he dwelt in his own hired house and received all that went in unto him. During this time he was interested in and in touch with many of his friends and churches, writing the letters to the Philippians, who greatly cheered him by sending him a gift (Phil. 4:18), and to the Ephesians and the Colossians and to Philemon, in which "Paul the aged" pours out his ripened instruction and tenderest affection and his mystic moods and deepest theology.

The strenuous period of battle, which he opened in the Epistle to the Galatians in which he fought for liberty in the gospel, has calmed down into the quiet and serenity of the evening time. He had fought the good fight of faith and won it. His thoughts turned to the deeper things of the spirit, especially to the cosmic Christ by whom "all things consist" (Col. 1:16-17), the immanent principle of the universe. These last letters are among the most precious portions of the New Testament.

Luke closes his biography of Paul at this point, and the best explanation of this fact is that he wrote his book while Paul was still in prison and he knew no more. Tradition, as we have seen, releases the great apostle from this first imprisonment to go out on further missionary service, during which he wrote I Timothy and Titus, and then brings him back a few years later for final imprisonment and death, at which time he wrote II Timothy, the last letter we have from his hand.

This letter is especially tender and earnest and rings with a victorious note as the grand old veteran declares, "I have fought a good fight, I have finished my course, I have kept the faith: henceforth there is laid up for me a crown of righteousness, which the Lord, the righteous judge, shall give me at that day: and not to me only, but unto all them also that love his appearing." How fitting and eloquent are these final words of Paul.

Yet Paul the aged has not lost interest in life. Affection is running deep in his soul and in his loneliness he yearns for the fellowship and love of his closest friends. Pathetically he records the fact that "only Luke is with me," and he bids Timothy to "Take Mark, and bring him with thee: for he is profitable to me for the ministry," a pleasant record as showing that the wound of the former separation was healed. He does not think he is done with service, for he wants Timothy to bring "the cloke I left at Troas with Carpus," and also "the books, but especially the parchments." Busy student and scholar and worker he was to the last, and how we would prize them if we could recover some of those books and parchments!

Some of the old fire also flashes out of him, for he remembers that "Demas hath forsaken me, having loved this present world," and he pays his respects to "Alexander the coppersmith," declaring that "he did me much evil" or "has done me a lot of harm": "the Lord reward him according to his works." These personal notes show how human he was to the last.

The Second Epistle to Timothy was the last writing from Paul's pen. He could calmly write, "I am now ready to be offered, and the time of my departure is at hand." The swift stroke of an executioner's sword, probably in the Neronian persecution of 64 A. D. and certainly before the death of Nero in 68 A. D., ended his life, his work as far as inspired history records it is finished, and the greatest man in the New Testament and the greatest leader since Moses passes from our view. But of hardly any other human being is it so grandly true that "he being dead yet speaketh."

We have concluded our study of the Making and Meaning of the New Testament: Its Background, Books and Biographies; its principal facts and features, cities and centers, program and personalities, origins and expansion of the gospel as traced in its pages, its truth and teaching and application for us, its words that are immortal spirit and life, its imperishable beauty and its transcendent blessings; and central and supreme in it as its chief value and vitality and glory its Master and Lord in whom all its rays converge and concenter as the express image and brightness of God and from whom they all issue as the Light of the World.

The study has surely caused the book to grow upon our understanding and appreciation until we realize it is beyond rival the greatest book in the world, incomparably the supreme literary treasure of the race. No one can afford to be ignorant of it even as a means of education and culture. In our translation it is the noblest literary monument in the English language. "Western civilization," says William Lyon Phelps, Professor of English Language in Yale University, "is founded upon the Bible; our ideas, our wisdom, our philosophy, our literature, our art, our ideals, come more from the Bible than from all other books put together.''

This is especially true of the New Testament. Its history and varied literature in Gospels and Acts and Epistles and panoramic Apocalypse, its stories and parables and prose-poems, its thrilling scenes and dramatic moments, its picturesque views and uplifting visions, its lucid streams and profound deeps, its vitalizing breath and victorious spirit, its great messages of salvation and hope, and withal the simplicity and charm and music and majesty of its style make it an education to the mind, culture to the heart, bread to the soul and victory to the spirit.

It is these contents and characteristics of the New Testament that prove it to be ''inspired of God and profitable for doctrine, for reproof, for correction, for instruction in righteousness, that the man of God may be perfect, thoroughly furnished unto all good works.'' The students that read, mark and assimilate this book will find that it will strengthen and enrich their souls and enable them to live a great life that is hid with Christ in God.

> Dear Lord and Father of mankind,
>   Forgive our foolish ways;
> Reclothe us in our rightful mind,
> In purer lives thy service find,
>   In deeper reverence, praise.
>
> In simple trust like theirs who heard,
>   Beside the Syrian sea,
> The gracious calling of the Lord,
> Let us, like them, without a word
>   Rise up and follow thee.
>   —*Whittier.*

INDEX OF SCRIPTURES

	PAGE
Gen. 1:1	117
Ex. 12:1-27	15
Ex. 23:12	168
Ex. 29:38-46	15
Lev. 1:2-3	15
Lev. 4:1-12	15
Lev. 5:1-6	15
Lev. 13—14	164
Lev. 16:5-15	15
Job 36:10	220
Ps. 22:18	228
Ps. 68:11	278
Ps. 81:10	180
Isaiah 1:1-18	183
Isaiah 9:1-2	63
Matt. 1:1-17	117
Matt. 1:18-25	118
Matt. 2:1-12	123
Matt. 2:23	125
Matt. 3:1-12	131
Matt. 3:7-12	49
Matt. 3:13-17	133
Matt. 4:1-11	134
Matt. 4:1-22	170
Matt. 4:3-10	49
Matt. 4:14	63
Matt. 4:18-22	156
Matt. 4:23	162
Matt. 4:25	23
Matt. 5-7	49
Matt. 5:1-12	172
Matt. 5:17	63
Matt. 6:5-15	175
Matt. 8:5-13	178
Matt. 8:14-17	158
Matt. 8:23-27	187
Matt. 9:1-8	164
Matt. 9:9	62
Matt. 10:2-4	169
Matt. 11:2-19	180

	PAGE
Matt. 12:15-21	63
Matt. 13:1-53	184
Matt. 13:55	104
Matt. 14:1-12	190
Matt. 14:13-23	192
Matt. 15:1-20	195
Matt. 16:13-20	198
Matt. 18:1-14	208
Matt. 21:1-11	212
Matt. 22:16	20
Matt. 23:4-17	17
Matt. 26:6-13	208
Matt. 26:17-36	217
Matt. 26:36-46	221
Matt. 26:57—27:31	223
Matt. 27:32-56	227
Matt. 28:16-20	233
Matt. 28:18-20	63
Mark 1:1-8	131
Mark 1:9-11	133
Mark 1-12-13	134
Mark 1:14-15	152
Mark 1:16-20	156
Mark 1:35-45	162
Mark 1:21	63
Mark 2:1-12	164
Mark 2:21-34	158
Mark 3:7	63
Mark 3:13-19	169
Mark 4:1-34	184
Mark 4:35-41	187
Mark 5:25-34	67
Mark 6:3	129
Mark 6:14-29	190
Mark 6:30-46	192
Mark 7:1-23	195
Mark 7:13	17
Mark 8:27-30	198
Mark 9:2-13	201
Mark 10:46-52	208

PAGE

Mark 11:1-11 212
Mark 14:3-9 208
Mark 14:22-26 217
Mark 14:32-42 221
Mark 14:53—15:20 223
Mark 15:21-41 227
Luke 1:1-4 70-72
Luke 1:26-38 118
Luke 1:28 119
Luke 2:8-20 121
Luke 2:39-52 125
Luke 3:1-20 131
Luke 3:7-9 49
Luke 3:21-22 133
Luke 3:23-38 117
Luke 4:1-13 134
Luke 4:1-18 184
Luke 4:3-13 49
Luke 4:16-30 153
Luke 4:22 70
Luke 4:31-41 158
Luke 4:38 70
Luke 4:42-44 162
Luke 5:1-11 156
Luke 5:12 70
Luke 5:17-26 164
Luke 6:12-19 169
Luke 6:20-23 172
Luke 6:20-49 49
Luke 7:10 178
Luke 7:12 70
Luke 7:18-35 180
Luke 8:22-25 187
Luke 9:7-9 190
Luke 9:10-17 192
Luke 9:18-22 198
Luke 9:28-36 201
Luke 9:38 70
Luke 9:51—18:14 72
Luke 9:51 251
Luke 10:1-24 208
Luke 10:38-42 208
Luke 11—18:8 50
Luke 17:11-19 208
Luke 18:18-23 208
Luke 19:1-10 208
Luke 19:29-44 212
Luke 22:7-30 217
Luke 22:39-46 221
Luke 22:54—23:25 223

PAGE

Luke 23:26-49 227
Luke 24:50-53 236
John 1:1-18 74
John 1:4 117
John 1:35-51 ....137, 170
John 2:1-11 141
John 2:13 59
John 2:13-22 143
John 3:16 ....75, 148
John 3:1-21 146
John 4:4-26 148
John 4:21 250
John 4:24 75
John 4:46-54 153
John 5:1 59
John 5:1-47 167
John 5:12-16 162
John 6:1-15 192
John 6:4 59
John 9:1-41 205
John 11:1-46 208
John 12:1 59
John 12:1-11 208
John 12:20 25
John 12:20-22 24
John 12:20-36 215
John 13:1-30 217
John 14:26 78
John 16:12-15 251
John 18:1 221
John 18:12—19:16 223
John 19:16-37 227
John 20:21 73
John 20:31 74
John 21:24 73
Acts 1:1 70
Acts 1:1-2 77
Acts 1:8 77
Acts 2:1-47 245
Acts 4:30 248
Acts 5:29 248
Acts 6:1 24
Acts 6—7 248
Acts 6:16 93
Acts 8:1-25 253
Acts 9:1-22 257
Acts 9:1-31 256
Acts 9:29 24
Acts 9:26-27 268
Acts 10:1-48 260

PAGE

Acts 11:1-18 263
Acts 11:19-30 265
Acts 11:27-30 ....83, 274
Acts 11:30 87
Acts 12:12 66
Acts 13—14 269
Acts 13:15-41 272
Acts 15:1-29 273
Acts 15:1-31 ....87, 274
Acts 15:30—17:13 276
Acts 16:4 87
Acts 16:10 ....69, 277
Acts 16:10-18 69
Acts 16:11-40 89
Acts 17:1-9 91
Acts 17:15—18:18 280
Acts 18:5 ....91, 282
Acts 18:23—20:3 283
Acts 19:1-41 88
Acts 20:5-16 69
Acts 21:1-18 69
Acts 21:16—26:32 286
Acts 22:1-21 ....256, 257
Acts 23:8 19
Acts 26:1-23 ....256, 257
Acts 27—28:16 ....69, 289
Acts 28:16-31 292
Rom. 3:25 26
Rom. 16:1 84
I Cor. 3:21-22 27
I Cor. 5:9 85
I Cor. 6:9-11 282
I Cor. 11:23-26 217
I Cor. 13:1-13 83
I Cor. 15:6 232
I Cor. 15:1-20 58
I Cor. 15:1-58 230
II Cor. 2:12-13 85
II Cor. 7:8-9 85
II Cor. 10—13 86
II Cor. 11:23-28 97
Gal. 1—6 269
Gal. 1:2 86
Gal. 1:6 86
Gal. 1:6-7 274
Gal. 1:7 87
Gal. 1:11-12 87
Gal. 1:12 99
Gal. 1:18 232
Gal. 2:1 83

PAGE

Gal. 2:1-21 87
Gal. 2:4 273
Gal. 2:12 275
Eph. 1—6 292
Eph. 1:1 88
Eph. 1:15 88
Eph. 3:2-4 88
Eph. 6:21 90
Phil. 1—4 292
Phil. 1:13 89
Phil. 2:24 89
Phil. 2:25-30 89
Phil. 4:18 294
Phil. 4:22 89
Col. 1—4 292
Col. 1:15-19 90
Col. 1:16-17 295
Col. 2:8, 18 90
Col. 2:9 90
Col. 2:10-17 90
Col. 2:16-17 90
Col. 2:20-23 90
Col. 3:10-11 90
Col. 4:7 90
Col. 4:9 90
Col. 4:10 271
Col. 4:14 69
I Thess. 1—5 280
I Thess. 1:8 91
I Thess. 4:13-18 ......91, 282
II Thess. 1—3 280
II Thess. 2:1—12 91
II Thess. 3:10 130
I Tim. 1—6 292
I Tim. 1:3 92
I Tim. 1:4-8 92
I Tim. 4:3 92
I Tim. 6:20 92
II Tim. 1—4 292
II Tim. 2:1-26 93
II Tim. 4:6-8 93
II Tim. 4:9-15 93
II Tim. 4:11 69
Titus 1—3 292
Philemon 1:1-25 292
Heb. 1:1-4 100
Heb. 1:9 240
Heb. 2:3 99
Heb. 10:1-2 100
James 2:14-26 101

PAGE

I Pet. 1:2-5 200
I Pet. 1:7 102
I Pet. 1:16 103
I Pet. 2:6 103
I Pet. 4:12-19 102
I Pet. 5:13 102
II Pet. 2:1-22 104
II Pet. 3:1 103

PAGE

II Pet. 3:15-16 103
I John 1:1 ....42, 103
I John 1:5 ....75, 104
I John 4:8 104
I John 4:24 75
Jude 1:4-16 104
Jude 1:9 105
Judge 1:14 105

INDEX OF SUBJECTS

Aaron, 194.

Acquila, 281

Acrocorinthus, The, 281.

Acts, The, date of, 54; authorship of, 77; purpose and characteristics, 77-79; omissions in, 79-80; continuation of the Gospels, 243-244; accuracy of, 272, 290.

Aeschylus, 22.

Alexander, the coppersmith, 296.

Alexander, the Great, 8, 23.

Alexander, 26, 266.

Amos, 8.

Andrew, the disciple, called to follow Jesus, 138; 156, 194, 215.

Annas, 223.

Annanias, 249.

Antioch, the gospel in, 265-268, 270, 272, 273, 274, 276, 283.

Antioch, in Pisidia, 272.

Antiochus, Epiphanes, 105.

Antonia, Tower of, 287.

Apocalypses, Jewish books, 20-21; in the Bible, 105.

Arabia, 259.

Army, The Salvation, 267.

Arnold, Matthew, quoted, 36.

Ascension, of Jesus, 236-240.

Assyrians, 18.

Athens, 91, 280-281.

Augustine, 108.

Background, of the New Testament, Jewish, 1-21; Greek, 22-28; Roman, 29-36.

Babylon, VIII, 2, 8.

Baptism, of Jesus, 133-134; meaning of the ordinance, 133.

Bar-jesus, sorcerer, 271.

Barnabas, at Antioch, 267-268; with Paul on first journey, 269-272; at Second Council in Jerusalem, 273-276; goes with Mark on missionary journey, 276.

Barnabas, Epistle of, 107.

Bartimaeus, 208.

Beatitudes, The, 172-175.

Bede, The Venerable, 110.

Beethoven, 124.

Berea, 91, 279-280.

Bernice, wife of Agrippa, 288.

Bethany, 208, 212, 217, 237.

Bethesda, pool of, 167.

Bethlehem, 5; Jesus born at, 120-121.

Bible, greatest book in the world, VIII; canon of, 107-108; Roman Catholic, 108, 110; translations of, 109-111; a book of principles, 238.

Birth, virgin, of Jesus, 119-120.

Cæsar, Augustus, 21, 120.

Cæsar, Julius, 115, 277.

Cæsarea, 5; Peter at, 260-261; Paul at, 287-289, 290.

Cæsarea, Philippi, 198-201.

Caiaphas, 223.

Calvary, 201, 227.

Cana, of Galilee, miracle at, 141-143; nobleman's son healed, 153.

Canon, of the New Testament, 43, 107-108; of the Old Testament, 108.

Capernaum, 5; headquarters of Jesus, 156; a busy day in, 158-161.

Carlyle, quoted, 130, 160.

Caro, Cardinal, 109.

Carpenter, Jesus the, 129-130.

Carpus, 295.

Carthage, Synod of, 108.

Christ, Jesus, outline of events of life of, 59-61; and Christendom, 116; life of, 117-240; the thirty "silent years," 117-130; genealogy of, 117-118; his humanity, 118; virgin birth of, 119-120; birth in Bethlehem, 120-121; angels and shepherds at his birth, 121-123; worshiping Wise Men, 123-125; childhood and boyhood, 125-129; the carpenter, 129-130; baptism of, 133-134; temptation of, 134-137; starting his kingdom, 137-141; first miracle, 141-143; first cleansing of the temple, 143-146; interview with Nicodemus, 146-148; conversation with woman of Samaria, 148-150; preaches at Nazareth, 153-156; headquarters at Capernaum, 156-158; a busy day in Capernaum, 158-161; missionary tour through Galilee, 162-164; strange things in Capernaum, 164-166; at pool of Bethesda, 167-169; choosing and mission of his twelve disciples, 169-172; the Sermon on the Mount, 172-178; the Lord's Prayer, 175-178; heals a centurion's servants, 178-180; how he dealt with John's doubt, 180-184; his parables, 184-187; stills a storm on Galilee, 187-189; feeding the five thousand, 192-195; breaks with the Pharisees, 195-198, with the disciples at Cæsarea Philippi, 198-201; his transfiguration, 201-204; healing the man born blind, 205-208; at the home of Martha and Mary, 208-210; at Simon's table, 210-211; the triumphal entry, 212-214; certain Greeks, 215-217; institution of the Lord's Supper, 217-220; in Gethsemane, 221-223; the trial, 223-226; the crucifixion, 227-230; the resurrection, 230-233; his Great Commission, 233-236; his ascension, 236-240; contrasted with Paul, 256.

Christian, the name first given at Antioch, 268.

Christianity, an historical religion, 41; struggle for freedom from Judaism, 82, 87-88, 100-101, 244, 250-251, 253, 263-265, 273-276; a rational religion, 188; universal religion, 235; starts on its world-wide march, 243-244; a "sect" in the Roman Empire, 294.

Chronology, of the Gospels, 53-54; of the birth and life of Jesus, 59; of Paul's life and letters, 83-84.

Church, The, in the teaching of Jesus, 152; the means of spiritual life, 159; it may be wrong, 166; the Rock on which it is built, 199, 200; in Jerusalem, 245-248, 286; struggle against Judaism, 263-265, 273-276.

Cicero, quoted, 24; 187.

Claudius, Emperor, 281.

Clement, of Rome, Second Epistle of, 107.

Codex, Sinaiticus, 108-109.

Colosse, 90, 94.

Colosseum, The, 29-30, 292.

Colossians, Epistle to, 80, 84, date, occasion and contents, 90, 90, 204, 205.

Columbus, 124

Communism, of early church in Jerusalem, 247-248.

Controversy, place of, in the church, 265, 275.

Conversion, nature of, 132, 152, 247; of Paul, 257-260; of Lydia, 278; of the Philippian jailer, 279.

Copernicus, 27.

Corinth, 91, 281-282.

Corinthians, I and II Epistles to, 80, 84, dates, occasions and contents, 85-86; 285-286.

Cornelius, and Peter, 260-262.

Council, First at Jerusalem, 263-265; Second at Jerusalem, 87, 273-276.

Coverdale, 110.

Crete, 94, 290.

Crispus, 282.

Cross, The, first revealed, 200; the principle of, 217; on Calvary, 227-230; meaning of, 230.

Crucifixion, of, Jesus, 227-230.

Crusades, 8.

Cyprus, 266, 267, 270.

Cyrene, 266.

Damaris, 281.

Damascus, 258, 259.

Daniel, Book of, 105.

Daphne, grove of, 266.

David, 194.

Deacons, appointed, 249.

Decapolis, 23, 198.

Dedication, feast of, 17.

Deissmann, Adolf, 26.

Demas, 296.

Demetrius, Ephesian silversmith, 284-285.

Demosthenes, 22, 115.

Derbe, 272, 276.

Diana, worship of, at Ephesus, 283-286.

Diatessaron, Tatian's, 108.

Didache, of the Twelve Apostles, 107.

Dionysius, 281.

Drusilla, wife of Felix, 287.

Domitian, Emperor, 105.

Doubt, how to treat religious, 180-184.

Ecclesiastes, Book of, 108.

Ecclesiastics, rarely the first to receive new truth, 121-122; often have been misguided, 166.

Egypt, 2, 7, 125.

Elijah, 8, 190; at the transfiguration, 202.

Elisha, 8.

Elizabeth, 119.

Emmaus, 231.

Empire, Roman, division of, 8, extent of, 30-31; its pagan religions, 31-33; its despair, 36; Christianity in, 243-244.

Enoch, Book of, 105.

Entry, The triumphal, 212-214.

Epaphroditus, 89.

Ephesians, Epistle to, 80; date, occasions and contents, 88-89; 294.

Ephesus, 88, 282, 283-286.

Epistles, Catholic, 99-105.

Epistles, Paul's, 80-98; circumstances, characteristics and contents of, 81-95; review of, 95-98; progression of ideas in, 96-97.

Esdraelon, plain of, 4, 126.

Essenes, Jewish religious party, 19.

Esther, Book of, 108.

Euripides, 22.

Euroclydon, The, 290.

Eusebius, 62, quoted, 63.

Ezra, 8.

Fairhavens, 290.

Farrar, F. W., quoted, 79.

Feasts, Jewish, 17-18; the four visits of Jesus to, 59.

Felix, governor of Judea, 287-288.

Festus, successor of Felix, 288.

Fiske, John, quoted, 248.

Forum, The Roman, 292.

Galatia, 272, 283.

Galatians, Epistle to, 80, 84; date, occasion and contents, 86-88, 96, 259, 272, 274, 295.

Galilee, district of, 15.

Galilee, Lake, 4, 5, 126; fishing

on, 157-158; a storm on, 187-189.

Genius, the Hebrew, 9-11; the Greek, 22-23; the Roman, 30-31.

Gentiles, their admission to the Christian church, 263-265; 273-276.

Gethsemane, 221-223.

Gnosticism, 93.

Gods, mythological, 31-32.

Golgotha, 227.

Gospels, The Four, general characteristics of, 44-60; historicity of, 44-47; interrelation of, 47-49; can they be harmonized, 50-53; dates of, 53-54; why four? 55-56; their different points of view, 55-56; miracles in, 56-59.

Government, church development of, 249.

Greece, VIII.

Greeks, the people, 22; their genius, 23; spread of their civilization, 23-24; their language, 24; certain ones desiring to see Jesus, 215-217.

Harnack, on date of the Acts, 54; on dates in the life of Paul, 83.

Headlam, Arthur C., quoted, 46-47.

Hebrews, Epistle to, 98, date, authorship, purpose and contents, 100-101, 108.

Hermas, Shepherd of, 107.

Hermon, Mount, 4, 201.

Herod, Agrippa, 288-289.

Herod, Antipas 14; 190-192.

Herod, the Great, 14, 59.

Herod, Archelaus, 14, 125.

Herod, Philip, 14, 190.

Herodians, Jewish party, 20.

Herodias, wife of Herod Antipas, 190-192.

Herodotus, 78.

Historicity, of the Gospels, 44-47; of miracles, 56-59; of the Acts, 272, 290.

Horner, Francis, 202.

Hospital, The, an annex of the church, 171.

Hugo, Victor, quoted, 202.

Iconium, 272, 276.

Immortality, 203.

Irenaeus, quoted, 69, 73.

Isaiah, 8.

James, brother of the Lord, 87, at the Second Council in Jerusalem, 275; author of the Epistle, 101-102.

James, the disciple, called to follow Jesus, 156; at the transfiguration, 201; 221; 231.

James, Epistle of, 99, authorship, purpose and contents, 101-102, 108.

Jeremiah, 8.

Jerusalem, capital of Judea, 15; condition in time of Christ, 143-144; university city, 170; why Jesus wept over it, 212-214; First Christian Council at, 263-265.

Jesus, See Christ.

Jews, history of, 6-8; racial characteristics, 8-9; religious nature of, 9-11; worship and life of, in time of Christ, 15-19.

Job, Book of, 206.

John, the Baptist, announcement of his birth, 119; preaching at the Jordan, 131-133; baptizes Jesus, 133-134; thrown into prison, 148; his doubt about Jesus, 180-184; death of, 190-192.

John, the disciple, called to follow Jesus, 155, 156, at the transfiguration, 201; 221; 231; on the morning of the resurrection, 231; at Samaria, 255.

John, Gospel of, relation to the other Gospels, 47; authorship of, 73-74; purpose and characteristics of, 74-75; contents of, 75-76.

John, I, II and III, Epistle of, 99, authorship and contents, 103-104, 108.

Joppa, 5, 260.

Jordan, The, 4; 131.

Joseph, of Arimathea, 230.

Joseph, husband of Mary, 118, 119, 120, 123, 128, 155.

Judaism, religion of, 15-19; struggle of Christianity against, 82, 87-88, 99-100, 244, 250-251, 263-265, 273-276.

Judaizers, 263, 273-276.

Judas, 170, 221, 223, 245.

Jude, Epistle of, 99; authorship and contents, 104-105.

Judea, district of, 15.

Jupiter, worshiped at Lystra, 272.

Justin, Martyr, 69, 107.

Justus, 282.

Kingdom of God, Jewish idea of, 20; how Jesus started it, 137-139; its place in his teaching, 152-153; his vision of, 180.

Knox, John, 132.

Lake, Kirsopp, quoted, 79.

Lamb, Charles, quoted, 199.

Language, the Greek, 24-26, 229; Aramic, 24-25, 222, 229; Latin, 229.

Lazarus, raising of, 208.

Lebanon, Mount, 4.

Leprosy, symbol of sin, 164.

Lincoln, referred to, IX, 51, 95, 115, 189, 238.

Livingstone, David, 269.

Locke, John, quoted, 274.

Longfellow, quoted, 33.

Lord, The coming of the, 91-92, 282.

Luke, author of the Third Gospel, joins Paul in the second missionary journey, 277; 290, 294, 295.

Luke, Gospel of, relations to the other Gospels, 47-49; date of, 54; authorship of, 69; characteristics of, 69-70, preface to, 70-72; contents of, 72-73.

Luther, 108, 132.

Lydda, 260.

Lydia, 278.

Lysias, captain of the Jerusalem police, 287.

Lystra, 272, 276.

Macaulay, 78.

Maccabaeus, Judas, 8, 17.

Maccabees, 19.

Macedonia, 277.

Machaerus, Castle, 190.

Magic, books of, burned at Ephesus, 283-284.

Malta, 292.

Manuscripts, of the New Testament, 108-109.

Mark, Gospel of, relation to the other Gospels, 47-49; date of, 54; authorship, 66-67; characteristics of, 67-68; lost ending of, 69.

Mark, John, author of Second Gospel, with Paul on first missionary journey, 270; turns back, 271; goes with Barnabas, 276; reconciled with Paul, 271-272, 295.

Martha, sister of Mary, 208-210, 238.

Mary, mother of our Lord, 79, 118, 119, 120, 121, 123, 124, 128, 141, 142, 154.

Mary, sister of Martha, 208-211, 238.

Matthew, author of the First Gospel, 62.

Matthias, 245.

Mercury, worshiped at Lystra, 272.

Messiah, Jewish idea of, 20; Jesus announces himself as, 151.

Miletus, 286.

Milton, 27.

Ministers, injured by mercenary

spirit, 172; yet should be properly supported, 172.

Miracles, their nature and historicity, 56-59; purpose of, 142.

Miracles, of Jesus, water turned into wine, 141-143; leper cleansed, 164; paralytic healed, 164-166; cripple healed at pool of Bethesda, 167-169; centurion's servant healed, 178-180; storm stilled on Galilee, 187-189; five thousand fed, 192-195; healing of the man born blind, 205-208; resurrection of, 230-233.

Mischna, quoted, 16.

Missions, foreign, 163, 269-270, 278.

Missions, home, 163.

Mithraism, 32.

Moab, 6.

Moffatt, James, translation of Luke's Preface, 71; his *New Translation* of the New Testament, 110.

Mohammedans, their conquests, 8.

Moses, Assumption of, 105.

Moses, law of, Pharisaic additions to, 15-17.

Moses, 194; at the transfiguration, 202.

Mozart, 124.

Myra, 290.

Napoleon, 115.

Nathaniel, called to be a disciple of Jesus, 140.

Nativity, Church of, 120.

Nazareth, 5, childhood of Jesus in, 125-127, his first sermon in, 153-156.

Neander, 78.

Neapolis, 277.

Nehemiah, 8.

Nero, 54, 292, 293, 294, 296.

Newton, 27, 35.

Nicodemus, interview with Jesus, 146-148; 230.

Olives, Mount of, 212, 237, 245.

Onesimus, runaway slave, 90, 94.

Ordinance, nature of, 133, 170, 197; baptism, 133; the Lord's Supper, 217-220.

Orontes, river, 266, 270.

Outline, of events in the life of Jesus, 59-61; of the life and letters of Paul, 83-84.

Palestine, the land of, 3-6; political condition in time of Christ, 14-15.

Pamphylia, 271.

Paphos, 270, 271.

Papias, quoted, 62, 66.

Papini, Giovanni, quoted, 143-144.

Papyri, 26.

Parables, of Jesus, 184-187.

Parthenon, The, IX, 281.

Passover, feast, 17, 218.

Paul, his Epistles, 80-98; his battle for the liberty of the Gospel from Judaic bondage, 82, 87-88, 250; as a letter-writer, thinker and theologian, 82-83, 97; chronology of his life and letters, 83-84; witness to the resurrection of Christ, 232; first appearance of, 252; his characteristics, 256-257; conversion, 257-260; called from Tarsus to Antioch, 268; his missionary journeys, 269-296; first journey, 269-272; at Second Council in Jerusalem, 273-276; second journey, 276-283; at Athens, 280-281; at Corinth, 281; third journey, 283-286; at Ephesus, 200-205; at Jerusalem and Caesarea, 200-209; voyage and shipwreck, 200-202; in Rome, 292-296; contrasted with Jesus, 256.

Paulus, Sergius, 270-271.

Peabody, Frances G., quoted, 97-98.

Pentecost, Day of, 245-248.

Pentecost, feast of, 17.

Perea, district of, 15, 208.

Perga, 271, 272.

Pericles, 22.

Persecution, in the early church, 253, 265.

Peter, the disciple, called to follow Jesus, 138, 156; his great confession, 199-200; his presumption and rebuke, 200-201; at the transfiguration, 201-203; 221, 222; on the morning of the resurrection, 231; 232; 232; preaches on the day of Pentecost, 247; in prison, 248; at Samaria, 255; and Cornelius, 260-262; at First Council in Jerusalem, 263-265; at Second Council in Jerusalem, 274-275.

Peter, I and II Epistles of, 99; authorship, dates and contents, 102-103, 108.

Pharisees, Jewish religious party, 19; in conflict with Jesus, 164-166; 168-169, 195-198, 207-208.

Phelps, William Lyon, quoted, 296-297.

Phidias, 22.

Philemon, Epistle to, 80, 84; date, occasion and contents, 94-95, 96, 294.

Philip, the disciple, called to follow Jesus, 140; 215.

Philip, the evangelist, in Samaria, 253-255; at Gaza, 255-256.

Philippi, 89, 277-279.

Philippians, Epistle to, 80, 84, date, occasion and contests, 89-90; 294.

Pilate, Pontius, Procurator of Judea, 15; character of, 224; at the trial of Jesus, 224-226.

Pindar, 22.

Plato, 22, 187.

Polycarp, 73, 107.

Pompey, captured Jerusalem, 14.

Prayer, the habit of Jesus, 162, 221; nature of true, 175-176; of Jesus in Gethsemane, 222; on the cross, 229; of Stephen, 252.

Prayer, The Lord's, 175-178.

Priscilla, 281.

Ptolemy, Greek general, 23.

Publius, 292.

Quelle, meaning of, 49; 71.

Ramsay, Sir, W. M., 87, 272.

Raphael, 124.

Reformation, The, 267.

Renan, quoted, 199.

Repentance, meaning of, 132; message of John the Baptist, 132; of Jesus, 152-153; on the day of Pentecost, 247.

Resurrection, of Jesus, 52; 230-233.

Revelation, Book of, 34; nature, authorship and date of, 105-106, 108.

Revival, Wesleyan, 267.

Robertson, A. T., quoted, 74; referred to, 118.

Romanes, quoted, 11.

Romans, Epistle to, 80, 84, date, occasion and contents, 84-85, 96, 286.

Rome, VIII, 30, 84, 100, 244, 265, 266, 289, 292-296.

Rubicon, The, 277.

Sabbath, Pharisaic restrictions on, 16; how Jesus used it, 154, 158-161; conflict of Jesus with Pharisees over, 168-169, 207.

Sacrifices, Jewish, 15.

Sadducees, Jewish religious party, 19, 228.

Salome, daughter of Herodias, 191-192.

Samaria, district of, 14; town of, 5, 149; conversation of Jesus with woman of, 148-150; the gospel in, 253-255.

Samson, 194.

Sanhedrin, supreme court of the Jews, 18; in the trial of Jesus, 223-224.

Sapphira, 249.

Schaff, Philip, quoted, 78-79.
School, the Jewish common, 18-19.
Sea, Dead, 4.
Seleucia, 270.
Seleucus, Greek general, 23.
Septuagint, 25, 109.
Shakespeare, referred to, IX, 124, 199; quoted, 6.
Sidon, 198.
Silas, goes with Paul on his second missionary journey, 276-279; 280, 282.
Simon, the sorcerer, 254.
Simon, the tanner, 260.
Simpson, James Y., quoted, 233.
Sinai, Mount, 7, 108, 201.
Slavery, Paul's treatment of, 94-95; Roman, 178.
Smith, Sydney, quoted, 202.
Socrates, 22.
Spirit, The Holy, power of, at Pentecost, 246-247.
Stalker, James, 60.
Stephanus, Robertus, 109.
Stephen, 202; appointed deacon, 249; began the battle for Christian liberty from Mosaic law, 250-251; his martyrdom, 251-252.
Stevens and Burton, their *Harmony of the Gospels*, referred to, 47, 48, 50.
Sunday, Palm, 212.
Synagogue, the worship in, 18-19; the Jewish common school, 18.
Syrians, 8.

Tabernacles, feast of, 17, 245.
Tarsus, 268-269.
Tatian, his Diatessaron, 108.
Temple, The, daily service in, 15; Christ's first cleansing of, 143-145.
Temptation, of Jesus, 132-137.
Tennyson, 27, 125.
Testament, New, best book in the world, IX; highly composite, human and divine; rooted in the Old, 12-14; Hebrew

contributions to, 1-21; Greek contributions to, 26-28; Roman contributions to, 33-34; books of, 41; order of its books, 43; canon of, 107-108; manuscripts of, 108-109; translations of, 109-111; characteristics and value of, 296-297.
Testament, The Old, background of the New, 11-14; quoted in the New, 13; translated into Greek, 25; canon of, 108; translations of, 109-111.
Testament, Expositor's Greek, quoted, 63-64, 232.
Theology, new, in the teaching of Jesus, 160-161; 251, 265.
Thessalonians, I and II Epistles to, 80, 84, dates, occasions and contents, 90-92, 282.
Thessalonica, 90-91, 282.
Thomas, the disciple, 231.
Tiber, river, 266.
Time, Fulness of, 35-36.
Timothy, convert of Paul, 276-277, 280, 282, 295.
Timothy, I and II Epistles to, 81, 84, 96; dates, occasions and contents, 92-94; 295.
Titus, Epistle to, 81, 84, date, occasion and contents, 94; 295.
Tower, The Black, 181, 190.
Tradition, its place in religion, 197-198.
Traditions, Jewish, 16-17; conflict of Jesus with Pharisees over, 195-197.
Transfiguration, The, 201-204.
Trial, of Jesus, 223-226; of Stephen, 250-252.
Troas, 89, 277, 295.
Twelve, The, choosing and mission of, 169-172.
Tychicus, 90.
Tyndale, William, 110.
Tyrannus, 283.
Tyre, 198.

Venus, 281.
Versions, of the Bible, Bede's,

INDEX OF SUBJECTS

110; Wycliffe's, 110; Tyndale's, 110; Coverdale's, 110; the Bishops', Reims and Douai, 110; Authorized, 110; Revised, 110; American Standard, 110; Moffatt's, of the New Testament, 110.
Vinci, Leonardo da, 124.

Wade, Dr. G. W., quoted, 233.
War, The Great, 8.
Washington, George, referred to, 115, 238.
Webster, Daniel, 202.

Westcott, Dr. B. F., quoted, 110.
Whittier, quoted, 297.
Worship, Emperor, 32.
Worship, true nature of, 150-151, 239.
Wycliffe, 110.

Zaccheus, 208.
Zacharias, 119.
Zealots, Jewish party, 20.
Zebedee, father of James and John, 138.
Zionist, Movement, 5.